Management Rights
and Union Interests

Management Rights and Union Interests

Margaret K. Chandler

Professor of Sociology
University of Illinois

McGraw-Hill Book Company
New York San Francisco Toronto London

Management Rights and Union Interests

Library of Congress Catalog Card Number 63–22727

10512

**To the memory
of my mother**

Preface

This book introduces an organizational analysis of management rights, an area chronically dominated by "legalistic" thinking. Contracting-out is the rights issue that serves as the test case, permitting me to pursue a detailed investigation of the effects of factors such as technology and structure. Too often, the bungling of the ill-fated manager who "gave away" his company's rights is accepted as an adequate explanation of events in this area. Other, more general studies of management rights have provided an overview of the field, but there has been a need for exploration in depth sufficient to furnish a satisfactory analysis of much of the behavior observed.

In order to avoid the bias inherent in a one-culture study, I have attempted to examine both the management rights question and the substantive issue from a cross-cultural perspective—a point of view which clearly indicates that the problems found in our society are far from inevitable and do, in fact, reflect certain cultural values, especially those relating to property rights and the nature of the employment relationship.

My research emphasized relationships ordinarily neglected in the literature. In this connection, I have been critical of the legalistic point of view and have tested some of its assumptions in the light of my findings. As an alternative, and I hope more fruitful, approach, I have embedded this rights issue in a technological and organizational matrix and have probed the operation of factors of this nature. This work also has contradicted the commonly accepted view of labor and management as two "united fronts," with the former securing rights at the expense of the latter. Instead, I discovered a complex system of interest groups and searched into a structure of cross alliances that involved elements both inside and outside the firm. Of necessity, many research efforts stop at the formal boundaries of the firm; but my problem provided an excellent opportunity to observe relationships extending beyond these artificial lines, and I have devoted considerable attention to the relations of "insiders" and "outsiders"—and to the significance of this status differential.

As a matter of fact, the rights questions studied were a product of changes in the organization of the work of the industrial firm, notably the tendency to assign increasing amounts of the firm's activities to outside specialists. I explored fully the conflicting property rights claims that resulted as diverse parties inside and outside the firm attempted to guarantee their "fair share" of the work in question. Competing and coexisting solutions to this problem were provided by interunion pacts, arbitration, collective bargaining, and governmental agencies. These were contrasted and evaluated critically.

Prediction of inside worker protest was another major phase of this research. In this connection, it was found that property rights in a job were not constantly asserted, even in the face of a threatened loss through outside contracting. Rather, the assertion of claims waxed and waned in response to specific organizational factors. A study of the management decision process over a period of time revealed that, ironically, certain of its aspects served as stimuli to these worker challenges to management "rights."

This book is based on research extending over a period of six years, from 1957 to 1963. I collected extensive empirical data in a representative sample of process and fabrication industry establishments and, in addition, conducted a study of the management decision process. Methodologically speaking, the second project introduced a fairly novel comparative analysis of the rates of change of factors that affect the course of events in industrial relations. These two formal studies were supplemented throughout the entire six-year period with observation in the field and extensive interviewing on a wide range of aspects of the general problem.[1]

---

[1] See further Chap. 1. _The Design of the Research._

This research has proved to be a valuable and enjoyable experience. In the future I intend to pursue a cross-cultural study of management rights and the organization of the work of the industrial firm, beginning this effort with a year as a Fulbright research scholar in Japan.

Much gratitude is due to all the persons in management and unions, both inside and outside the firm, who aided so generously in this research. As a neutral outsider in relation to all the groups that I studied, I was received graciously and helped by many who gave unstintingly of their time. In return, I hope that I have been able to provide answers to some of the questions they raised. I also wish to acknowledge gratefully the assistance of the Ford Foundation in supporting my work with a Faculty Research Fellowship grant in social science and business at the University of Chicago Graduate School of Business.

Many colleagues have encouraged my efforts. For my general approach to the problem, I am indebted to William Foote Whyte and my work with him on the University of Chicago Committee on Human Relations in Industry. My first interest in the specific field of management rights was stimulated by reading Neil Chamberlain's book *Union Challenge to Management Control,* and he has continued to encourage my work in this area. The present study owes much to earlier research on the Illini City project with Milton Derber, W. Ellison Chalmers, and others at the University of Illinois Institute of Labor and Industrial Relations. Leonard Sayles, of the Columbia University Graduate School of Business, was an early collaborator in the study of contracting-out and has served as a valuable adviser throughout this research. Henry Bobotek of the University of Illinois assisted in my work on the management decision process. In conclusion, I wish to thank Mrs. Jean Asato for doing an excellent job of typing the final draft of the manuscript.

Margaret K. Chandler

Contents

preface

part I A PERSPECTIVE ON THE MANAGEMENT RIGHTS ISSUE   1

chapter 1 The Approach: Technology, Structure, and Issues   3
A Perspective on the Rights Issue   3
The Substantive Issue   7
Inside versus Outside as a Rights Distinction   8
The Design of the Research   13

chapter 2 An Intercultural Perspective   *15*
Japan   16
Western Europe   19
The Soviet Union   21
A New Perspective on the Issue   23

xi

part II FACTORS IN THE EMERGING RIGHTS DIMENSION
          OF CONTRACTING-OUT   27

chapter 3 The Boundaries of the Firm   *29*
The Organization of the Work of the Industrial Firm   30
Patterns and Trends in the Contracting of Work   32
Summary   **39**

chapter 4 Economic, Technological, and Structural Factors   *41*
Economic Factors   42
Technological Factors   47
Structural Factors   53
Summary   58

part III MANAGEMENT RIGHTS: EROSION
           AND IRREVOCABLE LOSSES   61

chapter 5 Trends and Tendencies in the Management Rights Area   *63*
Management Rights: The Partisan View   63
Some Aspects of the Rights Issue in the Postwar Period   69
Research on Management Rights   73
*Some Technological and Structural
Components of the Rights Approach*   76
On the Permanence of Management Losses and Union Gains   78
Summary   81

chapter 6 The Preservation of Rights: Management's Defense   *83*
Defense Strategies: The Partisan View   85
Defenses for Contracting-out   88
The No Defense Firms   89
The Management-controlled Defenses   90
The Barter Defenses   97
Contract Clauses and Management Defenses   107
*Union Influence, Management Defenses,
and Organizational Structure*   108
Group Pressures and Management Rights   113
Summary   115

part IV THE INSIDE AND OUTSIDE FORCES   117

chapter 7 The Outside Forces   *119*
The Group Structure of Bargaining Issues   119
The Structure of the Outside Forces   122
Trends in Outside Management Organization   130
Summary   146

chapter 8   **The Inside Forces**   *149*
The Service Department   150
Inside Problems and Outside Contracting   160
Summary   164

chapter 9   **Inside versus Outside: Trends and Developments**   *167*
The Concepts Inside and Outside   167
The Changing Employment Relationship   168
Inside and Outside: Organizational Developments   169
Rights, Jurisdiction, and Technological Change   170
Inside-Outside Competition   172

part V   **CONCEPTS OF EQUITY**   177

chapter 10   **Rights and Equities**   *179*
Equity in What?   180
Who Divides the Work?   182
How Is the Work to Be Shared?   184
Interrelated Systems of Equity   185

chapter 11   **Rules for the Equitable Division of Work**   *189*
Interunion Pacts   189
Arbitration   203
Collective Bargaining   213
Equity through Legislation   232
Fair Shares and the Administration of Federal Labor Legislation   235

chapter 12   **Inside and Outside Views of Equity**   *243*
The Internal Service Department's Fair Share   244
The Contractor's Fair Share   247
Concepts of Equity: A Summary and Analysis   250
A Final Assessment   254

part VI   **MANAGEMENT RIGHTS AND THE DECISION PROCESS**   255

chapter 13   **The Management Decision**   *257*
The Real and the Ideal Decision   258
An Organizational Decision Model   259
The Research Design   267
Questions and Answers Regarding the
Management Decision Process   269

chapter 14   **Prediction of Protest**   *275*
Background Factors: The Character of the Work Group   276
Rate and Timing of Protest   278

Factors Predictive of Protest: General Findings   280
Cumulative Series Analysis   283
Management Control of Challenge   288
Prescriptions for Avoiding Challenge   290

**chapter 15   The Management Decision Process: Unity
and Diversity in Patterns   293**
The Decision Structure   294
Information Needs   296
Management Consensus   297
Summary and Analysis   303

Conclusion   307
Bibliography   313
Index   319

part 1

A Perspective on the
Management Rights Issues

chapter 1

The Approach: Technology, Structure, and Issues

A PERSPECTIVE ON THE RIGHTS ISSUE

In our property-conscious society, collective bargaining issues frequently are phrased in terms of the rights of the parties. In fact, rights seem to be a hidden dimension underlying all decisions in labor-management relations. The fact that labor-management questions are structured as rights issues is an extremely important facet of behavior in this field, for when one introduces rights, one conjures up a rigid legal framework for a given dispute. It can be assumed that this action, in turn, will affect the entire structure of bargaining and of the organizational processes related to the issue.

In other countries management rights may prove to be considerably less encumbered by "restrictions" than they are in the United States; but there are few, if any, places where these rights are extolled with greater vigor. For a parallel degree of enthusiasm, one may have to turn to the Soviet Union. In any case, it would be inappropriate to dismiss management rights as a withering straw man, for they reflect one basic set of American cultural values—the freedom to conduct one's own affairs—and they come into direct conflict with another set of values, the democratic ethos regarding the need for voice and representation for all concerned with a given problem.

In the United States the union has been the prime threat to management rights. According to the traditional model, management has a fund of rights, and the union proceeds to secure its rights at the expense of the rights of management. These rights are property and are held exclusively by one party or the other. There is no notion of coexisting bundles of rights. One party's loss is the other's gain. However, applying this model to other societies may lead to the erroneous conclusion that management rights are uninfringed because documents designated as collective bargaining contracts may be little more than empty promulgations by management. The important negotiations may take place between the government and the employers, and the meaningful rights issues then would be an aspect of these relationships. India provides a good example of this situation (Ornati, 1955).

Models that focus on a possessor of a fund of rights and an antagonistic force that chips away at his stock have obvious analytical limitations, as do intercultural comparisons that flow from this model. But, despite this fact, research in this area commonly has treated the rights issue as an entity having a self-contained, isolated, and mechanistic existence. Rights issues often seem to need no explanation but, rather, appear to lead an existence similar to that of a deity, independent of causal analysis. In part, this phenomenon is the result of the scholar's uncritical acceptance of the values and outlook of union and management practitioners.

Other researchers have attempted to clarify the murky waters surrounding definitions of management rights. Or they have probed the problem of defining the boundary line between "invaded" territory and remaining rights preserves. A traditional study in the management rights field might assess the impact on rights of factors such as past practices, arbitration decisions, and management agreements with workers and unions.

All these are legitimate questions, but in this book the author's approach has been both broader and narrower:

Narrower, in the sense that the analysis focused on a single issue in depth, the contracting-out of the maintenance and construction work of the industrial firm. Contracting-out is well qualified for this assignment, for it is fraught with property relations disputes and involves the rights of an impressive multitude of parties.

Broader, in the sense that this one issue was placed in an analytical framework that concentrated on the interrelationship of technology, structure, and issues. In this book, management rights is the main issue, with its substantive side, as indicated, the contracting-out of work. Our goal was the development of an organizational analysis of management rights issues. The organizational approach to the rights question has been neglected in the literature, as has the relationship of rights issues to factors such as technology and structure.

We were interested in the how, what, when, and why of these issues. We were especially eager to move from the traditional "how and what" aspects of analysis—identification, description, and classification of problems, attributes, and variables—to the "when and why" aspects, which involve prediction and the testing of theories, relationships, functions, and models. Needless to say, this investigation of these relationships represented only a beginning. As is so often the case in social research, much effort had to be devoted to spade work, but it was hoped that these efforts would serve to point the way to further fruitful avenues of inquiry. In brief, we examined the impact of the technical organization of work on this particular rights issue, focusing especially on the differences between process industries, characterized by continuous flow, and fabrication industries, which engage in the manufacture of discrete units. A related line of investigation probed the implications of technological change for issue creation. Structural factors involved, importantly, the alignments of organizational interest groups inside and outside the firm. We investigated the who, what, when, and how of splitting the industrial work pie, or, put more elegantly, of making agreements regarding the allocation of work opportunities. In addition, the research revealed dynamic factors in the management decision process that served to generate challenges to "rights."

In this book, we wanted to move away from the notion that collective bargaining over management rights issues, such as contracting-out, represents a special category of behavior with heavy political overtones. Instead, bargaining was treated as another example of organizational relations, of organizational process, which in turn is a function of technology and structure. In addition, we abandoned the purely legal-economic framework generally used in discussing contracting-out and, instead, viewed the contracting-out problem in the context of the organizational requirements of the firm.

The controversy surrounding contracting-out illustrates some of the fallacies inherent in abstract definitions of the organization and of collective bargaining as well. Relying on principles and armchair conceptions of the firm and union-management relations, one might conjure up a neat picture of a distinctly bound entity called the firm taking on as an adversary another distinctly bound entity called the union. In this case, as in many others, these boundary lines did not apply, for management is no unity but rather is comprised of special interest groups both within the firm and outside—maintenance and engineering departments conflicting with their own operating divisions and competing companies in the community seeking to obtain service contracts with the firm. The union, similarly, is made up of divergent and clashing groups in the plant and in the community. In reality, and as this study indicated, relationships stretching outside the legal boundaries of the firm are hard to distinguish in terms of frequency and importance from those taking place inside. And one or more unions at times are allied with groups in management in seeking mutual advantage, in contrast to the more familiar image of union-management antipathy and conflict.

The findings of this study contradicted the picture of industrial relations issues as entities having fixed characteristics. Most commonly, these issues have been treated in static terms such as rights and precedents. "Dynamism" has been introduced into such traditional analyses by including a separate treatment of union and management attitudes toward the problem. However, in this research it was apparent that attitudes toward contracting-out were secondary in importance to relations among interest aggregations both inside and outside the firm. With regard to rules and policies, rather than treating them as fixed entities, we probed their organizational functioning and their contribution to organizational process. Our findings suggest a modification of property-based concepts regarding the results of a particular dispute—the wins-losses, last-inning scorekeeping approach. Instead, we would substitute a focus on results in terms of organizational process, which proceeds by marginal increments. Inevitably, in this type of analysis, industrial relations tends to become less a separate and unique field and more an integral part of the study of organizational process and organization theory.

All of us have heard company officials mournfully exclaim, "Management has lost its rights." In a similar vein, this book might be regarded as a memorial to management rights. However, it was not intended as such. Rather, it was our purpose to analyze the consequences of the intellectual conception of the firm as somebody's property rights and to suggest a move from the rights philosophy to one based on organizational process—to move from management as a keeper of property to management as a promoter of process.

THE SUBSTANTIVE ISSUE

One of the most inflammatory issues in labor-management relations in the late 1950s and early 1960s was the firm's practice of contracting-out, giving maintenance and construction work to outside companies instead of assigning these jobs to the crew in the plant. According to classical economic theory, no issue should have existed, for this is a management decision governed by purely economic and technical factors. Moreover, it is the kind of decision that stands at the very core of the management function—coordination, the allocation of resources along various lines of investment. In organizational terms, it is part of the general problem of integration versus specialization. An integrated firm might operate a construction division to build its plants, while a specialist firm would be more likely to concentrate on its own product and assign the task of building to an outside contractor.

Industrial firms purchase a great variety of services. Thus, contracting-out is a process parallel to the buying of machine tools (subcontracting their manufacture) and to the hiring of consultants and outside research organizations. "Outside bureaucrats" are no longer a novelty in either government or industry (Alger, 1962). However, contracting-out had unique characteristics that served to distinguish it and to make it an infinitely fascinating and valuable subject for research on intergroup relations, for, in the case of contracting-out, the structure of competing groups inside and outside the firm led to unusually complex but nevertheless clear-cut interest conflicts.

An industrial firm that has never performed its own maintenance or construction work—and there are very few of these in the United States—would not have the specific "rights" problems that constitute the subject matter of this book. The dilemma began with existence of a competing element within the firm. If a contractor was hired, the managers in the plant who did not get the work faced a potentially severe loss of status. Decisions to contract-out may have served to reduce their department's size, budget, and power within the firm. The inplant workers were faced with the prospect of losing job opportunities to competing outside forces that were highly visible, for the contractors and their men came into the plant to perform their work. Though physically near, the contractor's force was managerially and organizationally different from the inside group, and in many ways differences regarding wage rates and work assignment placed the outsiders in an enviable position.

As inside workers generally were members of industrial unions and outside workers usually belonged to craft unions, contracting-out was a sore point in relations between these two organizations. This rivalry, in turn, could affect industrial management's position with regard to the issue, for management often was caught in the middle as both sides exerted pressure and sought agreements to bolster their respective positions.

Moreover, the maintenance and construction contractors were members of a specialized industry whose prosperity hinged on management decisions in this area. Companies that specialized in electrical work, sheet-metal, plumbing, and other maintenance and construction crafts were dependent upon a favorable climate for contracting-out, and they may have had little in the way of alternative employment if such a climate did not exist.

Generally speaking, relations of the firm to other outside groups who serve industry did not have contracting-out's potential for controversy. In tool and die subcontracting, the work moved outside the firm to the subcontractor's premises, where the workers may have been members of the same union that represented those in the client's firm. The outside management consultant and his inside counterpart may have competed on an individual basis, but they were not represented by competing external organizations, such as the craft and industrial unions.

The impressive array of competing "contracting-out" property claims served as the basis for this research. One of the elemental factors in this competition stemmed from differential evaluations placed on the positions of insider and outsider in this society.

INSIDE VERSUS OUTSIDE AS A RIGHTS DISTINCTION

With regard to most rights questions in the field of labor-management relations, membership in the category inside has distinct advantages over membership in the category outside. The permanent employees of a firm, whether they have the status of president or rank and file worker, traditionally have expected preferential treatment. In some societies, the lines between inside and outside have been clear and unquestioned, e.g., the distinction between permanent and temporary employees in Japan. (This point will be developed further in Chapter 2.) In the United States, the lines between the two groups have been less clear-cut. Where does one draw the line? Who is inside and who is outside in relation to the firm, and what is meant by this distinction?

When one considers the question of management's right to select an outsider, e.g., a maintenance contractor, and thus bypass the rights of the inside force, how does the distinction between inside and outside affect one's reactions? The job rights of the insiders were part of the structure of relationships in the firm although they may have been defended by an outsider, the union. Of course, the contractor and his men were members of an outside firm, and to accentuate this status, the contractor's men were represented by outside unions. One can readily see that, organizationally speaking, inside and outside have had quite different implications for behavior.

In our industrial system, the union has been regarded as the environing group that stands most completely outside, or apart from, the firm. As such, the union constitutes a kind of prototype for the outside element. The union may have represented inside workers, but this very act made them partially outsiders. As an outsider, the union commonly was assigned certain attributes that characterized this position. The objectives of the union were regarded as separate from those of management. The union challenged authority, particularly the prerogatives of the manager. Dealing with it involved negotiation rather than rational decision-making, and it served to extend the boundaries of the firm in an unpredictable fashion. An entirely opposite picture of inside relations emerged. Insiders in the firm were thought to have common objectives, to accept authority, use rational decision-making processes, and operate within clearly defined boundaries (see also Tannenbaum, 1950).

Outside groups were viewed in political rather than organizational terms. Thus, in the case of external relations, members of the firm raised questions of rights and inquired about potential shifts in the distribution of power. How much will the outsiders reduce the authority of the manager? This was the type of question that was asked. On the other hand, when management contemplated a new internal department, attention was focused on organizational matters. Will this move cut costs, increase efficiency, smooth out work flows, etc.? To whom will the new manager be responsible?

For internal relations, the manager had authority and responsibility; for external relations, the manager had rights. In terms of organizational relations, this was a basic and all-important distinction. The rights concept served as a handle to cope with external relations. It was one of a large number of tools of defense. However, by its very nature, it could not solve most of the organizational problems that involved the outsider, for these were not limited to property-oriented considerations. Moreover, the tendency to focus on matters of rights may have served as a block to the development of a satisfactory relationship. According to the commonly accepted picture of relations with outsiders, these relations typically were initiated via contract, and these contracts generally adhered closely to the narrow limits of the buyer-vendor relationship. Contracts with outsiders customarily contained guarantees that the vendor would not cause the buyer harm. Insiders also received contracts stating the terms of employment, but while potential damages may have been a concern in both cases, in the relationship with the outsider it was appropriate to make this concern a specific condition; in the case of the insider, it was not. Authority relations in the organization were supposed to cope with this matter. The contrast between the above view and reality will be discussed later in this chapter.

Managers in the firm who dealt frequently with outsiders, e.g., members of purchasing, industrial relations, and plant engineering staffs, at times found themselves in an ambiguous position. In the eyes of other insiders, they had become somehow tainted. It was not considered appropriate for those who conducted business with outsiders to act as neutrals in the fashion of an arbitrator. They were expected to defend the interests of the firm, but the outside contact almost inevitably seemed to take on a political flavor. It was hard to dispel the notion that some fancy dealing took place somewhere along the line.

Despite the commonly accepted picture of the outsider as a challenger of rights, there was an interesting paradox concerning the expectations of those in the firm who initiated contacts with outsiders. Those who promoted the relationship generally expected to be dealing thenceforth with a party whose property claims, in an organizational sense, would be much weaker than those of an insider. This anticipated weakness was partly a function of the outsider's initial lack of established organizational ties. In fact, their absence sometimes constituted a major point of attractiveness to the insider who sought the relationship. Through this relationship the insider could acquire new avenues of control. He could move outside established internal communication nets to bring in new information and skills. He could skirt around persisting and difficult internal problems, e.g., the pressures to use overburdened or ill-qualified personnel who would be in line for particular work if it were assigned internally. Thus, the outsider threatened rights on the one hand and served to reestablish controls on the other.

Moreover, another point of inconsistency appeared when one examined the industrial organization closely, for there was evidence of relationships that did not fit the initial conceptions of the differences between insiders and outsiders.

1. With regard to acceptance of authority: A service department (maintenance) complained that an operating division had usurped maintenance management's prerogatives by rejecting the work of the

maintenance staff without previously clearing the decision with the service group's officials.

2. With regard to rational decision-making: An operating division head attempted to negotiate with the plant manager for a better budgetary position.

3. With regard to common objectives: In order to show an operating profit, a service department gave preference to jobs that yielded the highest return on its bookkeeping costs. In the process, it neglected some work that was more urgent from the standpoint of the firm.

Another aspect of the interchangeability of the inside and outside patterns of behavior was seen in the increasing numbers of people in industry who have little direct control over internal groups upon whom they depend. Some executives sat in their offices with literally no one under them whom they could pressure. Members of their staff may have been working with others in different divisions, remote physically as well as in terms of control. In fact, the manager may have had control of a more direct sort over external forces, for while exerting pressure internally may have involved a complex and delicate organizational route, in the case of the outsider, he had available pressures reminiscent of the "old-fashioned" boss-subordinate relationship —the implied or actual threat of either failing to renew a contract or canceling it outright.

However, it should be noted that in the course of business dealings a goodly amount of nonthreatening interchange took place between persons such as plant engineers and outside maintenance contractors. The notion that relations between insiders and outsiders are legalistic, while those among insiders constitute a system of informal exchanges, is far from accurate. Agreements with outside contractors at times were verbal instead of written and loosely framed instead of detailed and specific. On the other hand, internal relations sometimes were conducted via formal devices such as work orders. In a few cases we encountered examples of these orders that closely resembled iron-clad legal documents. Situations in which insiders (manufacturers) have exerted strong legalistic pressures on outside contractors and related groups are well known, e.g., the automobile manufacturer and the franchised dealer (Rogers and Berg, 1961). Parallel instances with regard to strong economic pressures have been found in the relationship between manufacturer and subcontractor in the garment industry (Chandler, 1953). Yet the desire and economic need to continue a given relationship served as equally strong informal sanctions, controlling the behavior of both contractors and members of industrial firms. We found that in most cases the inside manager and outside maintenance and construction contractor were reluctant to resort to legal compulsion to enforce the terms of a relationship. Clearly, insiders and outsiders were not always willing to raise questions of rights in their dealings with one another, either in establishing a relationship or in handling problems that arose during its course.

Formality and legalism were not synonymous with situations in which insiders conducted business with outsiders. Rather, the legalistic approach was a function of factors such as the nature and duration of the relationship and the relative bargaining power of the parties involved. In other words, it was apparent that common organizational functions and processes were involved and that these superseded the distinction between inside and outside that might have been established on a strictly legal basis.

One could cite endless examples of management relations with outsiders that have many of the elements of the inside model, and vice versa. However, it is sufficient to note here that the stereotyped versions of these relationships simply do not hold water.

The concepts inside and outside as used in our research primarily served to distinguish inside (inplant) and outside (contract) forces in the service of the industrial firm. The work of all was connected with the operation of the firm, and the inside-outside distinction was based simply on the source and nature of the employment relationship. Socially determined elaborations of these differences constituted a superstructure supported by this primary distinction.

For many years, sociologists have analyzed relationships that parallel the inside-outside dichotomy. When the sociologist speaks of "associational," "secondary group," and "outgroup" relations, he assigns these the following constellations of characteristics: segmental roles (interpersonal relations serving a single purpose); impersonal, transitory, and superficial relations; lack of unity and cohesiveness; rapid change; low consensus and diversity in goals. These are similar to the socially determined elaboration of the category outside. On the other hand, communal, primary group, and ingroup relations tend to parallel the category inside. These are characterized by: inclusive roles (interpersonal relations serving many functions); personal, supportive relations valued for their own sake; group solidarity and stability; high consensus and common goals.

In the American culture, there has been a persistent bias in favor of the latter constellation, which depicts social relations of the more highly valued rural–small town type. The former constellation parallels the less favored urban pattern. This observation, in turn, suggests that popular sentiments favoring industrial relations of the inside type would predominate over those favoring the outside type. Some members of the "human relations" school of thought have advocated the application of the rural–small town model to American industry. But in industry this value system generally has been dominated by the values of competition and rational business practice. In order to gain a true perspective on the situation in this society, it is necessary to examine others. Chapter 2 will be devoted to this effort.

THE DESIGN OF THE RESEARCH

The data reported in this book were derived from two separate studies. The first was a 1958–1959 field interview survey, designed to explore the problem of contracting-out in a variety of industrial organizations. Data for this research were obtained from a stratified random sample of seventy-four plants located in seven metropolitan areas in the northeastern quarter of the United States. Our sample included thirty-one process industry establishments and forty-three in the fabrication category. The process industry group comprised five in food processing; one in textiles; two in paper; five in printing; three in chemicals; one in petroleum; one in rubber; six in primary metals; and seven utilities. In the fabrication group there were three in apparel; six in fabricated metal; ten in machinery; eight in electrical machinery; eleven in transportation equipment; four in scientific instruments; and one in miscellaneous industries.

Our sample was confined to plants large enough to have a significant potential interest in conducting an internal maintenance and construction operation. Details on the distribution of plant employment sizes are given in Table 4–1. Over forty different unions are represented. In 70 per cent of the plants the entire work force was organized by industrial unions or industrial branches of craft unions. Of the remaining plants, 20 per cent had a mixed industrial craft and 10 per cent a pure craft form of union organization. Some of the data relating to the substantive problem of contracting-out have been reported elsewhere (Chandler and Sayles, 1959; Chandler, 1962). Data presented in this book are largely previously unpublished materials that focus on the management rights question.

A second phase of the research involved a systematic study of the management decision process.[1] Results of the previous survey proved to be of value in pointing to significant variables for this later investigation, which was conducted in the years 1960–1962. In this book, we shall present aspects of this research that centered on the prediction of protest to management decisions. The design of this work specified the gathering of data for series of consecutive management decisions in order to observe the rate of change in various key factors.

[1] This research was supported during the year 1960–1961 by a Ford Foundation Faculty Research Fellowship grant in social science and business.

In addition, the author has conducted observations in the field and interviews, numbering in the several hundreds, with contractors, industrial managers at all levels, craft and industrial union leaders, and rank-and-file union members. Moreover, the author has followed current events closely and, whenever possible, has held discussions with leading figures in major contracting-out rights battles.

Work on this general problem commenced in 1957 and continued through the first half of 1963. During this time, we have had the opportunity of witnessing the development of the contracting-out issue and its emergence as a significant element in the management rights drama in the United States. In many cases, our limited descriptions of sources of data are due to the need to protect the anonymity of those who have cooperated so generously in this research.

chapter 2

An Intercultural Perspective

It is admittedly difficult to avoid cultural bias in an assessment of the contracting-out issue in the United States. In order to meet this problem, we have examined the situation here in the light of experience in other countries. A cross-national study of this area is badly needed. In its absence we have relied on interviews and on a variety of published materials and have attempted to derive from them implications for the problems in our society. Important among the sources used are the works of Levine (1958) and Berliner (1957). The presentation of materials with regard to the various countries is highly general, and it is recognized that, in reality, there are many variations on common themes. Moreover, change is proceeding at a rapid rate in some of these societies, and events in the 1960s may serve to alter patterns commonly held in the 1950s, the period to which this discussion primarily refers.

The American industrial system, with its strong emphasis on individual accountability in competitive enterprise, has tended to foster an acceptance of contracting-out, especially when this strategy has involved a competitive advantage. One immediately is led to inquire whether or not adoption of contracting-out has been more difficult in societies that do not accentuate individualistic values. And yet the attendant rights and interests battles that have taken place in this country may lead one to conclude that adjustment to contracting-out may have been easier in societies that did not have to cope with this aspect of the problem. Our management rights problems have arisen partly because of an impatience with opposition to rational requirements or change. If a situation has dictated contracting-out, then the American manager has tended to feel that, ultimately, the firm should accede to these demands. (Of course, managers of departments that compete directly with outside contractors generally would be exceptions to this rule.) While a firm may have made concessions to "violated" and abridged interests, these actions have been considered a secondary concern at best and an intolerable burden at worst. The above sentiments undoubtedly have been responsible for the managerial stress placed on problems of resistance to the exercise of rights. At the same time, the rights of the resisters—in this case primarily certain inside managers, workers, and unions—have been supported by American society, for these groups, too, have been held accountable for maintaining their own competitive position.

In other societies, American contracting-out has been viewed, not as a problem, but rather as a source of strength. The British Productivity Council report in *Industrial Engineering* (1954) cited the important part played by subcontracting and its useful contribution to the acknowledged success of American production in relation to that of the rest of the world. Whether a source of problems or prosperity, American practices are better understood in the light of an examination of the experiences of other countries.

JAPAN

Contrasting the American system with the Japanese, we noted an entirely different cultural and economic matrix for contracting-out. In the Japanese firm, the employment relationship is regarded as permanent and irrevocable.[1] There are exceptions, of course, but, on the

[1] Fujita noted that the concept of a permanent employment relationship had its beginnings in the early Meiji period of industrialization (1868–1880). Wakao Fujita, *Nihon Rodo Kyohyaku Ron*. Tokyo University Press, Tokyo, 1961.

whole, employment constitutes a life-long commitment between management and those who have gained the status of permanent worker.[2] The employee will not leave the firm, and the employer will not lay off or discharge the employee. Under this immobile system, labor cost is a fixed cost, and make work is an accepted way of life (Abegglen, 1957). This concept of the permanency of relationships is not limited to the firm. Rather, it pervades the entire Japanese culture.

It should be noted that Japanese firms have not been as large as those in the United States. The average small company employs a dozen workers. Companies having 250 to 500 workers are considered large, although some industrial giants employ over 1,000. It has been noted that even in some small shops, a worker will be retained at any cost. The owner of the business may have to go without food, but the worker will be paid (Bussard and Schlissel, 1961). Moreover, an elaborate system of fringe benefits exists. It is not uncommon for a worker to be compensated for his lunches and transportation to and from work. In addition, the employer may provide housing, schooling for the children, and other maintenance fringes of this type.

Even this short description suggests the need for certain adjustments to make this system workable. Thus, the Japanese manufacturer is reluctant to increase his permanent work force because of the difficulty of reducing it, should that step become necessary. He has attempted to adjust work load requirements to the work force, rather than vice versa. In the process, time limits may not have been adhered to rigidly. More significant for our problem is the very extensive system of subcontracting, which is partly the result of hesitancy to assume the burdens of paternalistic obligations to permanent employees. In addition, economic forces, such as the need to spread the risk of capital investment, have played an important role. In some cases, industrial management may have sponsored the contractor: in others, families may have established a business in order to supplement dwindling agricultural income. The wage levels of temporary and contract forces generally have been considerably lower than those of permanent workers (Ito, 1960).

In Japan, subcontracting and an allied practice, the hiring of temporary help, are not regarded as a serious threat to the firm's regular employees, as these practices often have been in the United States. Rather, these programs have served to support the permanent employee's status. The temporary employees usually do not belong to unions and often do not have a firm commitment to industrial work. They float back and

[2] Tsuda estimated that in 1960, 44 per cent of the nonagricultural employees in Japan were included in permanent employment relationships. Masume Tsuda, *The Basic Structure of Japanese Labor Relations.* University of Illinois Institute of Labor and Industrial Relations, Champaign, Ill., 1963 (mimeographed).

forth between family farm or shop and industry. However, in accordance with tradition, they tend to identify with a particular industrial firm. Competitive sentiments involving the permanent employees and the subcontractors and temporaries have been generally weak, and grievance activity has been rare. The outsiders tend to accept their role as buffers and also accept the primacy of the permanent relationship.

In Japanese enterprise unionism, each union consists of the permanent employees of a given company. Again, the primacy of the traditional attachment to the employer is apparent in its effect on union structure. Collective agreements define management prerogatives and union rights but say little about substantive issues. Wage payments still tend to be based on factors such as family size, social status, length of service, and age. Unions are not strong in the American sense. Horizontal, equalitarian bargaining relations do not exist. However, management has placed high value on the traditional worker identification with the enterprise and thus has not cared to upset unduly the traditional arrangements. The principal concern of the enterprise union is the protection of the permanent employees' status, but the leaders do not press for agreements to maintain or expand the core of permanent employees. They agree with management in not extending union membership or benefits to temporary workers. But attempts to dismiss members of the core group are resisted vigorously, and seniority systems have been rejected because these systems acknowledge management's right to reduce the work force (Levine, 1958).

The Japanese system offers a method of observing the job property rights of the permanent inplant force as well as minimizing the kinds of inside worker conflict with management and outside groups that have been found in the United States. In Japan, the traditional obligations of industrial management constituted "rights" the union sought to perpetuate. When the American plant union has attempted to reinforce this same right, it has been faced by the existence of another right, management's right to contract-out as a rational business practice. In addition, the plant union has encountered the job property rights of a strong rival union group representing the contractor's workers.

However, stable systems of obligations can become fragile items when they are not supported by the proper economic institutions. In Japan, subcontracting and the use of temporary workers have served to maintain the status of the permanent employees. At times in the past, Japanese management has attempted to "rationalize" the system. But challenging it has always been a hazardous process, and both management and union have veered away from this step. Nevertheless, economic forces may provide the impetus for eventual change. One of these factors is a growing labor shortage that could very well serve to stimulate worker pressures for interfirm mobility (Karsh and Levine,

1962). Moreover, if members of the buffer and fill-in groups become more completely dependent on industrial work as a source of income, their present way of life, alternating between family farm or shop and industry, may disappear, and with it their acceptance of the supportive role and its lesser rewards. Technological change and more complete mechanization of industry may increase management pressures against the lack of flexibility inherent in the permanent employment relationship. That the Japanese will adopt Western-type individualism and competitive patterns is far from certain, but there is an increasing possibility that the relationship between inside and outside and between temporary and permanent workers may undergo change as pressures for traditional security collide with pressures for mobility and flexibility.[3]

WESTERN EUROPE

During the postwar period, contracting-out has increased in Western Europe. However, the reasons for this development have been somewhat different from those which applied in the United States. The labor shortage has been one of the primary stimulating factors. In the future, the boom-determined labor shortages may level off if the sellers' market diminishes and competitive pressures increase. But contracting-out should continue to fulfill a function in these economies, especially if wages rise as a result of coercive comparisons with the United States. Then contracting-out may shift to another role, as a concomitant of automation, serving to keep internal labor costs down.

Problems have arisen in some cases where contractors have been Americans and the nationals of the European country in which these contractors operated objected to continued management by an outside group. But in Western Europe conflict concerning contracting-out has not assumed and probably will not assume the proportions it has reached in the United States. The labor shortage would tend to reduce worker conflicts regarding job property rights. However, there is a

[3] While in Japan in the fall of 1963, the author found that rising wage levels lessened the desirability of hiring new graduates who were potential permanent employees (*joyoko*). Moreover, a shortage of temporary workers (*rinjiko*) and dissatisfaction with their services made the hiring of outside contract forces more attractive. In the late 1950s contractor's employees who served inside the plant (*shagaiko*) began to be found in postwar Japanese industry. During this period of high economic growth, some Japanese industrial firms were diversifying into the service field, offering maintenance, overhaul, and construction work to other companies. In growing industries, pressures of technological change and competitive markets were leading to efforts to upgrade subcontractors' facilities. And as the traditional boundaries between permanent, temporary, and contract workers shifted, some signs of competitive sentiments did emerge in the relations among members of these groups.

more important reason for the absence of these conflicts. Working class sentiments have been stronger than in the United States, and in conjunction with this there has been a stronger feeling of membership in one labor movement. Thus the notion that certain work is the property of a particular union has been weak or nonextant. However, some milder forms of the American contracting-out problem may arise in England, where both jurisdictional conflicts and a deeply rooted sense of job ownership were found. British management has contracted-out but has been conscious of the dangers of raising the hackles of the traditionally solidaire inside forces (Field, 1955). On the other hand, outside craft forces in England have been known to protest the use of inside employees for construction projects.

The limited scope of European collective bargaining also has been cited as a factor conditioning the fate of the contracting-out issue. Thus McPherson (1962, p. 27) states that "European agreements place fewer limitations on the rights of management. Many subjects that are covered by American agreements usually remain within the realm of the prerogatives of European management. For example, an issue seldom is raised regarding job assignment, subcontracting, promotion, transfer, or the assignment of overtime." A related factor affecting worker protests regarding these matters is the reputed weakness of the unions at the plant level in countries such as France.

A consideration of management rights and rival unionism in France serves admirably to highlight various aspects of the American situation with regard to contracting-out. The status of collective bargaining in France well illustrates the point that the "rights" of management to change work rules in general, or to contract-out, are a function of the socioeconomic structure of a given society. In the United States, labor-management consensus regarding common values has been combined with some fairly effective labor challenges to management rights; in France, the opposite situation has prevailed. Class divisions run deep. For management and workers, there is little sharing of values, but this lack of consensus is not reflected in effective worker opposition at the plant level. Workers may have resented the "capitalist" who operates the business and questioned his right to function in this role at all, but nevertheless management could make transfers, introduce automation, or contract-out without interference from the unions. However, the manager has been restricted in a few areas, such as layoffs, which are regulated by legislation, and this factor, in turn, may have affected his policies with regard to matters such as the introduction of automation or contracting-out. The right to continued employment has been recognized as law for workers in France, but these legally enforced restrictions have not been as potent as they might have been, for sanctions generally have taken the form of small damage awards rather than reinstatement (Meyers, 1962).

Rival unionism has been strong in France, with the CGT (Confédération Générale du Travail), the FO (Force Ouvrière), and the CFTC (Confédération Française des Travailleurs Chrétiens) vying with one another for dominance. In a given factory, there may be several unions or none. Workers are free to join any union, and they join unions as one might a political party in the United States. Workers sitting side by side on an assembly line may be members of different unions. The fact that no one union has an exclusive interest in a block of jobs in the plant leaves job property issues such as contracting-out without a strong base for organizational protest or grievance action. Moreover, because no union has a fund of specific job rights to defend, there is little basis for battles over whose members will perform certain work. Thus, interunion rivalry is not expressed in competition for work at the plant level, as has been the case in the United States.

The absence of the familiar American patterns of rivalry and routes of challenge to management control must not lead to the conclusion that these phenomena do not exist in France. In France the avenue for challenge is political. If sufficient votes can be mustered, workers may be able to obtain legislative regulation of contracting-out and allied work rules problems. However, achieving the necessary political power is far from simple.

In summary, French management has retained its right to assign and allocate work, but at the same time it is faced with a potentially explosive worker discontent—a discontent thus far ameliorated by factors such as the postwar labor shortage. In the United States this right has been subject to piecemeal, plant-by-plant challenge, successful in some establishments and not in others. These piecemeal challenges on a substantive level, centered in particular issues, such as the contracting-out of certain work at a particular point in time, have served as a safety valve in a society that has required that the work one performs be needed but at the same time has provided the industrial worker with no assurance that such work will be made available to him.

THE SOVIET UNION

Obviously, the Soviet Union is not the equal of France as a source of comparative data regarding union rivalry and job property rights. While there is evidence that individual worker and union challenge of management authority has received encouragement in the post-Stalin era, the best insights from information regarding Soviet industrial relations arise in the opportunity to observe the functioning of some aspects of inside-outside relations in an economic system different from American "capitalism" (Brown, 1963).

In Communist countries, one might anticipate that no distinction would be made between inside and outside interests and that a sense of participation in a common economic enterprise would obliterate this difference completely. Nevertheless, this distinction does exist in the Soviet Union, where one can observe the impact of management and government essentially unmodified by the factor of independent union interests, a factor present in some form in all the other cases considered.

In Russia the government encourages the enterprise to seek contract work in order to make use of idle capacity, but this work does not count toward percentage of plan fulfillment. Therefore, the incentive to obtain such work is weak. Subcontracted work is considered a stepchild, and ministries support the efforts of their enterprises to conceal idle capacity in order to avoid such tasks.

When there is a need to conceal excess production wage payments, the internal maintenance and construction account provides the most popular vehicle for this practice. A work order is drawn up for a repair job, but while the worker is paid under this order, he spends his time on direct production. Bookkeeping and cost accounting in the construction departments of manufacturing enterprises tend to share the poor quality that characterizes cost records in the major construction enterprises. Thus, it is rather easy to confuse cost data to cover an expenditure of production wages. Another practice of the same type is the subcontracting of work budgeted in the enterprise's planned wage bill. This action frees funds to cover the overpayment of wages in production. Repair and small construction jobs are favorites for this purpose. On the other hand, managers do work that they are supposed to contract, but this step is taken primarily when they are unable to find a subcontractor (Berliner, 1957).

It appears that in the Soviet Union contracting-out and inside-outside relations are largely a management problem. While the gross structure of the economy is quite different from that in the United States, one observes some striking parallels when one approaches the finer points of organizational relations. For instance, in daily organizational life in both countries the internal maintenance and construction function serves as a favorite account-poachers preserve, and shifting work between inside and outside forces provides a valued source of budgetary leeway.

One can conclude that the managerial aspects of this problem area

—mediating the relationships between functions performed inside and outside the firm—are not unique to capitalism or uniquely a product of competition under the capitalist system. Rather, these data contribute to the feeling that one is dealing with common organizational problems that are found in industrial systems in various cultures and under various forms of government—in fact, wherever an organizational structure is erected for the accomplishment or the work of the industrial firm.

A NEW PERSPECTIVE ON THE ISSUE

The research findings presented in this book are based primarily on data regarding the industrial firm and industrial relations in the United States. In this type of one-country analysis lies hidden the danger of cultural bias. It is hoped that the foregoing brief survey of other countries will diminish this risk and provide a clearer perspective on the situation in the United States. If one inquires into the reasons for organizational struggles over contracting-out in this country, from an intercultural point of view these seem to be the salient factors on the American scene:

1. The potency of a sense of property rights in the organization for both management and labor. Compare Japan, where mutual obligations are emphasized.

2. The emphasis on individual accountability in competitive relations in the industrial enterprise. Compare Japan, where the individual is protected from the severe consequences of failure by group assumption of blame.

3. The institutionalized impermanence of the employment relationship. Compare Japan, where the permanent employment relationship has prime significance.

4. The lack of buffer groups of contract forces and temporaries. Compare Japan, where these groups assume a nonthreatening, supportive role in relation to the inside forces.

5. Rival unionism characterized by a clear-cut division into two powerful camps representing the inside and outside forces. Compare Great Britain, with its greater diversity of elements in the union movement.

6. Strong union organization at the plant level. Compare France, where unions are weak at this point.

In studying any one labor-management issue cross-culturally, one must not lose sight of the fact that he may be looking in the wrong places for evidence of the controversy in question. A given issue, or its cultural equivalent, can arise in a variety of ways—and can be coped with through a multitude of devices. Struggles may not take place on the plant floor, because broader cultural solutions provide the answer to a given problem. The absence of conditions approximating the American "syndrome" for contracting-out may be interpreted wrongly as evidence that a given party is in a weak position or that no pressures are being exerted. This point also serves as a caution against employing a narrow focus on a particular problem. This comparative analysis, limited though it is, has moved beyond contracting-out per se to societal value systems, to the nature of the employment relationship and work rules in general.

In the relationships cited above, one can note some distinctive modes of adjustment to contracting-out. The Japanese is the least turbulent, for the permanency of the inside employment relationship has been a cultural value adhered to by all the principal parties. A system of obligations has taken precedence over questions of rights. Thus, inside and outside groups have lived encapsulated existences, side by side, in a calm if not harmonious atmosphere that seems extraordinary in the light of experiences in American industry. Worker grievances exist, of course, but they are largely internal to the inside or outside system. There are few cross-system alliances or grievances, a phenomenon that again is part of traditional Japanese conservatism. Even the demands of the business take second place to the *inside security system*. This system has ensured the position of the inside group and has adjusted other practices to this prime requirement.

In the United States the situation has been markedly different. Neither inside nor outside forces have enjoyed a permanent commitment from the firm, and business requirements have been a significant factor in the management decision regarding the use of the two competing groups. In contrast to Japan, the issue has been phrased in terms of rights rather than obligations—management rights and labor rights. Also in contrast to Japan, the hiring of a contractor and his workers has led to their inclusion in a well developed system of competitive cross alliances involving members of the industrial firm.

The lack of a unified working class sentiment in the United States has been an essential condition for the existence of interunion rivalry for the work of the industrial firm. And when the rival unions have claimed exclusive property rights to specific jobs, the scene has been set for struggles over issues such as contracting-out. Thus, American management, which has benefited greatly from the lack of concerted, unified class struggle with labor, has had to contend with another source of limitations from rival segments of an upward-mobile labor movement, effectively organized at the plant level. Moreover, labor-management controversy has been intensified and moved into other arenas by these rival union groups, organized as two competing blocs, one representing inside and the other outside interests. The system found in the United States might be described as a *multigroup rights competition.*

It may be that the traditional Japanese inside security system represents one extreme type and the American multigroup rights competition its polar opposite. If this is true, then any number of variations could be expected to fall in between them. Thus societies in which paternalism and Western individualism coexist might fall in an intermediate category.

All the observations in this chapter should serve as a warning about the pitfalls of an ethnocentric point of view that might lead one to believe that certain problems inevitably become management rights issues, American-style.

part *ii*

Factors in the Emerging Rights Dimension of Contracting-out

chapter 3

The Boundaries of the Firm

Labor-management issues often are treated as though they were constant, unvarying entities—largely a matter of rights and precedents. As a matter of fact, these issues vary in intensity from time to time and place to place and are affected greatly by economic, technological, and structural factors. In its various forms, contracting-out is an old issue. The advocates and partisans of both integration and specialization have fought and argued with each other over the centuries. Since the late 1950s the contracting-out question has flared into prominence on the American scene, but it also was an issue in earlier periods—for instance, in the railroad shopmen's strike of 1921. All these disputes involved the question of the boundaries of the firm and the rights of those inside and outside these variously defined boundaries. If the boundaries were considered to be coterminous with the total activities of the firm, as they rarely have been, some of these issues might have disappeared. But usually the contested lines bounded an employment relationship or the legal limits of the firm, and conflict arose because the activities of the firm extended beyond them.

While the immediate parties at interest struggle over a historic boundary, action has been going forward on another stage. Economic, technological, and organizational factors have been shaping the pattern of the future—conditioning the long-range climate for contracting-out and incidentally promoting the cause of either the inside or the outside forces. In this section we shall examine these factors and use them to place our later study of the immediate issue in proper perspective. In the process we may obtain a clearer picture of the extent to which the inside and outside forces—the members of management, unions, and work groups directly involved in performing a function—could control their own fate and compete effectively for the work of the industrial firm. Certainly the pressure activities of some members of · these two groups—wildcat strikes, pitched battles at plant gates, and industrial and craft union pacts specifying formulas for dividing the work of the industrial firm—have given the appearance of considerable control in this area. Incidents such as those in which industrial management "pulled back" contracted work as a result of the pressures of the inside group have lent even greater weight to the impression of significant influence. However, one must assess the effect of these actions in terms of their potential ability to override major technological, economic, and organizational trends.

THE ORGANIZATION OF THE WORK
OF THE INDUSTRIAL FIRM

Studies of historic patterns for conducting the activities of the firm and theories based on these studies have stressed the importance of economic and technological developments in placing work inside or outside the boundaries of the firm. But the entire bundle of industrial activities has not responded to these forces in the same fashion. Some activities are fluid at particular periods, while others remain fixed. In this research we have assigned the work of the firm to three categories: a hard core of activities, always identified with the enterprise; a variable set, sometimes done by the firm and sometimes contracted-out; and a fringe element of functions that usually are performed by others. At times the formulation of this "mix" changes rapidly. On the other hand, it may be stable for long periods. It is a reasonable presumption that questions of rights arise in periods of change and are quiescent when the mix is stable.

In a given economy at any one period of time, industrial firms will exhibit different mixes composed of hard-core, variable, and fringe activities. These differences will be a function of factors such as industry type, technological change, ratio of labor cost to total cost, etc. It would be useful to classify firms according to content of mix and then endeavor to determine the specific factors responsible for the various patterns. Even more valuable would be research on changes in composition over time in a series of firms in different industries.

In our study the problem involved the movements of only one major function, maintenance and construction, among the three categories, core, variable, and fringe. In terms of Thorp's (1924) classification of the structure of manufacturing companies, maintenance and construction plays the role of a convergent function, an auxiliary service which contributes to the main activity of the firm, e.g., producing automobiles, but is not a direct part of it. Thus maintenance and construction is not inherently a basic core activity. In rare instances, some noted self-contained industrial empires, such as DuPont and Ford, may have approached this condition in the past. However, as a general rule the total function has tended to fall in the variable category—some of the work being done by the firm and some being contracted-out. Of course, when maintenance and construction is broken down into its component parts, ranging from major construction to routine maintenance, these parts fall in all three categories, core, variable, and fringe.

Historically, major construction projects most frequently have occupied the fringe area. Our survey of seventy-four plants in seven metropolitan areas revealed that roughly four-fifths of the firms contracted-out all their major construction. On the other hand, routine maintenance has tended to be a core function, although this pattern is changing. Three-fifths of the firms performed all their routine maintenance internally. Minor construction, modernization, and nonroutine maintenance have tended to fall in the variable category. Four-fifths of the firms contracted-out some of this work and did some with inside forces.

One would assume that moving work out of the core and fringe categories would be a most sensitive matter and that shifts of work traditionally in the variable category would not be as touchy because these jobs would not be fixed as firmly as the property of either an inside or an outside group. While these assumptions have validity, we found that conflicting property claims were by no means limited to the more sensitive changes. It also should be noted that the idea of a supportive or convergent function did not indicate properly the sensitive nature of transfers of the maintenance and construction function from one category to another. Labor has been an important component of this work, and thus empires of men as well as materials have changed hands. For instance, moving maintenance and construction jobs outside the firm has served to shift into the hands of outsiders a significant segment of territory encompassed by the crucial inside employment relationship boundary.

PATTERNS AND TRENDS IN THE CONTRACTING OF INDUSTRIAL WORK

Historical background

Historically, there have been marked changes in the overall mix of core, variable, and fringe activities in the industrial firm. Moreover, historical evidence reveals that the assignment of activities to the fringe category is not a new development. A classic case is the farming out of certain functions in the early stages of industrialization when a great demand arises for the services of those who are able to control scarce and badly needed resources. Labor is a significant item, for some means has to be found to lure workers from rural areas and villages to the centers of industry. Thus, the labor contractor, or labor boss as he is sometimes called, has been a familiar figure in this phase of industrial development. The sirdar in India is one example (Ornati, 1955). Another is the labor contractor who served British industry well into the nineteenth century. Technological and organizational factors made the contract system the most feasible method of bringing labor to the early English industrial plants (Bendix, 1956). The labor contractors were successful where other methods might have failed because they were able to maintain a personalized master-apprentice relationship with their workers. In both England and India these men often were regarded as ruthless exploiters, although in some cases they simply were passing on the hard bargains that industry had forced them to accept. Despite the fact that these men were at the economic mercy of the industrialists, they were known for their independence, another durable contractor characteristic that has persisted through the ages.

In the early period of English industrialization, subcontractors also organized the process of production, sometimes at the plant site, as in the metal industries, and sometimes serving as a link between scattered cottage workers and the entrepreneur. As part of the "putting-out" system, the subcontractors agreed to deliver a given quality and quantity of goods at a set price. Some cottage workers owned their equipment; others were forced to lease it at high charges. The form of subcontracting system depended on the technology and the consequent degree of concentration in particular industries. Early industrialists fought the move toward integration of the activities of the firm that eventually brought an end to putting-out. They feared the consequences of losing these contractor-sponsored buffer groups, who absorbed many of the risks of the market.

One can readily observe that the historic functions of contractors have persisted—risk-taking in periods of technological change and unsteady markets and the supplying and management of labor, especially when workers are difficult to enlist and control or are needed only seasonally or sporadically. In the past, these functions, by their very nature, seemed to lead to abuses, such as the exploitation of workers, which in turn encouraged repeated moves toward revolt and reform. But despite this fact, contracting has been a particularly durable institution, playing a continuing role as a component of the industrial scene.

It would not be accurate to refer to trends toward contracting-out in the late 1950s and early 1960s as a return to putting-out or labor jobbing, for subcontracting has served different functions at different stages of industrial development. Changing technologies and managerial requirements have necessitated changes in the relationship of the contractor to the firm. As will be noted in Chapter 7, in some cases the contractor has moved far beyond his basic role as a holder and organizer of a pool of labor and equipment—to more complex relationships wherein he integrates into the structure and problems of a particular organization.

Research and theory

The related questions of vertical integration, diversification, make or buy, and contracting-out have been discussed and researched periodically since the early 1920s. There was a spurt of publication in the early twenties (1924–1925); in the early thirties (1930–1934); in the late thirties and early forties (1938–1942); in the late forties and early fifties (1949–1951); and finally a more persistent interest in the late fifties and early sixties (1955–1964). Peak efforts seemed to coincide with periods when vertical integration and allied questions became political, legal, or collective bargaining issues. There has been relatively little in the way of further development based on preceding efforts, and, considering the significance of the problem, only a few examples of general theory relating to the organization of the functions of the firm. The work of Thorp and Crowder (1924, 1941), Stigler

(1951), and Gort (1962) constitutes the major interwoven chain of effort in the field. Of most direct interest for our problem were attempts to link the composition of the mix of core, variable, and fringe activities to both the stages of development of an industry and the phase of the business cycle.

Stages of development

With regard to economic theory-building in this area, Stigler (1951) probably has made the most important contribution to date. He used as his point of departure Adam Smith's theorem, "The division of labor is limited by the extent of the market." Stigler's law of vertical integration stems from the almost common-sense notion that, when industry can supply contract firms with an adequate volume of business, such firms will be established to serve industrial needs. In other words, a given function has to increase to a size sufficient to support a specialized firm. Thus, a new industry often must meet its own needs —design, build, and maintain its own equipment, for instance. A vertically integrated structure may be the only available organizational strategy.

On the other hand, the process of vertical disintegration—assigning functions to specialists—is characteristic of the middle period of vigorous maturity in an industry. Stigler concluded, "If one considers the full life of an industry, the dominance of vertical disintegration is surely to be expected." However, the process of disintegration will be reversed if an industry begins to decline. Forced to maintain constant overhead expenses with a decreasing volume of business, the firm in the declining industry may "pull back" work formerly contracted. Subsidiary, auxiliary, and complementary industries are affected adversely as the demand for their products and services diminishes.

Integration and diversification

The picture of movement between integration and specialization becomes more complex when diversification is added as a third strategy. The legal and employment boundaries of the firm may be extended by diversification as well as by integration. The integrating firm combines several stages of production, as these are variously defined, while the diversifying firm achieves a heterogeneous output in order to move into new markets. Gort (1962) has found a growing trend toward more diversification in large manufacturing firms—a trend that quickened in the 1950s. Integration reduces dependence on outside suppliers of goods and services; diversification reduces the firm's dependence on its primary product. The diversifying firm typically selects industries with a high rate of technological change and may be seeking to compensate for weaknesses in its primary field.

From the standpoint of our problem, contracting-out, Gort's excellent study produced a most interesting finding, namely, that integration and diversification tended to be alternate and competing corporate strategies. One can extrapolate from this result that diversifying firms may lose interest in large maintenance and construction divisions, preferring instead a hand in a number of product markets, with a neat, trimmed-down investment in each enterprise. The impetus to integrate in order to control one enterprise well may lose out to the managerial requirements of a diversified operation.

Specialization and diversification may prove to be interrelated organizational trends, but our research also uncovered an outlet for diversification that had its roots in integration. Firms were diversifying into markets for services that formerly represented integration activities. Gort found that, for his 111 large firms, entry into manufacturing operations was more common than entry into nonmanufacturing, but services represented one of the rising outlets for participation in nonmanufacturing activity. According to Gort's data, 13 of the 16 companies engaged in construction were members of process industries, and 8 out of 9 in the repair service field were in fabrication industries. He estimated that a majority of the instances of entry into nonmanufacturing represent integration, but our research indicated that some of these activities constitute a form of diversification. We found process firms, such as oil companies, diversifying into construction and maintenance services for others and fabrication firms, such as electrical equipment manufacturers, moving into the large-scale repair service field.

Theory and practice

After we had examined the diverse trends in the field, it readily became apparent that a theory concerning the structure of the firm would need a large body of principles to cope with a variety of situations—differences in industry type, rate of industry growth, state of technology, and the nature of specific activities. It was clear that no simple formula would serve the purpose, even when the problem was limited to the structure of the firm as it related to a single functional area such as maintenance and construction.

For instance, there have been some classic exceptions to the hypothesized trend from integration to specialization. Some activities and some whole industries, e.g., seasonal fabrication industries such as garment manufacture and construction, always have been organized on a contract basis. To accommodate fluctuating requirements in these fields, subcontractors have held resources and allocated them as demand arose. A pool of skilled labor has been a prime component among the items held in reserve. In addition, subcontracting systems were very much a part of early industrialization. In some cases, functions such as the employment relationship had a history of initial membership in the fringe category, moving only later into the hard core of internally conducted activities.

For a variety of reasons the infant industries of the 1950s and 1960s may not resemble their integrated counterparts of earlier days. In the heavily government-supported missile field, subcontracting has been required of prime contractors, in part to spread the work among a number of firms and geographic areas. Moreover, this industry did not have to await the appearance of certain contract services. On the contrary, contractors were ready and eager, and established contractor's associations actively pressured for installation work that was not contracted-out.

Parallel developments also have eliminated one of the prime reasons for self-sufficiency in new undertakings—the lack of suppliers of service facilities. Manufacturers of new equipment have diversified into maintenance operations in order to meet potential customer objections that purchase would entail heavy expenditure for a new maintenance program. In addition, widespread leasing of equipment has served to reduce the need for self-sufficiency at any stage of industry growth or decline.

In general, self-sufficiency has become less essential from the standpoint of industrial management, because of the marked increase in the available market alternatives to integration. This statement applies to the industrial maintenance and construction field as well as to others. An example of the scope of this trend is the development called "industrial contract maintenance." Under this system a large contractor may handle the entire function for the industrial firm, supplying labor, supervision, materials, tools, equipment, and even the planning and scheduling of the maintenance operation. The number and kinds of specialized maintenance companies have been increasing annually, and the services they offer cover almost all aspects of structural, mechanical, electrical, and process operations. Even the most menial of routine maintenance services are supplied by large organizations that specialize in the design and analysis of these operations as well as in their actual conduct.

On the whole, the above theories and data point to integration as a self-bounding process, paving the way for the advent of those who will turn various aspects of the total package into specialized industries. The lag in this process has been cut down by factors such as the diversification of large industrial firms into the service field, thus permitting this activity to keep step with the latest technologies. On the other hand, certain functions served by specialists may be more efficiently replaced by an integrated structure, not because of the decline of an industry but because of further technological change (see Chapter 9). The long-run bounding of integration clearly is a product of economic and technological factors. In the short run, one is more likely to be impressed by the organizational failure of the self-bounding process.

Many industries in our economy have reached the stage where the "dominance of vertical disintegration" could take hold. Unfortunately, from the standpoint of the logic of economic process, internal structures that may have been established in the infant stages of the firm, e.g., service departments, have had durable qualities, and thus the potential for disintegration has not been realized as rapidly in actuality as it is in theory.

According to one view, the failure of integration to give way to market specialization is a product of inertia in the system—temporary resistance on the part of internal forces that will wither away. In the course of our research we encountered cases in which the withering was delayed for a decade or more and the process was interrupted by periods of internal expansion rather than contraction. In this vein, some theorists have posited that integration also can be a cumulative, or self-reinforcing, process. In their study of the petroleum industry, DeChazeau and Kahn (1959, p. 43) speak of the "persistent flowering of integration in the face of a probable decline in the need for it."

The explanation for this phenomenon stands in sharp contrast to the rigorous economic logic often advanced for specialization. The self-reinforcing factors that promote integration tend to have the flavor of unreason. DeChazeau and Kahn (1959, p. 43) point to the role of cost calculations that obscure the actual expenses incurred by an internal operation, noting that "Common costs may make it appear uneconomic to slough off functions that standing on their own financial feet could not support their own required investment." Organizationally speaking, there were the familiar empire-building goals—management's pride in a growing function, with each extension broadening the scope of exposure to further extensions. Extending a function has also aided in the solution of a variety of managerial problems, such as the need to provide new opportunities for the advancement of subordinates.

Later chapters will present some of the findings of our research regarding the self-reinforcing process (see Chapter 8). The mere fact of empire-building may be dismissed as "old hat." However, the above account is interesting partly because it occurs in an economic rather than a sociological work. Moreover, important questions need to be answered. When does internal empire-building hold sway, and what factors serve to discourage it? In noncompetitive enterprises, such as public utilities, or in enterprises where the size of the labor force is not a key element affecting competitive position, one would anticipate a greater tolerance of the cumulative, self-reinforcing process in maintenance and construction departments; in competitive enterprises where the labor force is a key element, one might expect the self-bounding process to be more common. Some elements in this distinction seem to be reflected in differences between process and fabrication industries that will be noted in Chapter 4.

Business-cycle factors

A final body of theory has related shifts in the boundaries of the firm to the phase of the business cycle. Again, economists have emphasized the unreasoning nature of the response in the expansion period. In an early statement of this position Jewkes (1930, p. 633) notes, "A period of prosperity and expanding profits will tend to stimulate integration. Boom conditions will often weaken caution and lead to uneconomic expansion, both in degree and direction. More important still is the internal pressure which accumulated reserves exert in a concern which is flourishing and growing rapidly." Jewkes also finds that a period of depression has a reverse effect. This phenomenon is reflected in the decline of vertical integration in the 1930s. Oxenfeldt (1956) has observed the same pattern of response in the case of the "make or buy" decision.

Thus, there appears to be a cyclical or systematic bias with respect to the assignment of the work of the industrial firm to outsiders. The decisions to "make" and to do work with inside forces have tended to be phenomena of prosperous times. Conversely, the decisions to "buy" and to contract-out have tended to be more popular alternatives in times of economic adjustment or depression. However, during depressed periods, management may have made short-run adaptations that moved in the opposite direction by calling back work formerly contracted in order to minimize layoffs. But, inevitably, the pressure to become more efficient increases, and operations are subjected to cost tests and other proofs of effectiveness. Firms may well conclude that they can improve their position as buyer by contracting work formerly done internally, especially if this decision is reinforced by problems of skills and equipment obsolescence and the need for investment capital.

Oxenfeldt (1956) suggests an organizational explanation for the positive correlation between decisions to do work inside and periods of prosperity. According to him, the inside bias is partly a matter of the timing of these decisions. That is, they tend to appear on the agenda during prosperous times. Business is good, and to keep pace, the firm's requirements are increasing. At this point the decision to invest in more equipment often is accompanied by a decision to build new facilities or to institute new maintenance programs. The possession of surplus funds or the availability of attractive arrangements for borrowing them encourages the decision to expand internally—to add the new activity to the core group.

This prosperity-borne bias toward inside operation unquestionably has served to slow the process of vertical disintegration prescribed in the self-bounding theories and to strengthen the hand of the empire builder. Our research was initiated in 1957. Since that time, one recession has followed another, and there has been little opportunity to witness boom-inspired decisions to expand internal maintenance and construction programs. The recovery phases in the cycles have not lasted long enough to sustain themselves, and short periods of brighter economic outlook probably have not provided a sufficient base for an expansionist psychology to develop.

Economic forecasts seem to indicate that the decade 1960–1970 will continue to be characterized by frequent economic adjustments. Thus, there should be fewer optimistic actions to expand internally and more gradual moves to reconsider the current status of operations and to move activities from the core to the variable and fringe categories whenever this step seems advisable and feasible.

SUMMARY

This chapter has sketched the gross outlines of the competition between the inside and outside forces for the work of the industrial firm. As far as the rise and fall of the fortunes of the inside forces is concerned, their potential for advancement seems to be greatest at certain stages in the growth of the firm and industry and in certain phases of the business cycle. Despite a number of classic exceptions to the rule, the most favorable period for entrenchment as a core activity occurs in the initial stages of a firm's growth. In addition, periods of prosperity yield a variety of investment decisions that serve to accelerate the expansion of the inside forces. However, the initial advantage of the inside forces is becoming a less dependable phenomenon, because an increasing number of market alternatives to integration are available to the new industrial enterprise; e.g., a new chemical plant may install contract maintenance instead of hiring its own crew. Diversification also appears to be a trend that reinforces tendencies toward vertical disintegration.

It seems clear that, for the contracting-out problem, the relevant boundaries of the firm are not those set by the limits of its activities. The decision whether to invest in an inside function or contract-out involves the potential creation of another boundary. This boundary is based on the source of the employment relationship and separates the work of the inside and the outside forces. Activities located within the inside boundary of the employment relationship have had a strong self-perpetuating quality that has served as a brake on the operation of "normal" economic process.

However, a combination of economic and technological factors can promote an environment less favorable and perhaps even hostile to the inside forces. Issues are created as core work is assigned to the variable and fringe category. The inside forces are placed on the defensive— struggling to retain the gains they secured earlier. These are the gross outlines. Chapter 4 will supply some of the details of the competitive picture.

chapter 4

Economic, Technological, and Structural Factors

In this chapter we turn to some of the specific economic, technological, and structural factors in the competition between the inside and outside forces for the work of the industrial firm. These factors also have served to condition the climate for the management rights issue and have enabled us to predict when and where this issue is likely to arise. Some of the factors have been amenable to control by immediate members of the inside and outside forces; others have been a part of the larger matrix within which they conducted their efforts—matters to which they had to adjust in order to be effective.

ECONOMIC FACTORS

The cost picture

Logically, the relative costs of two alternative procedures should play a significant role in determining their respective competitive positions. Unfortunately, the price competition between the inside and outside forces has tended to be an abstruse matter. Management is not cued to this problem continually. In fact, day-to-day decisions regarding the use of either existing inside forces or outside contractors often have seemed to be bereft of computational elegance. As indicated in Chapter 1, the same situation apparently has prevailed on the other side of the Iron Curtain.

Certainly, any notion that every job is costed in detail to determine the exact amount of inside and outside charges is completely unrealistic. Our data on consecutive series of management decisions involving contracting-out indicated that detailed costs for the two alternatives were calculated, quite reasonably, when some question was anticipated in the form of pressures from either inside or outside groups (see Chapter 14). Thus, precise calculation may be a response to challenges to "rights." Some managers cited more rigorous cost computations as a side benefit of union challenge. More commonly, a cost estimate was computed for only one alternative. But even if calculations were made for both alternatives, these data may not have been the determining factor in the decision. An overwhelming majority, 88 per cent of the sample, stated that contracting-out might be chosen for reasons such as speed and efficiency even though it was not the cheaper alternative.

There was a substantial amount of variability in the rigor with which managers made their cost estimates. About 10 per cent made no appraisals, and 30 per cent made rough calculations that the men in the field designated as "guesstimates." Failure to estimate costs was not due to negligence. Rather, in these cases the nature of facilities or "political" factors meant that only one of the two alternatives was feasible. The remaining three-fifths of the firms moved above the guesstimate level to employ varying degrees of precision in their assessments of the relative cost picture. Various aspects of the cost question did prove to be related to technology and structure, but the above comments about union impact on costing behavior evidently referred to short-run effects. The relative complexity of the cost system apparently was an internal managerial affair and did not appear to shift in general character in response to union challenge or to become one of battery of management defenses in this area. Nevertheless, the data indicated that a picture of a universally casual approach to cost calculations would be an exaggeration, delightful as this prospect might appear to the confirmed institutionalist.

The kind of accurate assessments that are possible for production costs generally have not been feasible in maintenance and construction because of the lack of standardization in operations. Many managers expressed both considerable interest in more accurate cost data and discouragement about the possibility of obtaining them. Brandt's research (1960, p. 201) on contracting-out in refineries confirmed this point. He noted:

> It is difficult to assign decisive cost to a maintenance project but it is even more difficult to accumulate comparative costs on maintenance work because the rapid changes in a refinery are constantly changing the nature of the maintenance work to be done. Thus, a statement by a maintenance manager that his workers can perform work at a lower cost than contractors is a difficult statement to prove or disprove.

In other words, the problems associated with differentiating relative inside and outside costs have been part and parcel of a general measurement problem. However, developments that began in the late 1950s have increased the probability of reducing this area to measureable units. PERT (Program Evaluation Review Technique) and CPM (Critical Path Method) were developed to solve problems such as those involved in maintaining, operating, and managing increasingly complex chemical and mechanical processes. (Franklin, 1962.) Techniques such as these hold the promise of more efficient planning and scheduling and more effective cost control. In addition, developments involving the virtual elimination of the subjective aspects of job performance in advanced process technology should serve to increase the potential for accurate costing. Systems have been developed that provide automatic control of equipment maintenance through the use of modern data processing techniques to schedule, report, and evaluate maintenance plans and practices. Again, these methods should furnish a means for continual measurement and control in this area.

The impact of a potential revolution in determining the relative costs of the inside and outside alternatives could have a tremendous effect on the competition between the two forces. Much of what was observed in our study may pass on into the realm of folklore. The traditional organizational slack in the maintenance cost field long has provided judgmental leeway for decisions regarding contracting-out. This leeway has also had other organizational implications, for departmental heads seeking relief from budgetary pressures become dependent upon it. (This point is developed further in Chapter 8.) Thus, it should be noted that rationalizing the cost competition between the inside and outside forces may lead to the uncovering of a variety of other now hidden cost problems.

Given good cost yardsticks, economic logic dictates a rather simple process for resolving the competition between the inside and outside forces. Ideally, inside cost data would not be needed in many cases. If contractors were plentiful and competed with one another freely, the economic incentive for management to establish internal service departments would be reduced considerably. A firm normally does not integrate into a market in which it can buy unlimited quantities of a service at the going rate and in which suppliers are receiving either a normal or a subnormal return. However, a firm does integrate into a market in which services are scarce and/or expensive. If these latter conditions prevail, industrial management may then establish its own facility, which serves as a competitor of actual or potential suppliers of services. The firm's moving away from the outside market may have the effect of bringing the outside market into line. The mere threat of integration into a field may serve as a sufficient control, especially if the cost of entry is low. Moreover, contractors either would not enter or would leave fields in which they were unable to compete with the inside function.

It took little effort to uncover numerous troublesome points in this competitive model. Although contractors competed vigorously with one another on certain items, they failed to do so on others. The inside function often could not move readily into and out of its role as competitor in response to emerging shifts in the price differential. In addition, substantial information blocks existed. The contractor "on the street" was unaware of opportunities in the plant, just as the manager in the plant may have been unaware of the nature of the services that were available from outside sources.

Salient aspects of cost

Our research indicated not so much a managerial failure to consider costs as a selective bias regarding the elements considered. Other studies have produced parallel findings. While our data pointed to a selective emphasis on certain cost elements, another study revealed the existence of an overall cost bias. Among managers in a Middle Western metropolitan center, the details of the relative cost question were subsumed in an unfavorable construction industry cost image, dating back over the years. Despite the fact that prices apparently no longer were out of line, the high cost reputation was still alive. This study described the impact of the image as follows:

> While considerations such as cost . . . may be cited, they are frequently little more than rationalizations of attitudes currently held by plant management toward the unions and contractors. In other words, since even such items as cost, efficiency and quality are not completely objective,

they are interpreted within the context of the image of the construction industry and collective bargaining patterns [Sobel and Brown, 1960, p. 28].

Moreover, there seemed to be evidence that plants operating in the locality were influenced by this unfavorable cost image in their decision whether to contract-out or do work inside. It was found that one-third of the sample of sixty-one companies maintained that it was not possible for contracting-out to be cheaper than the internal operation.

Our own data indicated that for the various major maintenance and construction functions one-half to one-fourth of the firms held an image of the outside forces as being more costly. One-half took this position regarding routine maintenance, two-fifths for nonroutine maintenance, three-tenths for modernization and minor construction, and one-fourth for major construction. There was no indication that these estimates were as firmly held as those recounted above, but the data do provide an assessment of the extent of the cost bias against the outside forces. In addition, these figures might have furnished an estimate of the size of the management groups that did not regard themselves as having valuable rights regarding the contracting-out of work in various areas. However, data presented later in this chapter indicate that management positions on both costs and rights may be a function of underlying technological factors.

The findings of this and other research certainly have dispelled the notion that relative cost calculations are invariably precise. With technological advance, these cost data may constitute a generally available by-product of the computer, but, in the absence of such a source of data, in many cases it would be unreasonable for management to compute every cost differential or to exert the effort needed to acquire the requisite information. Especially if the potential gain is low, these data do not justify their expense in terms of managerial time and other scarce resources.

Relative wage rates

When we moved from cost data in general to specific items, the picture changed in the sense that selective biases were revealed. There were certain factors upon which management did focus, and the size of the outside craft rates was the prime item. Union and management members of the construction industry set these rates during the course of collective bargaining. As noted above, this industry is competitive in many ways, but the rates for labor are an outstanding exception to this rule. In effect, the unions control both rates and entry, and as construction is a local product, labor can effectively tie up the local market. In most cases, the rates of internal maintenance and construction workers were lower than those of the outside craftsman. Outstanding examples were instances in which low-skilled work such as building labor cost $3 an hour when obtained from outside sources and only $1.80 under the inside union's contract. Of course, in other cases the outside labor rates was $2.10, and the inside rate may have been only 10 or 20 cents below that. A notable exception to the prevailing direction of the difference in rates was found in the case of some outside maintenance services, especially janitorial work.

For our example, plant averages for six representative crafts, electrician, plumber, roofer, sheet-metal worker, painter, and building or general laborer, were compared with outside craft rates in each of the seven metropolitan areas included in the study. The differentials for basic wage rates ranged from $1.36 for the highest to $0.55 for the lowest. Outside craft groups have argued that industrial management should consider fringe benefits and a variety of overhead factors in computing these differentials, but in general little heed was paid to this admonition.

In our sample, one-fifth of the cases charged little or no overhead, and in three-fifths a moderate 15 to 50 per cent was charged. Only one-fifth exceeded this level (see Table 4–3). Thus, the overhead charge often did not serve to erase the wage rate differential favoring the inside group. In any case, the high visibility of the raw wage rate data was hard to combat. Interestingly, estimates of cost-related factors such as speed and quality of work generally did little to harm the position of the outside forces. With regard to speed, they were adjudged either as fast or faster in 79 per cent of the cases. The quality of the work of the outside forces was found to be the same as or better than that of the inside forces in 74 per cent of the plants. But management interviewees focused on the wage rate question. They stressed the absolute size of craft rates a great deal, pointing in dismay to "plumbers who earn more than vice-presidents." Another manager remarked, "They're getting five dollars an hour now and it'll be ten by the middle of this decade."

Some of the emphasis on high outside rates may have been self-serving, but this position also seemed to have an effect on actual behavior. It was apparent that for the industrial firm the most visible cost elements were those relating to outside craft and industrial plant wage rates. There appeared to be good reason for this quality of high visibility. While some factors were roughly equivalent for the two alternatives, labor costs generally were different and therefore they constituted a consistently relevant factor in the management decision. Moreover, labor constituted an important part of the total cost of maintenance and construction operations, and it also was an item for which comparative data on rates were readily available.

Our data seemed to confirm the existence of a community cost image for outside craft work. This image showed up very clearly in the extreme cases. In the area with the highest craft rates, this factor was mentioned almost invariably. At the same time, in the area where craft rates were lowest, appropriate recognition was given to this fact. Obtaining a measure of the effect of sentiments of this type is far from easy. Our data permitted the making of a rough estimate and, within their limits, seemed to indicate that there was some relationship to actual behavior. The average amount of maintenance and construction work contracted-out for the sample of plants in each of the seven metropolitan areas was related to the average craft-industrial wage rate for each community as these were reflected in our sample data. The Spearman correlation coefficient for the ranked data was −.76[1] Within the limits of these data, it appeared that, the greater the wage differential favoring the inside forces, the smaller the amount of work contracted, and vice versa. Even though the samples of plants in each metropolitan area were small in size, the range of plant employment size and industry type in each one was broad enough to enable us to dismiss these as factors possibly biasing the results.

It appears that, as long as wage rate differentials continue to exist between community craft and inside industrial workers, the size of these differentials will have some biasing effect on the decisions of management regarding contracting-out. It also seems clear that factors narrowing the gap between inside and outside rates will favor the cause of the formerly disadvantaged outside forces. This narrowing could occur either through increase in the inside rates or through efforts of the outside forces to become more competitive. Since 1955 continuing contract maintenance agreements for particular plants and projects have specified conditions which, in contrast to standard craft requirements, conform more closely to the inside union model. However the basic rates remained inviolable. The details of these agreements will be presented in Chapter 7.

TECHNOLOGICAL FACTORS

Technological change: the underlying thrust

While economic factors may have intensified shifts to contracting-out, there were many indications that technological change provided the underlying thrust. The increasing rate of this change should serve to open repeatedly the question of integration versus specialization and diversification. For instance, new technologies have been making pos-

---

[1] This result was significant at the 5 per cent level.

sible the fractionating of processes formerly necessarily conducted by one firm. At one time interruptions were costly, but now certain operations can profitably be turned over to others. In advanced process technology tasks have been rationalized to the point where contractors can enter with a minimum of disturbance.

In the past the shell was the main item requiring maintenance in a building, but gradually emphasis has shifted to the contents—to mechanical systems and utilities. The latter may need the services of specialists who can divide their attention among a number of industrial customers. In addition, interest in contracting-out has been stimulated by a reluctance on the part of industrial management to invest in equipment and methods that may rapidly become obsolete in an era of continued technological advance.

Process and fabrication technology

Historically, the maintenance and construction function has had a very different role in process and fabrication industries, and this difference proves to be significant for the contracting-out problem of our study. (Differences in managerial problems in these two types of industries will be treated in Chapter 15.) We found that in process industries, such as oil refining, the maintenance staff constituted 40 to 50 per cent of the force of hourly employees and maintenance work tended to be the equivalent of production in a fabrication industry. An additional difference stemmed from the fact that the process industries operated on a continuous flow basis. Stoppages typically incurred severe economic penalties. Fabrication involved the assembly of separate units of output and less severe penalities for interruptions. It was obvious that process technology provided the stronger base for union leverage. This vulnerability may be a prime explanation for the stronger management rights position found in process industries (see Chapters 5 and 6).

To ensure reliable performance in process plants, management has tended to employ large inside maintenance crews which handle a major portion of the work. In our sample, the average size of the maintenance and construction force in the process plants was 480, while in the fabrication plants it was 265. For the sample as a whole, the average crew size was 355. The sample had roughly equal proportions of process and fabrication plants in the various size ranges. Thus this result was not biased significantly by disparities in the distribution of plant employment sizes for the two major industry groups (see Table 4-1). Process plants has a slightly higher average size—4,400 as compared with 4,100 for fabrication. Maintenance and construction craft

Table 4-1 *Plant employment size and industry type*

| Plant employment size | Industry type | | | |
| | Process plants | | Fabrication plants | |
	No.	%	No.	%
1,000 and under	5	16	9	20
1,001–1,500	8	26	11	26
1,501–2,500	7	23	8	19
2,501–5,000	5	16	6	14
5,000 and over	6	19	9	20
Total	31	100	43	99

groups constituted 10.8 per cent of the total work force in process industries and a smaller proportion, 6.5 per cent, in fabrication.

As one might anticipate, process management in general was not a strong proponent of contracting-out. Only 26 per cent of the companies studied favored a policy of contracting-out as much as possible, whereas almost half the fabrication firms took this position. Seventy-one per cent of the process managements advocated contracting-out as little as possible. This view was held by only 40 per cent of the management groups in fabrication. Small proportions of both industry groups had no set policy or predisposition in this area (see Table 4-2). Translating policy into action, the thirty-one process establishments contracted-out an average of 29 per cent of the total dollar expenditure for maintenance and construction. The forty-three fabrication plants contracted-out an average of 48 per cent (see Fig. 4-1). The data upon which these estimates were based were variable in quality, as they generally are. Some sets of data were excellent and detailed; the quality of others was only fair. However, the direction of the results was unmistakable. Thus, maintenance and construction was more likely to be a core activity in process industries and a variable or fringe activity in fabrication.

Gort (1962) presents a similar finding in his estimate of the ratio of

Table 4-2 *Industry type and policy with regard to contracting-out*

| Policy | Industry type | | | |
| | Process plants | | Fabrication plants | |
	No.	%	No.	%
Favoring contracting-out	8	26	21	48
Favoring the internal function	22	71	17	40
No set policy	1	3	5	12
Total	31	100	43	100

integration employment to total employment for his 1954 sample of 111 large enterprises. He found the lowest average ratio, 9.7 per cent, in transportation equipment, a fabrication industry, and the highest average ratio, 67.3, in petroleum, a process industry. We used the data in Gort's table 29 (p. 81), The Relation of Integration Employment to Total Employment, to calculate an average ratio of 26 per cent for process industries and 17 per cent for fabrication. These data provided a measure that essentially represents the inverse of contracting-out. Therefore, they served as an indirect confirmation of our findings, for they indicated that the process industries had a higher average proportion of workers engaged in auxiliary "integration" activities.

Technology, cost behavior, and management rights

Fabrication and process management exhibited other behavior consistent with the pattern outlined above. The fabrication group studied seemed more likely to think in terms of individual job costs and to encourage competition between the internal operation and outside groups by opening more decisions to both alternatives. Nine of the plants in the sample employed internal profit and loss control systems for the maintenance and construction function, and all these were members of the fabrication category. (Under this plan, inside departments bid for work in direct competition with outsiders.)

The question of overhead charges also tends to divide process and fabrication industries. While one-half or more of both groups favored moderate charges of from 15 to 50 per cent, 80 per cent of those who charged either low or no overhead were process firms. Similarly, 80 per cent of those who charged high overhead were fabrication plants (see Table 4-3).

Consistent with this finding for the question of overhead charges is the process management's tendency to regard contracting-out as generally more expensive than the internal function. Only one-third of the managements took the opposite view that contracting-out was

Table 4-3 *Size of overhead charge in relation to industry type*

	Industry type			
	Process plants		*Fabrication plants*	
Size of overhead charge	*No.*	*%*	*No.*	*%*
Low	13	42	2	5
Medium	15	48	28	65
High	3	9	13	30
Total	31	99	43	100

cheaper, but almost half of the fabrication managements felt that it was less costly (see Table 4-4).

We were curious about the relationship between assessments of economic matters such as relative costs and "ideological" viewpoint. It was hypothesized that there would be some consistency between these two phenomena—that strong advocacy of management rights would have a logical economic basis, reflected in a position that contracting-out was cheaper. In Chapter 5 it is indicated that one-third (twenty-five) of the plants in the sample rated as strong traditional rights proponents with regard to contracting-out. An examination of these managements' positions on the cost question revealed that the group as a whole was split almost evenly—twelve maintained that contracting-out was cheaper, and thirteen held that it was more expensive. However, the latter group included 73 per cent of the strong rights managements in process industries and only 20 per cent of those in fabrication. Those viewing contracting-out as less costly included four process firms (27 per cent) and eight fabrication (80 per cent). Fabrication management seemed to be taking the more consistent stand that contracting-out was cheaper, and therefore it was insisting on its right to engage contractors.

However, it is probable that both the cost position and the rights advocacy of the strong rights groups in process and fabrication industries are manifestations of underlying factors related to technology and structure. In light of the present focus on technological factors, the process case is the more interesting at this point. Thus the process positions on rights and costs can be interpreted as two separate reactions to some of the aspects of process technology described above— primarily the need for an uninterrupted, closely controlled operation.

It should be noted that in some process industries, such as oil refining and chemicals, in which labor costs have been a low percentage of total costs (about 10 per cent), management has been less likely to maintain a close watch on this category and probably has been more

Table 4-4 *Estimation of the comparative cost of contracting-out and employing inplant forces*

| | Industry type | | | |
| | Process Plants | | Fabrication plants | |
Cost of contracting-out	No.	%	No.	%
Higher	20	65	10	23
The same	1	3	8	19
Lower	10	32	20	46
Don't know	0	0	5	12
Total	31	100	43	100

inclined to concentrate on matters such as the capital structure and the purchase of raw materials. Interestingly, in interviews and in response to questions, process management seemed to be greatly concerned about the matter of costs. However, the question of relative costs was more fully institutionalized in fabrication industries, and, in general, there was greater competition between the inside and outside forces.

Technological change and the organization of industrial work

All these findings would seem to indicate that the outside forces—the contractors and their men—should continue to focus on fabrication plants for advancement. But the period covered by our study is a discouraging one for persons attempting to draw definitive pictures. Recent technological change and the introduction of new concepts, such as industrial contract maintenance, have served to make the process field the site of innovations that may have far-reaching effects. Modern integrated process plants and older ones that have undergone conversion were especially amenable to the new arrangements. Moreover, in the more technologically advanced plants, the lines between fabrication and process, between inside and outside staff, and between production and maintenance were beginning to blur. As manufacturing made increasing use of automatic controls, it became less a fabrication and more a process operation. But this development did not mean a shift to the old process-type emphasis on internal forces, for as the costliness of stoppages increased and self-maintaining machines became available, plants were being engineered to go as much as two years between overhauls. Thus, it made less sense to keep a staff to take care of the major maintenance and more sense to hire a contractor to do it.

For instance, almost all the new oil refineries made extensive use of contractors for both turnaround and routine maintenance. Both our research and that of Brandt (1960) confirm this point. New refineries were generally more highly automated and integrated, so that a shutdown on any unit for more than a few hours required a shutdown of the entire plant. Formerly, a single unit could be closed down, permitting a distribution of the work load throughout the year, but in the integrated plant the whole plant was shut down for turnaround (major overhaul), creating widely spaced peak demands for labor. A good example of the impact of technological change on the organization of work was found at a modern integrated refinery, where the entire maintenance program was handled under contract maintenance. A basic crew of 200 to 300 men took care of all but heavy seasonal work loads. This contract force was enlarged temporarily to meet the demands of major overhauls. An "old-fashioned" refinery would have employed an internal force of about 5,000 to do this work. This contractor had similar arrangements in the chemical, rubber, and cement industries.

The process plant, until the 1960s the special preserve of the inside forces, exhibited the greatest potential for change as well as the greatest potential for creating rights issues in the struggle over work formerly allocated to inside crews. This is a prime example of the execution of the sensitive shift of an activity from the core to the fringe category.

It is highly possible that under complete automation the shift from core to fringe may be reversed. As the organization of work becomes fully integrated, some elements may be returned to the core category and others may be eliminated entirely. Even routine maintenance tasks will be greatly altered in factories that house machines rather than both machines and people. Thus, the contractor may again be serving his traditional role of taker of risks in periods of technological change. The potential impact of this development on the inside and outside forces will be dealt with in Part IV.

STRUCTURAL FACTORS

Plant employment size

In generalizing about trends in the organization of the work of the industrial firm, there is a tendency to ignore the fact that these trends have a differential effect on firms with varying technological and structural characteristics. Some aspects of the technological side of this question were presented in the preceding section. In this section we shall examine differences which are a function of structural factors, primarily plant employment size. It seems to be almost self-evident that the extent to which a firm engages in internal maintenance and construction work will be related to the size of the establishment. In our sample, plant employment size ranged from 230 in a food processing concern to 21,000 in a giant electrical machinery factory. Thus, the study did not include plants that were small, according to the commonly accepted criteria for membership in this category.

Adelman (1955, p. 320) hypothesizes that "The smallest firms appear to be specialists in a particular process." If this statement were generally true, then one would anticipate that the small plant's internal activities in the maintenance and construction field would be rather limited, especially in cases in which fifty or fewer workers were employed. However, during the 1960–1962 phase of this research, we encountered cases that proved to be exceptions to this rule. A striking

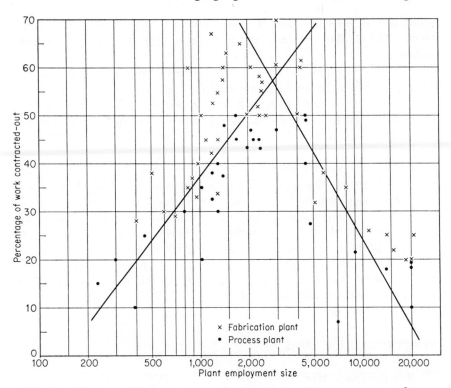

Fig. 4-1 *Plant employment size and percentage of maintenance and construction work contracted-out.*

example was a family-operated plant with a staff of about twenty-five workers. By working week ends, the president and two vice-presidents built a substantial addition to the plant. Similarly, the maintenance operation was conducted by younger members of the family.

An analysis of the relationship between percentage of the total dollar value of maintenance and construction work contracted-out and plant employment size indicated that "small" and "large" plants were the stronghold of the inside forces, while "middle-sized" concerns had a distinctly higher rate of contracting-out. These distinctions regarding size of establishment are appropriate only within the limits of our data (see Fig. 4-1).

In examining the data regarding the percentage of work contracted-out and plant employment size, we found no indication of a simple inverse linear relationship, with the proportion of work contracted-out decreasing as plant employment size increased. We had anticipated this inverse relationship, but instead there seemed to be two distinct forces in operation. The data could have been described by one continuous parabolic function, but, in view of the above observation, two separate functions seemed to be more logical. Percentage of work contracted-out proved to be a linear function of the $\log_{10}$ of plant size. The proportion of work contracted-out increases as we proceed from small to middle-sized range. Thus, for plant size 200 to 2,000, percentage of work contracted-out $= -93.3 + 43.6 \log_{10}$ (plant size). From middle to large size, the slope of the curve is negative. Thus for plant size 2,000 to 20,000, percentage of work contracted-out $= 271 - 61.7 \log_{10}$ (plant size). The straight line was drawn to approximate the mean position for each major plant size category. From the standpoint of the management rights focus on contracting-out, the second equation was the function of primary interest and also the one that promised to be the center of significant change.

The small plant

The first function reflected the need of the small plant to utilize fully its internal force by providing the essential core group of maintenance and construction employees with as much work as possible. In slow periods, maintenance and construction jobs were used as a fill-in for production crews. When work was scarce, union leaders were willing to relax the sacred dividing line between production and nonproduction tasks. Moreover, this general strategy enabled the small establishment to charge some capital improvements as current expenses.

Plants in this category tended to make full use of existing personnel, especially in the conduct of functions peripheral to the core purpose of the firm. New functions in the maintenance field were heaped on the shoulders of staff members who generally served diffuse (many-functioned) rather than specific (single-functioned) roles. In these companies, top management often was enthusiastic about this practice, but the head of maintenance sometimes responded in a fashion that was contrary to his traditional role of organizational empire-builder. Several mentioned the possibility of contracting-out as a means of reducing a burgeoning work load, some of which was outside the realm of competence of the staff. Empire-building seemed to be more commonly a forte of management in larger plants where new functions meant both new management positions and staff. Despite the case of the family-operated plant mentioned above, smaller plants, employing, say, fewer than fifty workers, probably would have difficulty in following the example of some of the "small" plants in our sample because of the almost complete lack of functionaries who could assume the additional tasks.

The head of a small metal products company, employing 400, with a maintenance and construction staff of 35, explained his position on contracting-out as follows:

We lost a contract six months ago. That cut our production work, so we put our men on carpentry. They made a 50 by 75 foot building to house a new machine. On another occasion when we didn't have enough orders for a two-shift operation, our nightshift workers were given the job of painting and cleaning the plant and making repairs. Some of them fixed the roof. We get other benefits from doing this. It enables us to retain a low capital investment, and we have to do that.

The manager of a food processing plant employing 26 maintenance and construction workers in a total staff of 230 expressed this opinion about contracting-out: "Contracting-out is an overhead cost, another expense to be paid out without receiving anything in return. Our men handle all routine maintenance and 90 per cent of the minor construction jobs. It is company policy to keep our force occupied."

The middle-sized plant

Plants in the middle-sized range were not so fully committed to the inside function (see Fig. 4-1). Their volume of business was adequate to permit them to specialize and to realize savings by contracting-out part of their operations, especially an auxiliary function like maintenance and construction. A case of this type was found in a medium-sized machinery firm that employed 1,900, with a staff of 40 maintenance and construction workers. In explaining the basis for his firm's policy, the plant manager remarked:

> Contractors can provide us workers with special skills. We find the cost of training these men prohibitive. Our own efforts to hire specialized craft labor haven't been successful. Besides, contracting takes care of our work load variations. Our staff cannot keep up with its regular maintenance work and also finish a special job fast enough. When our men do a job, it's a big headache for our plant engineer. They say they will pull off a couple of men to take care of it, but then something else comes up in the plant, and they give that preference. It shoots his schedule all to hell. Besides, there's the overtime. At time and one-half a job can run into a pretty penny.

The large plant

The second logarithmic function reflected the fact that, as plants become sufficiently large, they are able to support a continuously operating maintenance and construction function which supplies a substantial portion of their needs. Economies of scale can be realized. They might even form a subsidiary that offers services to other firms. Operations of this type were found in both process and fabrication industries. It can readily be seen that the forces acting on the large plant were quite different from those which induced the small establishment to favor inside performance of maintenance and construction work.

A large, self-sufficient plant in the transportation equipment industry employed 14,000, including a maintenance and construction force of 1,000. The plant manager gave the following description of the company's program:

> We have always done as much as possible ourselves. We have our own maintenance training program, and it has been extremely successful in increasing the abilities of our men. We feel that a big crew is necessary. We have the work, and we get what we want. We can do a better job, and the men are always there when we need them.

These data substantiate the point that, if and when shifts to contracting-out take place, the large plants should be the sensitive spots in future competition between inside and outside forces. While small plants may turn increasingly to contracting-out, it is doubtful that they will become the focus of equivalent intergroup conflict.

Future trends

There seems to be little doubt that plant employment size will drop drastically in the 1970s. According to a *Factory* survey of 952 manufacturing plants, a force of 1,000 workers may be close to the upper limit. This survey produced the following prediction regarding the plant of the future:

> Few new plants are expected to employ more than 1000 workers, and most new plants are trying to limit total employment to the 500–750 range. . . . In many new plants, management is building up its work force slowly to guard against inflated start-up employment. . . . The desire to hold actual employment to a minimum shows in extensive use of subcontract services. [2]

Thus, in years to come, plants with employment sizes as large as some of those included in our sample may be nonextant. It is of interest to speculate on the future relationship between plant employment size and the proportion of maintenance and construction work contracted-out. It may be that the answer to this question is rather simple —namely, that it is the wrong question to ask. For instance, a small automated operation, such as a paper mill, may be just as likely as its larger counterparts to contract infrequent overhauls or even the entire maintenance operation. In fact, the acceptance or rejection of contracting-out may very well lose its relation to plant employment size and focus only technological requirements.

[2] *Factory*, 1962, 120 (5):71–72.

SUMMARY

The competition between the inside and outside forces for the work of the industrial firm is shaped by economic, technological, and structural factors that also serve to condition the climate for the management rights issue. Providing a definitive picture of the action of these factors is difficult in view of the dynamic nature of the elements involved. Some of the relationships that appeared to be significant in our research may eventually either change or disappear.

The situation with regard to managerial assessment of the relative costs of the two alternatives, contract-out or use inside forces, is not so chaotic and imprecise as some have pictured it. Precise estimates of the cost of both alternatives tend to be made infrequently, generally when some question is anticipated. There is substantial variation among firms in the rigor with which cost calculations are made. In addition, there is considerable evidence of a selective bias regarding the cost elements considered. Industrial management seems to focus particularly on the size of the wage rate differential between the inside and outside forces.

While economic factors may have served to intensify shifts to contracting-out, there were many indications in our study that technological change provided the underlying thrust. From the standpoint of our research, one of the most interesting phenomena was the impact of technological advances in the process industries, the long-standing stronghold of the inside forces. Historically, the maintenance and construction function has had a very different role in process and fabrication industries. To ensure continuous and reliable performance, process plant management has tended to employ large inside maintenance crews to handle a major portion of the work. Our research findings indicated that, in contrast to process management, fabrication management was a strong proponent of contracting-out. Translating policy into action, fabrication companies contracted-out a larger proportion of work than those in process industries. Various organization costing practices of the two groups were related to these differing orientations. In general, the question of relative costs was more fully institutionalized in fabrication firms, and there was a greater encouragement of competition between the inside and outside forces.

Process management's position both on the relative cost question and on management rights seemed to be related to the underlying technological realities of these industries. However, recent technological change and the introduction of new concepts, such as industrial contract maintenance, have served to make the process field the site of far-reaching innovations. The trend in the early 1960s was toward greater emphasis on contracting-out, but under full automation some aspects of this trend may be reversed in both modern process and fabrication plants.

With regard to structural factors, we found that within the limits of the plant employment size range of our sample, 230 to 21,000, small and large plants were the preserve of the inside forces, while middle-sized concerns had a distinctly higher rate of contracting-out. It was predicted that this relationship of proportion of work contracted-out to plant employment size should gradually give way to one based almost entirely on technological factors.

From Chapters 3 and 4 it is apparent that economic and technological trends in the late 1950s and early 1960s served the cause of the outside forces more than that of their inside counterparts. Moreover, the relative positions of these two groups regarding shares of the work of the industrial firm were influenced significantly by factors outside the realm of control of either one. In contrast to the magnitude of these forces, the efforts of specific individuals and groups to pursue their respective interests seemed puny and ineffectual stopgaps at best. The process of technological change was a major factor in permitting the job property rights of both groups to revert to the control of industrial management.

Only some aspects of the cost picture and of organizational structure were under these groups' control to a significant extent. These, then, defined the area for effective competition and for the reassertion of job property rights. With regard to wage rates, a major cost item, both inside and outside union groups had considerable voice through collective bargaining. The fact that the rate per se rather than any more complicated calculation was the focus of the industrial manager's attention tended to give the inside forces an advantage. Conceivably, either group could proceed to cut rates as a means of driving the other from the field, but prospects for this eventuality were slight to say the least. Small adjustments in wage-related items probably represent the outer limits for concessions in response to pressures to remain competitive. Another alternative, agreements between the two groups that would serve to eliminate competition, is not an easily achieved solution in view of their long history of conflict. A development of this type undoubtedly would have to await prior changes in their organizational structures—changes that would provide for a closer amalgamation of the two groups or even an elimination of their separate identities. (The efforts of the inside and outside forces to create "cartel-type" divisions of the work of the industrial firm will be presented in detail in Part V.)

Apart from the dollars and cents aspects of the competition, the other phase over which these groups could exercise control involved some aspects of organization structure. In changing times, the main organizational virtue is flexibility, and the most beneficial activities from the standpoint of advancement are those which serve to promote ready adaptation to new requirements. This aspect of relations between the two competing forces will be discussed fully in Part IV.

This chapter concludes the general presentation of the larger inter-cultural, economic, and technological matrix within which the parties to the management rights and contracting-out issues were operating. These materials will provide a valuable background as we turn to the legalistic, organizational, and collective bargaining aspects of these problems. We shall continue to bring into our analysis the factors that constitute the larger matrix, for they will serve as a basis for placing realistic limits on assessments of specific events that might otherwise be judged out of proportion to their actual significance. Of course, this is a constant problem in the evaluation of elements in the atmos-phere of strong advocacy that surrounds issues in labor-management relations.

part iii

Management Rights:
Erosion and Irrevocable Losses

chapter 5

Trends and Tendencies in the Management Rights Area

Contracting-out involves a complex interest group structure and, as a result, an equally complex structure of rights and job property claims. In our study of this problem from an organizational viewpoint, the commonly accepted version of labor and management as two giant forces standing in opposition to one another proved to have little meaning. There were no united fronts in the contracting-out issue, but rather conflicting interests—diverse systems of rights and equities within each major group. For example, the inside engineering and service departments, the inside industrial unions and outside craft unions and contractors all asserted specific rights or property claims in

63

this area. Members of industrial management sought affirmation of their rights in alliance with the cause of either the inside or the outside unions, and the inside and outside unions took diverse positions regarding the rights of management.

The contracting-out issue has been fought on many fronts. Each front, legal, economic, or organizational, has its own specific history and system of logic, and each provides a different picture of contracting-out as a problem. In this chapter, the legalistic argument will be explored. When the rights aspects of an issue are abstracted from the total complex of elements that it represents, then substantive matters become the vehicle for expressing conflicting property claims. Thus, according to some lines of reasoning, management's failure to inform the inside union of its intent to contract-out diminished the firm's legal title to the action. Moreover, when contracting-out was reduced to the status of a rights issue, a substantial number of economic organizational data were thrown away in the process. What was the effect of this distortion? What were the implications for the quality of the ubiquitous legalistic solutions to contracting-out problems? Common conceptions in the management rights area were evaluated in the light of our empirical data regarding a specific problem. What was the value of these concepts as tools of analysis and guides to reality?

In line with our general plan of analysis, we shall examine the relationship of the rights issue to technological and structural factors. With regard to general structural factors, a legalistic position obviously is not self-enforcing. It must have available a means for defending its holder against challenges and "invasion" by contrary interests. In the United States, there was a strong theoretical approach to management rights, but in practice other, fairly similar societies, such as Canada, seemed to provide a firmer basis for the defense of these rights.

In Canada one found a mechanism that has tended to uphold the legalistic approach. Legislation requiring compulsory arbitration and no strikes during the life of a collective bargaining agreement was part of the pattern. Another aspect involved the use of judges and lawyers in the arbitration process. Judges comprised over four-fifths of the arbitrators in Ontario, and judges and lawyers combined accounted for four-fifths of the members of this group in Quebec (Woods and Ostry, 1962). In practice, the great majority hewed to a narrow interpretation of the contracting-out issue. A prime example of this position is found in the decision of Judge H. D. Lang in *United Auto Workers vs. Ford Motor of Canada*.[1] He stated that "The Union claims that if the company decided to contract-out this and that job and all jobs piece-

[1] *Labor Facts*, 1962, 13(5):9.

meal it would gradually eliminate the bargaining unit. That could be and there is nothing in the contract to prevent it." One Canadian author concluded that the contract was the guide to the decision because arbitrators gave little consideration to factual elements (Verge, 1962).

Of course, a legalistic structure can be used for the benefit of the challenger as well as the holder of rights. In general, Canadian unions have tended to operate within the legal framework by attempting to "tighten up the agreement," and in the early 1960s efforts were made to interpret section 10A of the Quebec Labour Act as both a restriction and a control on contracting-out. This section of the law provided protection of the bargaining rights of workers involved in a transfer of company ownership. The interpretation in question extended this point to include protection in situations in which work was transferred to units outside the company.

Across the border in the United States, the legalistic approach did not lack partisan support, but it was less well buttressed by appropriate enabling structures. Legislation gave fuller course to "free" collective bargaining, and arbitrators serving under specific agreements were more evenly divided between strict legalists and those who "examined the entire case." In addition, many of them could not be classed as members of either school of thought. In their decisions regarding contracting-out, arbitrators often side-stepped the rights issue, and governmental bodies tended to do the same. This greater diversity in interpretation of role, in part, may have reflected the origins of the occupants of these positions, for in the United States the legal profession shared this function with college professors and other labor relations experts.

In the United States, the legalistic approach to contracting-out encountered the multi-interest group structure (see Chapter 1), and was shaped and in a sense absorbed by it. Strict legalism lost out as a vital force, for bargaining over contracting-out rights was a diffuse process, spreading far beyond the confines of legal and/or formal structures. Moreover, many of the resulting solutions were inconclusive or related to organizational problems of a short-run nature. The question of principle rarely was touched on—or at most only the surface was skimmed. All these factors introduced a great deal of uncertainty into the process. Accurate prediction of outcome seemed to be much less possible than it would have been in societies that employed a thoroughly legalistic approach. These points may serve to clarify some otherwise puzzling aspects of the management rights culture in the United States.

MANAGEMENT RIGHTS: THE PARTISAN VIEW

Interestingly, one can pick up a piece of management rights literature dated 1946 and another dated 1963 and find almost the same concepts, sentiments, and conclusions. Apparently, the rights question leads a most sedate existence. But as rights are considered a form of property, one would have anticipated a conservative, static treatment. In addition, the rights literature tended to take the place of the institutional supporting structures that the larger society supplied only to a limited extent. The constitutional manager (Dunlop, 1958) who fell afoul of the multigroup interest structure could seek in the literature confirmation of the significance of his submerged self, the manager with complete discretionary powers.

In the management literature, a simple model was used to describe the process of challenge to rights. It was elegant in its simplicity. The main actors were management and labor. Labor stood in opposition to management. Management had a fund of rights and a solemn obligation to protect it. The union, which represented labor, was the challenger, and when successful, it secured rights at the expense of the rights of management. All other actual sources of challenge were ignored, as were the divisions within these groups.

The erosion model

In the immediate post-World War II period, the literature expressed fears of imminent drastic inroads into management's fund of rights. For instance, one management journal predicted that "There is going to be a managerial revolution in the United States if organized labor can bring it about. The revolution will take the form of a drastic restriction and redefinition of the rights of management."[2] Conservative management publications did not deviate from their basic position in the ensuing years, but their view of the process became more sophisticated. The notion of complete takeover was supplanted by a theory of gradual erosion. The concept of catastrophic change proved to be inconsistent with actual experience, and thus the process through which rights were lost came to be characterized as erosion, a gradual wearing away. One management study describes this phenomenon as follows: "You aren't often asked to give up a right in toto. More likely you are confronted with a demand to give up just a little piece of that right . . . you are asked that no work presently being performed in the bargaining unit ever be taken out of that unit . . . the signing of such a provision is nothing more than a nice gesture" (Torrence, 1959, p. 3). This conceptualization of the process of losing rights was so prevalent

[2] *Factory*, 1949, 107 (8):101.

that the author found inside union leaders also complaining about the "erosion by arbitrators" of union-won contractual rights regarding contracting-out.

The concept of loss of rights through erosion called attention to serious managerial problems. In the world of loss via erosion, simple day-to-day acts assumed tremendous significance. Small concessions became permanent road blocks. Thus one was confronted with the plight of the manager who made a nice gesture to the inside forces only to find later that he was completely blocked from hiring a contractor when this course of action became economically advisable. In general, either losses of rights were considered irrevocable or, if lost rights were to be retrieved, management had to resort to drastic measures. Moreover, rights came to be regarded as an all-or-none determinant of a prescribed course of action. According to this line of reasoning, if rights were not intact, contracting-out or any other desired managerial program was not possible.

The doctrine of individual responsibility

In the light of this theory, mistakes in judgment inevitably had the most serious consequences. And, interestingly, the blame for these errors was personalized. The full burden was assigned, not to the organization, but to the individual manager. Possible sharing of the burden was largely ignored. As noted above, the rights-affirming legalistic approach did not have a strong system of supporting structures outside the firm. Thus, the manager was viewed as the only person who could defend rights conclusively and block the entry of a decision into the uncertain rights-threatening world of worker protest action and third-party dispute settlement. His actual ability to function effectively in this manner was not questioned. For instance, organizational imperatives may have dictated a concession. In spite of this, losses were regarded as something the individual manager caused and that he could prevent. Torrence (1959, p. 7) stated that ". . . it is safe to say that practically all of the rights which have really been taken away from management are those which management itself has given away, deliberately or otherwise." This statement reflected the general American practice of assigning responsibility to the individual in competitive enterprise. Ensuing sentiments of guilt were well expressed by a manager in a large automobile firm, who remarked, "I gave up part of a management right to contract-out. I didn't intend to, but it worked out that way."

The manager could take small comfort in the fact that the Torrence study divided his losses into two categories, those committed knowingly and those perpetrated inadvertently, unknowingly. Clearly, actions with unintended consequences had full sway in this area. A manager could watch the sales chart to judge his performance in the field of marketing, but how did he know when he was sacrificing a member of that abstract category, rights? To remain blameless, the manager needed, among other qualities, the astuteness of a rising member of a law firm. Moreover, one found a parallel to the doctor's advice to keep fit through regular exercise, for the manager was exhorted to use rights "frequently in order to hold our franchise" (Klassen, 1958). Skills in offensive as well as defensive strategies were required. The manager had to move away from the situation in which rights were perceived clearly only in retrospect.

The manager's rights dilemma

The rights dilemma of the manager has been outlined briefly. As later chapters in this book will indicate, the theory of individual responsibility ignored some of the realities of organizational life. However, on the assumption for the moment that the theory was valid, what would be the consequences of complete ineptness on the manager's part? Would anything in the way of rights ultimately remain? Is the entire managerial function potentially erodible, or is there something that the manager cannot surrender, wittingly or unwittingly? Some theorists have held that, as long as management is defined as decision-making, there can be no end to union penetration, because unions and other outside groups potentially can exercise authority and influence in the case of any and all managerial decisions.

However, an end to the erosion process was found in a redefinition of the concept, management. By defining management as the coordination of activities in a formal line of authority, one could obtain a core of unfettered inside function, unerodible by definition. The union was assigned to the position of regulator. Regulators were distinct from managers, for they were external to the firm and had different goals. While they regulated managers through influence and authority, they did not manage (Tannenbaum, 1950). The facts of union "invasion" were among the items that the manager must coordinate into a coherent, smoothly functioning program of operations, directed toward the enterprise goals. A wag might envision a situation wherein the union, in effect, is running a plant but management remains supremely secure, coordinating the entire effort. But even if one accepts the line of reasoning that separates out a completely distinctive management function, a problem still remains. Coordination is far from being a unitary function. It, too, is subject to considerable shackling from sources both inside and outside the firm.

SOME ASPECTS OF THE RIGHTS ISSUE
IN THE POSTWAR PERIOD

As the post-World War II period progressed from the late forties to the late fifties, some observers perceived a shift in the institutional roles of union and management. The union, formerly the challenger of management rights that were embedded in the past, became the defender of the *status quo* in its battles to preserve traditional conditions against the onslaught of a management striving to introduce change. Thus, management's former right to preserve the *status quo* became the right to initiate change. It should be noted, however, that the interest in change actually did not represent the conversion of management to a new line of reasoning. Rather, management was responding to demands dictated by the pressures of competition and new technology, and the reversal of the parties' institutional roles actually was a function of powerful external forces acting on both of them. In view of the strong pull of vested interests, it is safe to say that probably only small segments on either side could be classed as being enthusiastic about change or the prospect of change.

The shift from status to power emphasis

The actual shift in management position that occurred in the postwar period might better be described as a change from status to power emphasis. This switch was noted in the case of the "right to contract-out." In the early postwar period, concessions to the union were viewed largely as a status threat. The economic aspect of the problem was neglected. Concession represented a symbolic rather than a dollar loss. A manager in a metal-processing firm remarked, "In '49 we stiffened up, but it wasn't out of the conviction that the roof was about to fall in. We didn't want them telling us how to run the business." Unionists who obtained concessions during this period reported that "They were easy to get. We just had to twist their arm a little."

At the turn of the fifth decade there was a shift to concern about management control over contracting-out. At the time, some management informants attributed the change to the interunion pacts of 1959, dividing the work of the industrial firm between the craft and industrial segments of the labor movement. Although the effect of this action was more imaginary than real, it symbolized a complete loss of management rights. More significant were pressures generated by technological change and recession-inspired economy drives. One manager noted, "We bargained away too much on subcontracting. The profit statement obscured the fundamental matter of control." Another remarked, "Contracting-out is in a state of anarchy. We let things slide, but we are in the process of making some changes now."

Technological and economic transformations were much more a part of life in the early part of the sixth decade than they were in the relatively stable and prosperous fifties. Thus the situation with regard to the union-management power structure became dynamic. The erosion model implied that management must recoup its power or right to contract-out from the unions—that this was management's only recourse. Actually, the key to changing the situation lay in the introduction of new plants, new processes, new organizational structures for which there was no body of traditional management or union practice. (This point will be developed further in case materials in Chapter 9.)

Rights battles in the public arena

However, thinking based on the erosion model did have an effect on the behavior of the parties during the period of shift from status to power emphasis. In line with the feeling that drastic measures were needed to recoup rights, management conducted a series of massive appeals for public support. The best known of these was the management drive to change work rules in the 1959 steel negotiations. Limitations on contracting-out figured significantly as one of the local working conditions that management wanted to alter in its campaign against section 2-B of the contract. The bitter struggle and long strike spotlighted the management rights issue but hardly illuminated it. Contracting-out was cast in a prominent role in almost all the notable work rules battles of the late fifties and early sixties. It played a prime part in railroad disputes in this area and was a key issue in the Pennsylvania Railroad strike of 1960. The same was true of the steel negotiations of 1962 and 1963. (Details of some of these contract settlements will be discussed in Chapter 11.)

As far as the management rights issue was concerned, the public airings accompanying the above negotiations were not very instructive. Interviews with participants in these work rules battles indicated that the settlements typically were inconclusive. However, this finding revealed more than at first was apparent about rights issues, that is, that there is no satisfactory alternative to winning outright. Wage negotiations involve a scale of values along which the parties can move until they reach a settlement. Wage-related items, such as vacations and seniority provisions, are other issues that fall in the class of "measurables." While neither party may be satisfied with its present location on a given scale, a feeling tends to exist that "we can make it up next time." But no graduated scale applied in the case of bargaining over rights issues. Rights were scaled as black-and-white, all-or-none factors. A continuous numerical scale precludes firm commitment to a position, whereas the lack of one fosters this commitment. This fact, in turn, tended to move rights out of the bargaining arena proper, for bargaining implies the possibility of some concessions.

Movement out of the bargaining arena has often taken the form of public relations campaigns via full-page newspaper advertisements. These appeals may constitute not bargaining, but rather an attempt to avoid bargaining by seeking public confirmation of the rightness of one's position. There must be the hope that the public sitting in judgment will confirm management's initial bargaining posture and thus bring the union into line to accept an initial "no yield" stand as the final result. Unions have countered with the same kind of publicity. Thus the rail unions met railroad management's 1959–1960 public relations campaign against featherbedding with the "poverty myth exposé" of 1962.[3]

The public did not prove to be the unflinching ally of either side, partly because the communiqués contained very little information that might have led to understanding. A steady diet of strong emotional appeal probably satisfied partisan groups, but it is more than likely that to the average citizen this approach indicated only that (1) a dispute existed and (2) the stakes were high, or else the parties would not have been spending so much money on advertising. Plant-based rights issues displaced to the public arena tended to be devoid of meaning. All means for settlement were absent. And, as a matter of fact, plant problems regarding rights issues such as contracting-out have not been resolved in these debates.

The above analysis serves to explain why these major rights battles teach the student so little about the issue in question. In order to gather meaningful data about a rights issue, a study has to be conducted at the plant level, where the issue has its roots, and the subject must be probed in depth. Such a study must be much more than an inventory or a survey of a miscellany of rights questions. This counsel applies to both the practitioner and the scholar seeking solutions to problems in this area.

A history of major management rights battles that have been fought on the public stage would be interesting in and of itself. But, the probability that these performances will become an institutionalized ritual in the pragmatic business world is small, in view of their low productivity. It is a fairly certain prediction that this tactic will be abandoned, either completely or in favor of campaigns directed at specific audiences. As an institution, these public battles could be traced in origin to notions of the permanent character of rights losses

[3] *Railroad "Poverty" Myth Should Be Exposed*, Railway Labor Executives Association, 1962.

and of the need for drastic action to achieve a reversal. Management feelings of guilt and responsibility for losses provided another stimulus for this behavior. In effect, management was saying, "The odds against us are overwhelming. The unions have us at their mercy. Only a major public outcry can save us." (The above is an actual quotation from an interview.) But a collective outcry probably never will be heard, for the public is much less of a unity than either labor or management. As successive managerial groups take up the cudgels on the work rules issue, it is to be hoped that a shift will take place, away from the campaigns and toward more constructive activities.

The symbolic content of issues

Our study of management rights issues in the public arena revealed that not all of them had the same qualities of communicability and appeal to sympathy. Issues have a symbolic as well as an objective content. In some, the lines of battle are clear-cut and the roles of the parties simply defined. Thus, in the case of featherbedding, management is the underdog and the union the exploiter, demanding pay for work not performed or not needed. In the case of plant relocation, the roles are reversed. The worker is the victim of social injustice as his livelihood and equity in a community are pulled out of his reach. By comparison, the contracting-out issue has had little popular appeal. While this issue was the center of strong sentiments among the inside and outside parties directly concerned, it has never received wide publicity as one of the offending work rules.

Contracting-out often served as a stimulus for conflict, but it was not a popular vehicle for expressing sentiments of righteous indignation. The management advocate of contracting-out rights also had to face up to breaking the "we take of our own" tradition. The industrial unionist who insisted on doing work inside was blocking employment opportunities for fellow craft unionists in the same community. Each advocate was both defendant and plaintiff. The strong, clear-cut position had its roots in the organization but with removal from this base the overall ambivalence of a given position became all too apparent. Not many issues impart a one-sided picture to the outsider. Featherbedding and plant relocation may come closer to this standard than most. But the greatest number of substantive rights issues are like contracting-out. They are tied to a specific organizational base and, unlike general problems such as the rights of citizens, do not communicate readily beyond that limit.

Communications problems often forced both partisan and publicist back to the general question of management rights. This question may not convey abundant information, but it has the proper ring of a clear-cut, simple issue. Moreover, it permits special advocates to tie in with a cause larger than their own. The legal basis of these rights well may be challenged (Young, 1963). Nevertheless, they constitute a significant part of managerial ideology. In a commonly accepted interpretation, they occupied a place on the other side of the coin, democracy. In the words of one management writer, ". . . the source of management's responsibility to manage is that duty of trusteeship which business management was created to fulfill. Management alone is the balance wheel of distribution—alone capable of seeing to it that a fair share of created value . . . goes to investors, employees, consumers" (Klassen, 1958, p. 90).

The author does not wish to conclude this discussion of trends in management rights in the clutches of a vague generality, and yet somehow this is an appropriate position. Even when the subject of violent attack, the rights issue never moves far from dead center. The prerogatives issue per se apparently is the symbol of power but not the substance. It flares into prominence in periods of change when the balance of power becomes unsettled. However, after the shouting has died down, the observer may feel little wiser than before. The study of major events leaves one far short of the goal of understanding what has been happening in this extremely important area. In an attempt to find definitive answers, one generally turns to the work of researchers. But, despite the widespread interest in management rights, there has been surprisingly little systematic work in this field.

RESEARCH ON MANAGEMENT RIGHTS

Our review of some of the major studies of the postwar period revealed a convergence about a central problem and design. Chamberlain's *Union Challenge to Management Control* (1948) still stands as the classic work in the field. This research investigated the degree of union penetration of six major areas of management responsibility. The writer concluded that there were no firm bounds to the areas of mutual or exclusive interest for either management or unions. Unions did not have the conscious goal of penetrating management functions as such. Rather, they challenged management authority whenever they perceived that the interests of the workers were involved. Therefore, the situation was dynamic, and it was impossible to specify a limit to this interest.

In the same year Turnbull (1948) published an interview study of union and management views on the prerogatives issue. The most interesting finding involved the detection of a difference of management sentiments in large and small plants. Management in smaller plants seemed less concerned over the matter of sharing control with the union and felt less certain that the union had curtailed management's effectiveness.

Turning to major research of a later date, we noted first the work of the Illini City group (Derber, 1960; Derber, Chalmers, and Edelman, 1961). The members of this group made significant advances in the direction of refining measurements of union penetration into management areas. Interviews in thirty-seven Middle Western plants in 1955–1956 and again in 1959 led these authors to conclude that the unions were sticking close to the traditional approach of job-conscious unionism and were not preparing any full-scale advances into management territory. Interestingly, contracting-out was one of the few dynamic areas, and, in fact, it led all others in positive changes in scope of union participation.

The study also indicated that a sizable proportion of managers would have preferred having unilateral control in all areas. Contracting-out was one of three areas in which management objected most strongly to union participation. According to the writers, "The expressed desire of the union leaders for additional areas of participation was much weaker than the managerial desire for decreased union participation" (1961, p. 89). Contracting-out was the only item with a substantial union interest. The researchers concluded that their data confirmed the notion of a hardening of the management position on rights during the late fifties but cautioned that the scope of this trend might have been exaggerated. Thus, a management hardening on a few issues, such as contracting-out, was extended to the entire universe. It is also possible that the generalized rights issue simply became the vehicle for the ready communication of these specific complaints.

The Impact of Collective Bargaining on Management, the mammoth study of Slichter, Healy, and Livernash (1960), examined nineteen management rights issues in 150 plants. In assessing the influence of the union, the writers concluded that there had been some narrowing of the scope of management discretion and a trend away from the exercise of judgment and toward the application of simple principles. On the whole, they characterized the period of study as an era of adjustment via contract administration. However, they noted that the process of adjustment was neither complete nor uniform. Subcontracting was one of four areas in which adjustment was less well developed. They also found that "Conflict over employee performance and subcontracting has intensified in recent years." Both this and the previous study confirmed the notion that contracting-out is a crucial area for the investigation of the dynamics of the rights issue.

It is interesting to note how closely the models for the above research projects parallel those discussed earlier. The challenge, penetration, and impact models are close kin to the partisan's erosion model, although scholarly objectivity replaced more biased interpretations. In addition, the models of the researchers were more sophisticated, but basically all were dealing with a process in which the union nicks away at a fund of management rights in order to obtain its own capital. In contrast to the partisans who viewed the situation with alarm, the findings of the researchers seemed to provide assurance that management rights were not in dire straits. However, conclusions of this type served only to confirm a basic acceptance of the scorekeeping, wins-losses approach. While the latter constituted a legitimate basis for investigation, one wonders at the lack of attempts to construct an organizational frame of analysis.

As a matter of fact, academic interest in the management rights area has ebbed and flowed with that of the partisans. Great surges of activity took place in the immediate postwar period of the late forties, and again in response to the economic and technological changes of the late fifties. Moreover, members of the partisan group have adopted the researcher's survey approach. A fairly elaborate scheme of this type was suggested in a Bureau of National Affairs manual (Torrence, 1959). It supplied an inventory form listing twenty-seven different rights. The manager was advised to use this form in making a study of all divisions and departments to determine which of these rights had been given away and which were still retained by the company. Of course, for his part the academic researcher would class a strict, legalistic approach of this type as an extreme case. Perhaps in accordance with his own "ideology," he tended to place a majority of rights issues, and the relationship between the partisan contenders, in a category such as "accommodation" or "adjustment," indicating the existence of some common meeting ground, although not necessarily a cordial one, between the two sets of management and labor interests.

On the whole, it would be fair to characterize management rights as an area marked by very few systematically gathered empirical data. With the exception of the work of Chamberlain and Derber and associates, most of the research has been rather rudimentary in nature. The lack of adequate information may account for the unnecessarily legalistic treatment of the area and for the tendency to handle rights questions as though they were isolable from all other organizational behavior—or, even worse, as an entity with a completely separate existence.

Any and all organizational behavior can be examined from the viewpoint of an underlying rights dimension, but this approach does not provide a meaningful or realistic treatment of organizational process. An informant stated that legalistic decisions and agreements had created a critical dilemma for his company. Part of this dilemma lay in a treatment of contracting-out problems that focused on static legal concepts and that failed to recognize and study organizational and technological factors that could serve to outline the shape of future developments. It should be added that all the other interested parties, inside and outside the firm, shared management's dilemma in this regard.

Nevertheless, it would have been foolish to deny the importance of the rights approach and its effect on management, union, and worker thinking and action—to write it off as a useless question. As indicated earlier, the rights that management and labor, respectively, have claimed are uncertainly held in American society. In the absence of strong external supporting structures, these rights have become primarily a part of a bargaining process in which claims to rights far outnumber instances in which these claims have been accepted. The real-life elusiveness of this process challenges the ingenuity of the researcher and, in a sense, defies anything but a pedestrian approach. The remainder of this chapter will be devoted to an exploration of the relationship between the rights approach and some aspects of technology and structure and to the testing of some of the assumptions of the legalistic model.

SOME TECHNOLOGICAL AND STRUCTURAL COMPONENTS OF THE RIGHTS APPROACH

In this part of our inquiry the general position of management in particular companies was measured against the traditional legalistic approach. In other words, we were asking to what extent management subscribed to a behavioral model stressing rights as a guide to organizational policy and practice regarding contracting-out. Key components of this model were the notion that management possessed a bundle of contracting-out rights, potentially subject to erosion from one outside source, the union. Moreover, union entry involved irrevocable losses of rights.

Industry type

It might be assumed that, as fabrication industries have a higher rate of contracting-out than process industries, fabrication management would be a stronger proponent of management rights. However, we found the reverse to be true. General management in process industries was significantly more inclined to have a strong orientation toward management rights in contracting-out work, whereas fabrication management was more likely to view contracting-out as a labor-relations problem. Forty-eight per cent of the process industry managements and 23 per cent of the fabrication managements took a strong position on the rights issue. Undoubtedly, and as noted in Chapter 4, the importance of continuous operation in a process plant underlay the greater insistence on the right to manage. Strikes and allied forms of protest action traditionally have had the most serious consequences, although the advent of the day when a few supervisors can operate a plant may eliminate the potency of this type of threat.

Plant size

However, size also was a factor that served to determine position on the rights issue. Management in large plants with large internal maintenance and construction forces tended to take a strong rights stand. Sixty-eight per cent of the twenty-two plants employing over 4,000 fell in this category, and these included 70 per cent of the rights-oriented fabrication plants and 53 per cent of the process plants of that type. Thus, for process plants, greater size did not appear to be so consistently a concomitant of a strong position on the rights question. For the sample as a whole, members of groups that contracted-out lesser amounts of work, process plants and large plants, were more traditionally rights-oriented than those who farmed out larger amounts.[4]

These findings seemed to point to the conclusion that those who practiced their rights customarily seemed to be less rights-conscious than those who did not. Those who did a fair amount of contracting accepted labor problems as inevitable but realized that their goals could be accomplished successfully. This situation underlined the fact that in contracting-out, as in other areas on the shadowy boundaries of collective bargaining, one had a "right" to do the things one had done customarily and therefore one did not feel so strongly about the matter of prerogatives. It is safe to venture that persons with no interest in an activity also show little concern about their right to engage in it. Thus, the fact that process industry management had some technologically determined reasons for a pronounced general rights orientation was not a sufficient explanation for a stand on a given issue. However, at the time of this survey, process industry management as well as management in large firms with large internal maintenance and construction departments were becoming interested in contracting this work. Reactions involving strong rights positions evidently occurred as moves away from the prevailing pattern of behavior were con-

---

[4] For a further discussion of this group of plants, see Chaps. 4 and 7.

templated. In this light, rights became a defense in advance of action, a bargaining posture in the stages before bargaining actually had begun.

It is interesting to note that some of the anticipated pressures were a function of inside interests that flourished in the light of infrequent exercise of the contracting-out "prerogative." General management's discussions of rights frequently turned to anticipated opposition from the heads of the inside maintenance and construction function. However, the potential internal challenge was not interpreted as a rights matter. Instead, the rights issue was focused on the appropriate outside group, the union.

ON THE PERMANENCE OF MANAGEMENT LOSSES AND UNION GAINS

An assumption of traditional thinking in the management rights area concerns the permanent character of management losses and union gains. One of our cases provided an interesting example of what happens when this line of reasoning is applied in practice. A metal-products plant followed the prescription to take an inventory in each department to determine what had been lost, and what remained, in the way of rights. The inventory seemed to indicate that the right to contract-out was largely a matter of past history. Some concessions had been made at some time on every hand. However, the amount spent on contracting maintenance and construction work ran into the millions that very year. Evidently, some of the lost rights were still viable.

The permanence of union-management agreements

A systematic examination of our data indicated that notions about the permanence of losses and gains were inaccurate. The data indicated that agreements between management and union that certain categories of work belonged to the internal forces did not constitute permanent commitments against contracting-out. Even when formally worded, these agreements seemed to be not definitive settlements of an issue, but rather temporary solutions, largely applicable to the case or cases that originally prompted them.

Thus, management was as likely to contract-out work governed by these agreements as it was to contract-out work to which they did not apply. And unions were just as likely to grieve about the contracting-out of work that was not governed by special agreements as they were about work that was. In other words, the existence of a special agreement did not serve to predict either management behavior or union behavior. Patterns of grievance activity proved to be attributable to dynamic organizational factors that superseded the influence of the workers' rights secured in these agreements. (The full data on this point will be presented in Chapter 14.)

Even impressive union gains (and management losses) have been confronted with substantial contracting of maintenance and construction work—contracting that subsequently was upheld by arbitrators. If management losses were impermanent, obviously this generalization also applied to union gains.

The permanence of arbitration awards

The fact that the parties did not adhere strictly to a bargained agreement—even though it involved rights to certain work—was not unduly surprising in this era of general sophistication about organizational behavior. But arbitration awards have a sacrosanct aspect that enhances the aura of permanent impact. However, even in the case of arbitration awards, we noted flexibility in organizational adjustment that often was ignored in the literature. This statement applied not only to practices subsequent to the impact of a particular award but also to the method of carrying out the award itself.

Ten of the seventy-four plants in our sample had had one or more arbitration cases on contracting-out. Four of the ten lost their cases and presumably were saddled with the task of adjusting to a loss of rights following the union's victory. In all cases of loss, some immediate adjustments were made, but these did not necessarily constitute complete compliance with the letter of the award. For instance, in one of the cases, an arbitrator sustained a union grievance regarding the contracting of some new janitorial maintenance work. Management felt that the workers who had filed the grievance were not competent to handle the job. Therefore, the company hired some more highly skilled persons to perform the new work and relegated the others to less crucial positions in the back of the shop. Subsequently, janitorial work was contracted-out in other parts of the plant. Moreover, the union failed to object. Yet persons reading this case might cite it as "another instance in which management lost its right to contract-out."

To summarize the results of arbitration in all ten of the plants that had such cases, two of the four that lost their cases found that the union victory had no effect on the company's ability to contract-out work. The firm described above experienced some temporary decrease in ability to contract-out. The other firm represented a special case of impaired right to contract-out that could not be attributed clearly to the effect of this specific arbitration decision. For years, this company had been remarkably self-sufficient. When it finally began to contract

work, it was faced with considerable opposition from interests within
the firm, management as well as union. Grievances were frequent, and
a complex apparatus was established for handling the cases. Many
hearings and many levels of management were involved. A manager
who wanted to contract-out was faced with close examination of his
entire procedure. Members of management maintained that the red
tape that contracting-out often involved was a much more potent
deterrent than the outcome of the arbitration case in question.

The six firms that won their arbitration cases presented much the
same picture of inconclusive results. Five found that the decision had
no effect on ability to contract-out. One experienced some slight
"increase" in this ability because, apparently disappointed by the loss,
the union shifted its pressure to other issues. Had all ten managements reacted according to the pattern found in the management rights
literature, one would have anticipated a high valuing of wins and a
very negative reaction to losses. "No effect" responses would have been
completely absent.

Thus, prescriptions such as the advice to take an inventory in order
to determine what rights remain emphasized a characteristic of finality
that concessions, agreements, and awards simply did not possess. One
study (Dash, 1963) divided arbitration awards into two categories,
"Right to Contract-out Retained with or without Limited Qualifications," and "Full Right to Contract-out Not Retained." Again, one notes
in this language a tendency to extrapolate from the immediate instance to an indefinite period of time.

In making a decision about a grievance on contracting-out, the arbitrator in effect is taking a unit out of a continuous process and
treating it as a discrete item. He issues a decision—grievance sustained
or denied. In assessing the effect of the decision, one is in error if he
continues to deal with it as a discrete unit. One tends to forget that,
when the decision reenters the organizational process from which it
was detached, it will be molded and shaped by this process in the
course of everyday events.

The assumption that an agreement or award automatically favored
one side or the other, labor or management, also contributed to the
false notion that gains and losses were permanent. The diversity of
interests within each group undoubtedly was a crucial factor in explaining why agreements and the more elegantly phrased arbitration
awards had largely short-run effects, for these pronouncements took
little account of the fact that they rarely pleased either all workers or
all on the management side. For instance, inside construction and
maintenance departments, displeased by an arbitration award uphold-
ing management's right to contract-out, continued to exert pressures on
their own behalf.

Moreover, our data indicated that the attention of the various parties was not focused continuously on rights issues, but rather only at select intervals, for instance, when a crisis was imminent. At these times their orientation was toward the seeking of short-run settlements—not toward the implications of long-run trends. The "wins" of a particular party at interest were temporary, almost by implicit understanding. However, formal recognition of this fact has been slow to come.

SUMMARY

This chapter has set forth the legalistic argument in the management rights area. In the United States bargaining over management rights has been a diffuse process, spreading far beyond the confines of legal structures. In fact, the legalistic approach has been shaped and, in a sense, absorbed by interest groups in the process of day-to-day organizational life. At the same time one cannot ignore the effect of a treatment of management problems in terms of static legalistic concepts.

The basic components of the legalistic argument were found to be two united fronts, labor and management. Labor gained rights at the expense of the rights of management in a process characterized by the erosion model. Assessment of the results of the entire process involved a wins-losses, scorekeeping approach to bargaining over rights issues. As results were assessed as gains or losses of rights, these gains and losses tended to be regarded as permanent entities. Managerial skill in battling with the union was crucial, because wins and losses were credited or debited to the individual manager's account. However, the legalistic approach overlooked the importance of the technological and structural matrix in which an issue was placed.

Our data revealed that management position on the rights question was a function of technological and structural factors as well as of organizational position with regard to potential change in an area. Far from being an automatic response, managerial adherence to the legalistic model had organizational roots. Moreover, while in the process of solution an organizational problem might be transformed into a question of rights, the reverse of this process took place when losses and gains of rights were returned to the organization. Diverse—not united—interests within the organization molded the output of the legalistic machine and translated what this machine labeled long-run effects into short-run effects.

These findings raise a crucial question regarding the effect on the organization of operations conducted within the legalistic management rights framework. The organization may not conform to the legalistic specifications, but it cannot very well ignore them. To what extent does this focus cause the manager to fix exclusive attention on winning the game at the expense of missing the point of playing the organizational process and concentrating his efforts on long-term goals?

chapter 6

The Preservation of Rights:
Management's Defense

The internal procedures by which management defends its rights provide an excellent vantage point from which to study the intermixing of the organizational and legalistic approaches to a given problem. A legalistic approach dictates the need for defensive counterstrategies to prevent the ceding of management territory to the opposition. From an organizational standpoint, the goal of a defense also should be the promotion of a smooth-running and efficient operation. As observed in our study, what happened when the organization simultaneously attempted to meet the demands of these two objectives, efficient operation and retention of rights? Did one aim inevitably dominate the other? Were the two goals mutually compatible? What tended to be the underlying logic of the firm's defensive strategy—legalistic, pragmatic, responsive, or chaotic? Did procedures tend to be rigid and constricted, or were innovations common?

Management's defensive procedures are no longer a private affair. These actions have become matters of public concern. Legally, a defense must not constitute an "unfair labor practice." The National Labor Relations Board has distinguished between management "defenses" and "offenses." A defense is aimed at the unauthorized actions of the other party and is considered a lawful activity. However, moves directed against the legitimate functions of a union are considered offenses and are subject to challenge by the NLRB. In 1962 the Board designated as an unfair labor practice "no discussion," one of the most rigid and legalistic defenses presented in this chapter[1] (see also Chapter 11). It is significant that the Board's action chastised not innovators in this area but rather those who cling to rigid legalism. In many ways, legalistic defenses have been the most vulnerable to formal attack, literally victims of their own medicine. Innovative defenses, although not common, have been at a premium and have more readily eluded efforts at control.

Defenses are shaped by the character of the particular problem that is the object of defense. In a highly bureaucratized area, a defense may consist largely of formal procedures. At the time of this study, contracting-out issues existed in a semibureaucratized state, with many relevant variables uncertainly specified. Thus, this managerial problem was open to a variety of informal "power struggle" defenses. If contracting-out eventually were reduced to a system of rules, its defenses would, of necessity, be organized quite differently.

Moreover, in common with most other organizational programs, defenses have their unintended consequences. One such consequence, observed in our study, was the movement of the problem in question into a more highly structured environment, where it became more readily accessible to attack by prospective invaders. Despite attempts to conceal defensive tactics, by their very use they became known and thus available to others in the organization, members of both management and union. In this manner, a defense eventually can create new organizational problems as the opposition adopts a defense originated by management and uses it for its own purposes. Other defenses were converted into requirements of the legal structure, and thus they completely lost their private character.

[1] *New York Times*, Nov. 21, 1962, p. 21.

DEFENSE STRATEGIES: THE PARTISAN VIEW

As one might have anticipated, the management literature featured extensive recipes for defending prerogatives against attack. In line with the theory of managerial accountability for loss of rights, these defenses involved personal actions of the manager and depended upon his skills. In general, actions that he initiated and controlled were favored over "responsive" defenses that indicated that one or more other parties were playing a determining role in the situation. Many of these defenses constituted rigid, uniformly applied plans of action. No questions about basic strategic design were asked. It was assumed that one was defending the right territory against the right invader.

A survey of the literature indicated that recommendations for the defense of rights fell into three categories: more astute collective bargaining, better personnel practices, and the education of subordinates in the proper approaches to rights issues. Of these three, more astute collective bargaining seemed to receive the greatest stress. The following were key points in the "better bargaining" defenses:

1. Management must take greater initiative in bargaining and not simply react to union demands and pressures (Drucker, 1950).

2. Management should consider union demands in terms of their impairment of management functions and agree to demands only when there is reason to believe that they will not interfere with the efficient running of the business (Caples, 1955).

3. Management must be especially sensitive to union demands for joint action and mutual consent and also must avoid making all "foot in the door" concessions (National Association of Manufacturers, 1956).

4. Management should leave no loopholes in agreements. Terms should be spelled out in clear detail. The dangers of loose and ambiguous language should be recognized [*Factory*, 1949, 107(9): 106–109].

5. Management rights should be spelled out in detail in the contract (O'Shaughnessy, 1957). No specific areas should be listed as management rights. Management must retain the right to initiate action in all areas (Justin, 1960).

6. Management should handle grievances involving management rights with special care, making no mention of the company's right but instead endeavoring to persuade the employee that the action is necessary and reasonable (Torrence, 1959).

In addition, the authorities recognized that defending rights in formal bargaining over contracts and grievances was not enough. Rights had to be protected on a day-to-day basis, and this need could be met through programs in which the lower levels of management were alerted to their responsibilities.

1. Management should train supervisory personnel in the "occupational techniques of labor relations" so that their actions would not add to or modify bargained agreements (Justin, 1960).

2. Management should educate the entire managerial force so that supervisors at all levels are aware of the importance of management rights and can quickly spot a situation in which these rights are involved, thus avoiding the dangers of engaging in practices that could in time establish unhealthy precedents (Torrence, 1959).

The defensive programs described above clearly were based on the wins-losses, erosion model. In general, the dominant message could be summarized briefly as follows: "Pin everything down. Then take steps to ensure that members of your organization do nothing that might pave the way for losses of rights." However, a dilemma existed. This dilemma stemmed from the feeling that spelling out rights might be a form of self-erosion. (Sentiments of this type were expressed by the authors of items 5 and 6.) A counterstrategy involved keeping rights out of the bargaining arena. According to this counsel, the manager should neither discuss rights nor specify what they were. Some of this confusion disappeared when these defensive strategies were placed in their appropriate organizational context. As our research data indicated, the "no discussion" and "pin everything down" defenses were not mutually contradictory. Rather, they represented steps along the way toward increasing managerial involvement in the defense of rights.

The creators of these defenses steered clear of complicating organizational factors, such as the diversity of interests within the managerial group. A weak defense was attributed not to the existence of different positions on the rights question but rather to ignorance that could be cured by educational programs. On the whole, the partisan approach to management defenses operated within a framework in which limited questions were asked about a very limited number of the total relevant data. Even so, no one was able to produce a simple, all-embracing formula for a legalistic defense.

Dissatisfaction with the legalistic defense of rights prompted some authorities to recast the problem in a broader framework. Solutions were sought in personnel and human relations programs aimed at both workers and unions. Some recommended techniques were designed to include the members of these groups in the management circle. The following were examples of this approach:

1. Management can instill in employees a greater appreciation of the role and functions of management by associating employees with various kinds of management functions (Drucker, 1950).

2. Management can prevent rights-challenging issues from arising

by developing adequate personnel policies and procedures and by practicing consultative supervision (Bergen, 1940).

3. Management should establish cooperative relations with the union, which in turn will encourage the development of responsible actions on its part (Lipstreu, 1956).

4. Management should create a system of industrial democracy which would give the organized work force some responsibility for the enterprise and its relations to the economy (Brown, 1948).

Advocates of the above programs pointed to the fact that management had to secure cooperation from the work force; so why argue about rights? Forget about management rights, and instead establish good relations. This approach judges as irrelevant legalistic warnings that extracontractual conversations with union members could lead in time to binding practices.

Thus, there actually seemed to be two grand stategies in the rights field, defenses through legalistic and defenses through human relations routes. Both offered formulas for maintaining effective operations— careful bargaining and good personnel relations. These are worthwhile goals, but their advocates overlooked the fact that these panaceas may have little impact on rights problems which are embedded in complex organizational matrices, notable for their diversity in technological and structural components.

Turning to the literature on contracting-out, one found that much of it seemed to indicate that a strong defense of some kind was necessary. This theme was repeated so consistently that the reader obtained the impression that trouble was endemic to the process of contracting-out work. One writer recommended a kind of last-ditch defense that serves to underline this statement: "Finally, be sure to provide a hole in the maintenance contract so you can get out fast if serious trouble begins to brew."[2]

Failure to pursue a strong legalistic defense was most frequently cited as the reason for management's difficulties: "Your union contract, your union's attitude, the way an arbitrator is likely to react to your situation, your past practices—all these will determine what you can or can't do."[3] This article recommended the usual search of the contract and side agreements to determine what remained in the way of rights to contract-out. However, the writer offered some hope for the man with a poor legal defense—the climate for contracting-out might be right. Needless to say, the pursuit of a good contracting-out climate was one of the major concerns of the manager in organizing his defense.

[2] *Factory*, 1959, 117(7):214.
[3] *Ibid.*

The ensuing sections of this chapter will present actual defenses used by managements in the plants under study. These defenses offered interesting contrasts and parallels to those recommended in the literature.

DEFENSES FOR CONTRACTING–OUT

As indicated above, the character of a defense is dictated in part by the problem at issue. In Chapter 5 it was noted that contracting-out was not amenable to easy control by unions, and our study of these defenses revealed that the same generalization applied to management. In common with all other labor-management issues, contracting-out had its own particular cadre of defensive strategies. When the firm farmed out work, the flow of interaction that followed involved certain sensitive points. At these points the parties became aware of certain inequities and at times proceeded to challenge decisions. Various interests in industrial management, the contractor and his competitors, the inside and outside work forces and unions took part in this process. To smooth the entire operation, defenses had to be pin-pointed to control events along the route or, in traditional terms, to prevent the loss of management rights.

One might have anticipated finding an endless variety of defensive techniques as one moved from firm to firm. Each industrial establishment might have had its own peculiar assortment, but this eventuality did not occur. Various patterns of defense strategies were found, and these could be explained on a rational basis. In part, they were a function of the technological and structural aspects of the particular case in question.

Our study investigated the defensive strategies employed in each of the firms at a particular period of time. But these defenses must not be conceived as rigid devices. They changed over time. In general, there appeared to be a progression from more preferred to less preferred strategies. The process of change more often than not constituted a managerial response to threats in the environment. A picture of managerial initiative and overall planning was missing. Nor did managers adhere rigidly to their avowed defenses. The tidy and consistent approach advocated in the partisan management literature was absent.

The defenses observed in action were a curious blend of the legalistic and personnel approaches and the application of organizational know-how—playing the organizational process. As anticipated, management almost universally preferred defenses that were under its exclusive control in the sense that the activity did not go beyond the bounds of management's private communication networks. Gaining flexibility or "preserving rights" in contracting-out by resorting to contact with the union or creating potentially bargainable categories of work was definitely a less preferred strategy. In essence, some defenses constituted managerially initiated equivalents of union "invasion," but these actions were classed as defenses if management employed them unilaterally with the goal of maintaining control and preserving its right to contract-out.

Defenses were divided into two major categories, "management-controlled," programs initiated and regulated unilaterally, and "barter," defenses in which management traded less-valued goods for rights. With few exceptions, management goals in erecting a defense were the preservation of managerial initiative. Even in the case of defenses that approached bargaining with the opposition, the anticipated consequences often were viewed in narrow, legalistic terms. The high value of unilateral action was underscored by the fact that the most popular defenses were those under one-sided control, and progressively less popular items involved increasing degrees of movement away from this standard.

THE NO DEFENSE FIRMS

Nine of the companies in the sample employed no defenses to protect their right to contract-out and therefore, in a sense, did not belong to the population of rights defenders. These plants formed a fairly homogeneous group. They were members of the fabrication category, performing work that could be described as light rather than heavy—garment, nuts and bolts, electrical appliance and gear manufacture. These firms had uniformly small maintenance and construction departments and contracted-out an average of approximately 60 per cent of their work. Thus, there was little internal pressure for work, and little need for a defense, because, organizationally speaking, the right to contract-out was well in hand.

In seven of these nine cases, the lack of a defense evidently represented a historic *status quo*—a long tradition of contracting the work in question, with little opportunity for the development of opposing interests within the organization. Two cases deviated from this pattern. As a result of past difficulties, an electrical appliance firm reduced its maintenance force by a factor of one-half by failing for a period of ten years to replace those who retired or resigned. This policy was no longer in effect, but the company now was enjoying the fruits of its former efforts. A history of prior defensive measures resulted in a situation where none were needed. The other "deviant" firm manufactured record changers. It was organized by the Electrical Workers, who had insisted early in the relationship that all electrical work should be done with inside forces; in return, any other work could be farmed out if management wished. Usually, concessions of this type served to stimulate further defensive measures on management's part, but this cession of a small part of the rights territory apparently eliminated the need for such programs. Even the ceded territory proved to have more symbolic than real meaning, for when special jobs arose, the union did not object to the use of organized electrical contractors.

The above descriptions of plants in the no defense category may disappoint advocates of the personnel approach, for membership in this group seemed to be a product of factors other than good human relations techniques.

THE MANAGEMENT–CONTROLLED DEFENSES

The no discussion defense

As indicated above, the most popular defenses belonged to the management-controlled category. The first involved a strict legalistic "defense of territory"—maintaining the right to contract-out without justifying one's position. In its purest form, this defense condoned no discussion whatsoever of contracting-out decisions with workers or union officials. A manager in a metal-processing plant stated this position as follows: "This is our decision. If management surrenders the full right to make it, we might as well give the business to the union. They would be running it. Talking to someone implies that he has an equity in the matter. Discussions are bound to lead to concessions, and we must avoid concessions to the fullest extent."

Holding to a strict no discussion line of defense had obvious difficulties, both legally and organizationally. Yet sixteen plants, eleven process and five fabrication, declared this to be a basic defensive tactic. This group essentially concurred with one of its member managers when he remarked that "The union has no business in this field." The relatively small proportion of proponents—21 per cent of the entire sample—indicated that this position no longer represented a majority viewpoint. This proportion is close to that found by Derber, Chalmers, and Edelman (1961) for a similar area, technological change. Sixteen per cent of their firms retained this type of strong control.

The number of plants relying exclusively on this defense was very small—four process firms, three small and one large, and one large and one small fabrication firm. These managements were strict legalists in action as well as in theory and were numbered among the twenty-five described as strong rights advocates in Chapter 5. These firms also were potential candidates for changes toward more contracting-out—and toward possible difficulties. But at the time of the study the defense was working well. The inside unions had little or no voice in the area. An additional ten firms, seven process and three fabrication, maintained an equally strong no discussion defense, but they fortified it with organizational strategies that were a part of the second management-controlled defense.

Although a strict no discussion defense was limited to a minority of the plants, a much larger proportion used modified versions of it. These included 48 per cent of the process plants and 44 per cent of the fabrication. The modified versions usually involved moving away from "none of your business" in practice but not in spirit. One manager explained, "we do it discreetly. You just can't refuse to talk, but we draw the line." Another manager commented, "If they ask, we try to show them why, but we won't justify our stand. We are firm on that."

Limiting a response to a complaining worker or union official to an explanation that involved no justification—drawing the line between these two categories of behavior—was clearly a difficult assignment. For instance, if management explained that work was contracted because it could not be scheduled properly, the union sometimes suggested that the workers' normal activities could have been rescheduled or that the workers could have accomplished the task in question through overtime assignments. Thus, a veritable Pandora's box was opened in the face of the "rights defender." It was little wonder, then, that most managements combined this defense with others designed to compensate for its obvious inadequacies. That is, it functioned well only when decisions were not challenged or when challenges could, in effect, be ignored.

The avoidance defense

The second management-controlled defense was classed as "avoiding borderline cases"—controlling pulse-raising sensitive points in the flow of interaction that characterized the contracting-out process. If a decision was to be contained within the management circle, it was simpler to take steps to avoid the occasion for challenge than to cope with challenge after it had been initiated. Moreover, avoidance could be accomplished unilaterally, whereas, in the case of the first defense, action beyond refusal to talk and literally closing the door inevitably involved participation by the other party. The avoidance defense demanded greater managerial skills than the no discussion method because it required a sensitization to danger signals and to blocks to the smooth operation of organizational process. However, it had the desirable qualities of being both amenable to unilateral management control and effective in a nonthreatening manner. Defenses based on a strong legalistic rights position often resulted in highly negative worker and union reactions. Avoidance was less conspicuous and less controversial, simply a demonstration of competent management.

Ideally, avoiding sensitive situations involved a continual checking on organizational processes in order to keep all potential trouble elements under control. In practice, avoidance strategies did not favor this middle road. Rather, these strategies seemed to run to extremes. Executives tended to be oriented either toward controlling one element at a particular point in time or toward making drastic changes in structure. Legalistic reasoning which advocated either blocking day-to-day challenges or moving for the wholesale regaining of rights undoubtedly contributed to the development of this pattern. In addition, lack of time, energy, and awareness prevented the great majority from monitoring the gradual build-ups in critical factors that often led to challenge (see Chapter 14). The nature of organizational structure and communication networks probably was equally important in promoting the use of strategies at either extreme, for necessary information often was unavailable to those who needed it in order to monitor continuously (see Chapter 15).

The avoidance defense was used commonly. Forty-eight of the seventy-four plants employed it—70 per cent of the process plants and 60 per cent of the fabrication.

Avoiding coercive comparisons

Specific avoidance defenses often were designed to keep the peace by not cueing the parties involved to inflammatory differences in the wages and working conditions of the inside and outside forces. A very popular strategy tackled this job at an elementary level. Management simply arranged to *separate the two groups physically*. In part, this action reflected a general desire, as one manager put it, "not [to] make the presence of a contractor overly apparent." In other words, the goal was to keep the fact of contracting hidden from a variety of competing interests, management as well as workers.

Tactics included working contractors on week ends and during vacations, the use of separate entrances and facilities for the men, and actual separation on the job. In one case, in order to facilitate the "no contact" program, partitions were erected around a contractor's prospective work site prior to his entrance into the plant! In a metal-processing plant, separation was accomplished by assigning different times for work. To avoid possible jurisdictional conflicts over a job in a storage area, the contractor's men did their part of the work during the week, and the inside men were brought in on Sundays.

The multipurpose function of physical separation also was indicated by the fact that it served to control challenges from the outside craftsmen. After a survey of activities in the plant, the outsiders sometimes questioned management's "right" to assign inside forces to tasks that fall within the outside craft jurisdiction. One manager explained, "We don't want them comparing wage rates, and then too, we don't want the contractor's men to see ours doing more than one job. There is no point in inviting trouble. We keep them as far apart as possible."

There were obvious practical limits to the use of this defense, but thirty-one firms employed it whenever possible. These included 34 per cent of the fabrication plants and 51 per cent of the process establishments.

The separation defense was illustrative of a whole battery of others designed to avert challenges to management rights as a result of coercive comparisons of the relative well-being of inside and outside forces. For instance, peaks rather than troughs in the work load were selected as propitious times to contract-out. Occasionally contracting was deferred or rejected if inside men were on layoff, and, conversely, periods when internal forces were busy were selected as a propitious time for contracting. In the latter case, the customary questions of rights and equities in the work involved could be set aside in the light of the pressures of a short-term emergency.

Restructuring work and the work force

The avoidance defenses also involved long-run programs designed to institute structural changes. In contrast to the above "subtle" controls on the distribution of workers and work loads in space and time, these defenses had a basic impact on the organization of the work force. One such plan called for the *minimization of craft differences* in the internal staff. The goal was a reduction in property-conscious attitudes toward particular work. Thus, craft lines were erased, and the men were identified as maintenance mechanics rather than as electricians, plumbers, and carpenters. A small, flexible internal force then could be supplemented by outside specialists, who no longer were direct competitors. This defense had a defect from the cost standpoint if there was no saving on the number of labor units employed, for the general mechanics would receive their regular wage rate for low- as well as for high-skilled tasks. From the standpoint of preservation of rights this strategy was better suited to a new plant, lacking in traditional practices, than to an old one, where it simply could result in trading one source of challenge for another. In inside departments structured along craft lines both managers and workers tended to resist the demeaning designation "mechanic." Only three companies were using this particular defense.

An even more drastic restructuring involved decreasing the size of the inside maintenance and construction forces through a process of *attrition,* failing to replace those who had retired or resigned. Thirteen of the seventy-four firms had instituted such programs, six in process industries and seven in fabrication. One manager explained:

> We want to eliminate jobs through attrition, deaths and retirements. Our thinking does change though. We have considered keeping a group of people for emergency work. We can keep 200 men busy, but we want to get away from the difficulty of having these restrictions on contracting-out. The union screams about this. The smaller these departments, the freer we are to contract when we want to.

A similar plan was discussed by another executive:

> We need increased flexibility. We want to get the whole unit down to just enough men to meet our continuing needs in each plant. We can end layoff and seniority problems by keeping these departments small and then contracting-out the balance.

Programs of this type often were stimulated by economic and technological changes (see Chapter 4). In turn, these programs were fairly certain to stimulate vigorous challenge from members of the inside crew. The question of management rights entered the picture in full force, although if "rights" were regained, this result generally was a by-product rather than a prime purpose of such major organizational changes. However, if carried through, these changes permitted a new assessment of old borderline and sensitive situations.

An interesting case of this type was encountered in a fabrication (machinery) plant, where the installation of manufacturer-serviced automatic equipment had been accompanied by a reduction of the maintenance staff from sixty to forty men. Under these new circumstances, management sought to redefine the prior territorial claims of the inside forces. As the plant manager described the situation, "We look for borderline cases. We generate them for educational purposes and to clear up understandings." The remaining internal staff had more work than it could handle. Thus, these management-generated cases represented a kind of symbolic regaining of lost managerial ground. This plant presented a unique reversal of the avoidance defense. In light of the opportunity provided by the staff reduction, management used borderline situations as an excuse to "go to trial" on the contracting-out issue.

Restructuring also involved moving work from claimed to unclaimed territory. Thus, in some cases the right to contract-out was defended by converting ground appropriated by the inside forces, e.g., truck driving, into virgin territory, e.g., sales work. When new uncontrolled areas appear, as they inevitably do in times of technological change, the opportunity to convert "A" to "not A" offers itself quite frequently.

In this regard, in the highly legalistic railroad industry, the shop unions have accused management of transferring the ownership of property to others in order to contract-out and avoid the controls of the Railway Labor Act. According to one union account:

> Subcontracting is responsible for the abolition of thousands of railroad shop jobs. Some carriers have all but given up repairing their locomotives. These carriers turn over locomotive upkeep to General Motors Corp. or some other contractor, taking work traditionally performed by railroad machinists and other shop crafts out from under the Railway Labor Act.
>
> Railroads use such devices as sale and repurchase of equipment and a variety of leasing arrangements when they subcontract maintenance work. [4]

Summary

Altogether, twenty firms limited their use of defensive measures to the above management-controlled strategies. Six firms (four process and two fabrication) held to the legalistic rights approach; four firms (three fabrication and one process) used the avoidance defense solely; and ten (seven process and three fabrication) had a combination of the two defenses. Thus, the management-controlled defense group included 39 per cent of the process establishments and 18 per cent of the fabrication. These figures reflect the bias of the process firm toward a strong rights position.

However, the relationship between a strong rights position and a management-controlled defense was not a simple one. Factors other than management philosophy played a determining role in the ability to cope with invasion of rights without moving into the barter defense group. With the exception of two large plants in the no discussion defense group, the others fell structurally into positions where the defenses employed served adequately. To amplify on the point about structure, with regard to size the members of this group fell primarily in the middle range of the total sample. The process firms averaged 2,400 in employment size as contrasted to 4,400 for the entire process sample, and the fabrication plants averaged 2,500 as contrasted with 4,100 for the fabrication sample as a whole. Moreover, internal maintenance and construction staffs constituted a somewhat smaller than average proportion of the total in both groups. In the process plants, the crews averaged 9 per cent of the total employment size, in contrast to 10.8 per cent for the entire process sample, and the fabrication

[4] *The Machinist,* Nov. 15, 1962, 17(37):5.

crews averaged 5 per cent, in contrast to 6.5 per cent for the group as a whole. In addition, plants in these two groups contracted-out more than the average for their overall category—roughly 8 per cent more than the average for process and fabrication firms.

The weaker commitment of these firms to the inside function did not encourage the growth of a strong inside interest group devoted to maintaining and expanding its position in the organization. Inside union voice in the contracting-out question was either very weak or nonexistent in all cases.

It was clear that the use of the avoidance defense, either alone or in conjunction with the no discussion approach, was a function of a total situation favorable to contracting-out. The great majority of companies would have preferred the exclusive use of defenses of this type, but a variety of factors limited their feasibility. Some of the minor and major avoidance defenses operated smoothly to forestall confined onslaughts but could not cope with massive opposition from well-fortified internal groups.

It also should be noted that these defenses were not sure-fire formulas for protection of rights. Of course defenses were not subject to continual testing, for they rarely were used consistently. For instance, other pressures might lead to contracting despite layoffs. Moreover, although these defenses grappled with some aspects of the workers' equity in the job, they ignored others, such as an interest in overtime as well as in steady work. It also has been observed that these defenses either focused on controlling single elements at a particular point in time or were associated with drastic changes in structure but that they did little to cope with problems inherent in the gradual build-up of critical factors.

Management in four companies disagreed with the notion of an exclusively management-controlled defense. The no discussion defense was anathema to them, although they used avoidance defenses to good purpose. But a program such as regular notification of the union was regarded as a healthy move. These were fabrication firms that contracted an average amount of work, and their managements felt that the union should be included in the process. These exceptions to the general rule advocated the following: "The union has a right to question our decisions." "We believe in working with the union rather than pushing power down their throats." "We take up the whole thing with them." These companies manufactured either electrical machinery or scientific instruments, and contracting-out was not the center of a power struggle in any of them. One of these plants employed 1,300 and had a maintenance and construction crew of only 19. Thus, in these cases, movement toward the barter defenses did not have great implications for loss of control.

Apart from these few instances, the other companies that moved into the barter defense area seemed to do so with varying degrees of reluctance.

THE BARTER DEFENSES

Notification

The first steps away from the purely management-controlled defense involved embracing measures to inform the inside union of a move to contract-out work. In seven establishments, notification clauses appeared in the collective bargaining contract, and of course these were not considered management defenses. To qualify as a defense, notification had to be a voluntary management program designed to protect the "right" to contract-out. In all, thirty-five companies employed this defense, just under one-half of both the process and fabrication plants. In nineteen cases, this was the sole defense added to the management-controlled group. In fourteen cases additional barter defenses were added to this one. In two plants notification was part of a strictly barter defense program.

There was a good deal of uneasiness about this defense. It symbolized bringing an outside group into the inside circle, although management rather consistently claimed that it retained complete initiative in the act. Notifying was believed to head off rash protest moves and "quickie" walkouts by preparing the inside workers for the coming event. Once informed, union officials could proceed to gain the cooperation of "fireballs," who might otherwise be inclined to start rumors that the contracted work was their work or a job that they easily could perform.

Despite these advantages, officers in the twenty firms that confined their strategy to the management-controlled defenses expressed fairly strong reasons for not adopting notification.

Management in a food-processing plant explained, "We'd rather not notify them. The union might stick its nose in where it's not concerned. This way we keep control."

Management in a refinery commented, "They find out anyhow. It would just open the door for a grievance."

A transportation equipment executive remarked, "Notifying them would be acquiescing to the union."

Finally, in a utility company, the following comment was made: "Notifying is too close to asking for approval."

In the literature one found some emphasis on the positive gains to be achieved through notification. An engineer writing in the *Maintenance Engineering Handbook* cited numerous benefits:

In dealing with your own people, it is advisable to tell the plant union committee what work is to be contracted and why. Telling them ahead of time is an excellent way of determining their attitude and while they may not like it, they usually can be made to understand the value of employing a fixed number of people versus a fluctuating one, the need for special equipment or skill or the need to complete a task within a specified time limit. Telling them ahead also makes them feel they are being taken into a confidence and that their opinions are weighed and considered as they should be [Starr, 1957, pp. I-89–I-91].

Other experts have assured management that informing the union need not lead to disaster. One authority noted, "Discussing your intentions with the local union does not jeopardize your inherent right to act regardless of acceptance or not. If you can present an honest, convincing justification for contract work so that your men will not fear the loss of job stability, you have solved 99 per cent of your problems" (Dobe, 1963).

However, the dilemma of weighing this advice and then making a theoretical decision about the wisdom of notifying the union often was resolved by an incident that precipitated the adoption of "informing in advance." An industrial relations manager explained how one particular experience had led to his firm's embracing a notification policy:

Before we bring in a contractor, we notify the union committee. Now we don't ask their permission. It is strictly a matter of telling them who is coming in and why. Usually, we do this with the local people, but with an important job, we will want to have some higher officials in and sometimes we will even take it to the international headquarters. They can calm down these local hotheads. We started doing this about five years ago. We were hit for a bill of $28,000 in back wages. That is what made us change our minds. It was a grievance over some electrical work. We hired a contractor, and our electricians said the work belonged to them. We could have taken it to arbitration but there were some loopholes in our case. They (the plant industrial union) could have gotten us on the local conditions and practices clause. We paid up instead. With all the overtime, it amounted to $28,000. After that we started notifying them. It wasn't one of their demands, but we decided we had to do it to protect ourselves.

With 47 per cent of the companies in the sample using the notification defense, it could no longer be classed as an unusual or radical practice. However, some users expressed considerable doubt that they were realizing the gains predicted by the experts. Only 35 per cent felt that benefits had been realized. Some of these firms approached the task with the enthusiasm of a salesman. For these firms, notification seemed to result in greater flexibility in operations and better relations with the union. A plant manager remarked, "It seems to help in keeping union confidence."

The remaining 65 per cent voiced doubt about the efficacy of notification—doubts that often were reflected in the manner in which this defense was administered. The administrative problems were similar to those encountered by managers attempting to carry out modified versions of the no discussion defense. Maintaining the integrity of the rights territory while engaged in interaction with a potential invader created dilemmas for managers and led to the development of behavior patterns that symbolized managerial retention of control.

In two process firms notification was withheld until the moment when the contractor entered the premises. Thus, the notification function was stripped to its bare bones. If the inside union leaders tried to "expand" the process by issuing complaints, they might have obtained the same information by simply looking around the plant. A manufacturer of resistors made a point of notifying the company foremen and the union simultaneously. Contacting the union at the same time as a low-level management group served to dispel the notion that officers of that organization were being included in upper and middle management circles.

Other firms stressed the importance of underplaying notification by "keeping it informal." Managers eschewed arranged meetings in favor of casual mention during the course of everyday affairs. An officer in a transmission factory remarked, "Telling them is good business, but you shouldn't make too much of it—blow it out of proportions. It should be done casually not formally—when you run across them in the plant." Thus the timing and setting of notification were geared to fit the requirement that it be essentially a low-key performance. In addition, most users stressed that the practice was employed sporadically. A manager explained, "You can't do it too often. It takes time." Another said, "We say we do this, but we get careless. Usually we will if it's something big or we expect trouble."

Even more perplexing problems arose in turning from questions of the timing, setting, and frequency of notification to the actual verbal content of these sessions. A sharp line was drawn between informing the union and seeking its approval, but how did one draw the line in practice when one was seeking the other party's cooperation? One solution involved the transposition of a labor-management problem into the language and context of a less controversial field, marketing. As one manager phrased it, "We do a super-selling job." A more conventional approach involved establishing a set of rules or guidelines specifying the kind of information that could be imparted. For in-

stance, conversation was to be limited to the facts of the contract work
—when it would begin, how long it would take, and the nature of the
job in brief. One manager in a steel company explained. "This is good
human relations, but you must never let them think this is to be used
as a channel for influencing your decision. You must stand firm. They
get the bare facts and that is all."

Drawing the line between informing and seeking approval is not
a problem unique to labor-management relations. When the president
of the United States Steel Company called on the President of the
United States in April, 1962, with the news that his firm was going to
raise steel prices, he emphasized that he was not seeking presidential
approval of the action but rather was simply imparting information
(Blough, 1963).

No matter how the notification defense was administered, most of
these programs had a common goal, to exclude the union via a process
of inclusion. In many ways, the informant who described notification as a superselling effort came close to describing the real purpose of this defense. Instead of figuratively slamming the door as in
the no discussion defense, the manager kept his foot in it and attempted to engage the union's attention. He wanted the prospective
customer to be satisfied, but he did not want to answer all the customer's questions or to permit the customer to challenge his claims.
Therefore, it was difficult to make a sale or to guarantee satisfaction,
and the effort may have produced more harm than benefit. A basic
conflict arose between achieving the desired results on the one hand
and executing the defense as a unilateral action on the other. To contrast process and fabrication plants, process management seemed
more likely to hedge this defense with side defenses designed to prevent its becoming a bargaining wedge for the union.

Old versus new work

The old versus new work defense involved establishing categories of
work that served to define and thus to limit the job property rights
claims of the inside forces. In addition to limiting job property rights
claims, this practice also was designed to gain for management predictability and freedom from challenge. Some of the headaches of the
notification process were traded for a system that placed less emphasis
on managerial skills and substituted instead a formula for determining
the proper owner of the work in question. In essence, a commonly
accepted version of this formula held that old work, e.g., work on old
buildings and facilities, belonged to the inside forces and new work, on
new construction, could be turned over to outside contractors. In terms

of the erosion model, one part of the management rights territory was ceded in order to protect another.

Nine process and nine fabrication firms employed this defense, but only two of the process firms were satisfied with the results. Establishing categories of this type often appeared to be an attractive strategy in periods when management had no intention of contracting-out old work, for then the only result was greater freedom in the new work area. But in the face of developments favoring the contracting of functions falling in the old work category, this defense lost much of its appeal. Significantly, the two companies that expressed satisfaction with this defense traditionally had followed the old work-new work formula in assigning activities to various groups and had not at the time developed any reasons for changing this procedure.

The other companies that used this defense found it unsatisfactory for a variety of reasons. Bureaucratizing the decision process by developing a set of rules had resulted in a loss of flexibility. Inevitably, these categories had to be communicated to the union, and then they often became the basis for bargaining and establishing claims. An electrical-equipment manufacturer reported that the workers finally struck over what they considered an erroneous application of these management-devised rules. Drawing the line between informing and seeking approval had a close second in the perplexities of distinguishing between old and new work. The installation of old machinery in a new building could prove to be an exquisitely complex problem from the standpoint of job property rights.

These management-generated attempts to develop rules for dividing work between the inside and outside forces were not unique. Other notable efforts were made by national craft and industrial union leaders (see Chapter 11). As indicated elsewhere, most of these rules have tended to be both arbitrary and unrealistic (see Chapters 11 and 14). Yet, those who rejected the use of these rules took this stand not on the grounds of impracticality but largely because they felt these procedures would lead to a loss of freedom.

Management in the nineteen plants that employed notification as their sole venture into the barter defense territory opposed a system of new and old work categories. Officials in a steel mill stated, "We try to run our own business. Distinguishing between old and new work would be restricting ourselves. We want to maintain freedom of action. We want to be able to contract any work."

Actually, the old work–new work system was typical of other attempts to devise functional classifications. Some managers said they used categories based on the size of the jobs: "Small jobs are inside work. Big jobs go outside." Any reason for contracting could be reformulated into a rule of this type. One manager in a fabricated-metal plant noted that he had two categories, "work our men can do, and work our men are unable to do." He reported that thus far the men had accepted this distinction, but he was afraid that they would begin to bargain about it.

One manager summed up the whole situation by saying that he would favor using a system of categories, "if someone could think up one that nobody could question."

As in the case of notification, this defense was used sporadically. A plant engineer remarked, "It works when the men are busy." It was applied, not uniformly, but rather whenever it promised to be useful in a particular state of affairs.

Equalizing conditions for inside and outside forces

As noted earlier, sensitive points along the route in contracting-out work involved the emergence of inequities in the conditions for the inside and outside forces. From the standpoint of the inside forces, some inequities were more provocative than others. Heading the highly provocative list were occasions when the contractor's men received overtime at double time. Separating the inside and outside forces constituted a first line of defense, but when inside worker pressures broke through this barrier, a new solution was required. To cope with these emerging inequities, some firms used a form of the avoidance defense. Despite the inconveniences that were incurred, some highly visible sources of inequities were forbidden. Thus, contractors working for a fabricated-metal concern were not allowed to work their men on an overtime basis.

However, a bartering solution also was available to management. Dollars could be exchanged for freedom to contract. Equalization usually involved giving inside workers overtime pay whenever this type of compensation was earned by their counterparts in the contractor's forces. This defense was not common, but seven companies, five process and two fabrication establishments, used it. Some of the uneasiness that characterized the notification process was missing. While this device cost money, it did not involve the discussion of decisions with the union. On the other hand, the great majority of the firms that rejected this defense described equalization as "featherbedding" or "paying tribute to the union." An industrial relations manager in a refinery commented, "It amounts to an implicit contract." In dismissing this plan, a manager in a chemical firm noted, "There would be no point to it. We contract to avoid overtime."

Those who used this defense regarded it as an uncomplicated means of making contracting-out palatable to the inside crew by converting this activity into a source of potential gain. The equalization defense was employed only in the case of need. These funds were offered to the inside forces infrequently—when trouble seemed imminent. In order to avoid making this action a matter of contract, management in a machinery-manufacturing firm said that they "tried to do it informally." This, of course, was a recurrent theme in all these defenses —to keep them casual and unplanned in appearance.

Related management defenses represented variations on the equalization theme. For instance, management might guarantee that the inside forces would receive a certain number of hours of work per week or per year. In some cases the guarantee included eight hours overtime per week. It was assumed that, if this guarantee was met, workers would cease to complain about contracting. Moreover, if complaints should arise, they could be countered with the "full employment" argument.

Only one firm in the sample used this defense, but a few other managements expressed interest in it as a possible way of "retaining our rights." The food-processing company that employed this defense guaranteed its craft workers 2,000 hours of work yearly after they had completed one year's service. Although this program was a fairly recent introduction, the plant manager credited it with having forestalled union penetration into the contracting-out area. One of the chemical plants in the sample formerly had guaranteed a full week's pay in order to obtain a free hand in contracting-out. However, in the later fifties the inside workers noticed that management was assigning increasing amounts of work to contractors. Therefore, the union demanded compensation for all the potential overtime that the plant crew had lost as a result of contracting. This demand was "traded off" for other concessions, but the case illustrates the instability of barter defenses of this type. As management proceeds to take advantage of its newly found "freedom," the inside forces recalculate their notion of a fair share in terms of the now-prevailing situation.

Letters of intent

Letters of intent constituted a last-ditch defense before complete surrender in the sense that a contract clause signified capitulation. The letter had the appearance of being a management-initiated act rather than a bargained agreement, although in content it may have differed very little from a contract clause. Therefore, the form of the letter was a point of great importance. One manager noted that he might be willing to send the union a carbon copy of an internal letter that was written by the plant manager and addressed to the head of maintenance and construction. In his eyes, a letter directed to the union was the equivalent of a contract clause.

Ten plants, three in process and seven in fabrication industries, had issued such letters. Half these firms had signed collective bargaining agreements on contracting-out in addition to the letter, and these managements were not strongly opposed to letters of intent, for they viewed these letters as a means of excluding further concessions from the contract. Some thought that provisions in the letter might not spread to other plants of the same firm as rapidly as those in a contract. Others hoped that the letter would not be considered arbitrable, thus serving to exclude disputes from arbitration proceedings.

The letter was much more distasteful to those managements for whom it represented the first item in writing on the subject of contracting-out. One large fabrication company discharged a vice-president who issued such a letter in answer to a union complaint. This letter promised notification in advance and stated that, if comparative costs were equal or less, work would be given to the inside forces. The director of industrial relations explained the situation as follows: "Management wanted to kill the vice-president after he issued the letter. The whole idea of it was distasteful. They never refer to it." He also remarked that the conditions specified in the letter did not represent a radical departure from actual practices. As he noted, "These things were done, more or less, anyhow." But the letter itself served as a symbol of defeat and resulted in a firm resolve, unbroken for eight years, "never to put another line in writing on the subject of contracting-out."

The letter of intent was significant in the study of the management defense process because it represented a first formal statement of practices that were deliberately administered in an informal and casual fashion. The existence of a letter was an indication that a company was fairly well into barter defense territory. The crystallization of defensive practices in the form of a letter was the result of another exchange in which the formal statement was traded for a valued "right," the right to avoid a contract clause. Of course, companies that used only management-controlled defenses regarded such a letter as a major threat to prerogatives. The industrial relations manager in one of these firms stated, "Anything in writing represents a basic weakness in exercising prerogatives." For those who employed a battery of barter defenses, the letter represented another step in the trading process. In this respect, some regarded it as no better than a symbolic gain over a contract clause. A manager in a metal-processing plant commented, "You are just kidding yourself when you write one of those letters.

You can pick up a copy of the contract and say, 'See we haven't lost any ground,' but I say it has the same effect as a contract."

The barter defense firms

A small group of five companies, three fabrication and two process, employed only barter defenses. Management was no longer concerned with the problem of unilateral control or the avoidance of sensitive borderline cases, for almost all cases fell in this category. The union had a moderate to strong voice in the decision, but this fact was not the basis of a full explanation of the defense pattern. All these plants had a past history of "do-it-yourself" operation. This policy was abandoned, but the entire responsibility for the decision remained where it had been, at the middle and low operating levels in the organization. Top management considered the problems that arose "housekeeping matters" and instructed officers at the operating levels to "work things out with the men." While decisions involving major expenses were made at the top levels, these, too, were to be implemented on the above basis. Experiences from the do-it-yourself days definitely affected the manner in which the men at the operating level carried out the defense of management rights. Defenses of management rights were by no means abandoned: rather, they were reduced to a pragmatic level.

All the barter defense firms automatically used notification as their first line of defense and proceeded, as a plant engineer in one of the companies noted, "to argue it out with them in advance." There was no question of making notification a unilateral process, with management retaining complete initiative. In three of these cases the defense involved assiduous efforts to gain acceptance of the management position, but through means that would have horrified staunch advocates of management rights. On occasion, the reverse of the "none of your business" approach was employed. Data, including cost records and bids from contractors, were presented to the workers, and if they did not accept the idea that a contractor could do the job faster, better, and cheaper, at times they were given an opportunity to try their hand at the assignment. If the men "botched" the work, management then turned to a contractor. The mechanical superintendent in one of these firms described the manner in which he regained his "right" to contract-out a tile job:

> I let them get involved. Once they wanted to lay a tile floor in the basement of the general office. The basement is a kind of showplace. We have lounges down there and we want it to look nice. Well, they said

they could do the job, and I thought, "You can't, but I'll just let you try."
I even came down Saturday morning to see how they were getting along.
Well, you never saw a mess like that. They had the tiles crooked, and
black tar was oozing all over. They had said, "Oh, everybody lays that
tile," but it isn't easy to do a professional-looking job. You have to know
how. I thought I'd let them continue, let them get themselves in a little
deeper. I didn't know if the general office would get on my back for it,
but I let them work on until 5. Then Monday morning I called in the
union steward and the local president, and we went over and showed
them the job. We told them we were going to call in a contractor that
very morning to rip up their work and do the job over. We asked them
if they had any objections, and they said, "No, you don't have to show us
any more." They had all sorts of excuses. This was wrong and that was
wrong. The tar was no good. But they weren't putting up an argument.
Now we contract tile jobs whenever we want. Of course you can't run an
experiment all the time. This one cost us maybe three or four hundred
dollars, but when it runs to much more than that, the lessons are too
expensive.

Thus, when a defense began with notification as a first step, the
whole tenor of the defense changed. Notification became a matter
of striking bargains and winning points, and arguments were carried
from the office to the work site. Those who favored trading on a case-
by-case basis eschewed the use of rules for barter. One of the maintenance managers explained his position:

> I believe each job should stand on its own feet. If certain work becomes
> contract work, or if you pay your men for overtime just because a con-
> tractor's men received some overtime pay, it looks like you are buying
> freedom, but it seems to me that you are losing it. You are bribing your
> men and you are committing yourself to a policy of contracting in certain
> cases, regardless of cost and other important considerations.

While three of these managers preferred case-by-case barter, management in the other two companies emphasized barter via rules. But
these rules were quite different from those based on gross distinctions
such as old work–new work. These rules often focused on standards
for the inside forces' fair share of work of various types. Negotiations
associated with this process were complex and time-consuming and involved a continual shifting of position and remaking of rules in the
light of the current situation.

Some management experts would view these cases as examples of
a healthy democratic process, while others would regard them as
examples of near chaos. The managers in charge of these operations
were less than enthusiastic about the time and energy absorbed, and
they attributed mounting backlogs of work and inefficiency to the
slowness of the process. They also presented a notable contrast to the

commonly accepted picture of the lower levels' sabotaging management rights by active collusion with the internal crews. Saddled with responsibility and groping for an adequate approach, these managers seemed anxious for more support and a stronger stand on the part of the upper levels of management. On the other hand, a strong stand by top management may have stimulated collusion between lower management and the work force.

CONTRACT CLAUSES AND MANAGEMENT DEFENSES

Defenses did not include bargained agreements, but rather measures that management instituted unilaterally to defend its "right" to contract-out and to avoid the onus of a formal bargained agreement. In an area that has been covered extensively in collective bargaining, it would be difficult to distinguish clearly between defenses and agreements. In the case of contracting-out, bargaining had not reached this stage, and therefore it was possible to draw the line and to isolate management defenses as an entity for separate study.

Interestingly, contract clauses often represented nothing more than a formal statement of one of management's avoidance or barter defenses. Our research also indicated that converting these practices to a contractual basis did not involve drastic changes in managerial behavior. Whether in the form of a defense or a clause, these programs tended to be adhered to in an inconsistent fashion. Twenty-four firms in the sample had signed union-management agreements on contracting-out. These included 28 per cent of the fabrication companies and 16 per cent of the process, excluding those in the utility industries, where special conditions prevailed. All the utility firms had these clauses, and when they were included, the proportion for process industries rose to 39 per cent.

Only one of these agreements moved beyond the stage of formalizing a measure used by the firm in question or by others as a defense. Typical examples specified notification of the union before or after the letting of a contract and the avoidance of contracting if inside men were on layoff. The single exception to this rule involved a reverse agreement in a plant organized by craft unions. All nonproduction work was to be contracted-out! (A specific discussion of these agreements will be presented in Chapter 11.)

The signing of a contract clause proved to be a far from perfect indicator of a complete loss of management rights. The majority (three-fifths) of the firms with clauses reported no real sense of restriction in their operations. On the other hand, about one-fourth of the firms without agreements reported restrictions by the inside unions.

Obviously, and as numerous other studies have pointed out, one had to look beyond the contract to obtain an accurate picture of the influence of a union on a management decision. However, the existence of a clause certainly constituted reliable evidence of union interest. In addition to the twenty-four clauses that unions successfully negotiated, there were sixteen attempts that failed before the final round of bargaining. Thus a total of 55 per cent of the firms in the sample either had agreements or had unions that had some interest in obtaining agreements.

Clearly, formal contracts did not mark the end of the trail for management rights—or the end of management defensive measures. On the contrary, all the companies that had signed clauses also continued to employ a variety of defenses. The great majority (three-fourths) of these firms used a mixed management-controlled and barter defense. Two had purely barter defenses and four a purely management-controlled defense. Of the specific defenses, the management-controlled "avoidance of borderline cases" was the most popular. It was used in eighteen of the twenty-four cases. Although barter defenses were not abandoned, the formal clause seemed to encourage attempts to check the points at which the operation of the decision process had been faulty, e.g., choosing inopportune times to bring in contractors. Two firms proceeded to ignore the agreement and retreated to a modified no discussion defense. They preferred to take their chances on the union's inability to enforce the contract.

UNION INFLUENCE, MANAGEMENT DEFENSES, AND ORGANIZATIONAL STRUCTURE

Contracting-out proved to be a management area that was not easily converted into a controllable state. Putting the problem in contractual language was the beginning rather than the end of the process. Or perhaps this act might be described as merely a step along the way. The real key to the process of "infringing" on management's right to contract-out lay in devising effective means for control within the industrial organization. Organizational structures that favored this effort and the existence of managerial allies played an important role in the union's success in this regard.

Measuring the union's achievements obviously required more than a rating based on contract clauses, letters of intent, and other informal agreements. Therefore, we devised a means for scoring each establishment on the actual ability of the union to affect or influence the management decision regarding contracting-out. Each company was scored on a six-point scale, with a score of 6 indicating "no influence" and a score of 1 indicating "complete control." On this basis it was found that twenty-five unions had absolutely no influence (a score of 6); twenty had only weak influence (a score of 5); fifteen had moderate influence (a score of 4); and ten had strong influence (a score of 3). Two unions were rated as having very strong influence (a score of 2); and two had almost complete control (a score of 1).

Union influence and organizational structure

Like management defenses, union influence proved to be a function of organizational structure. The amount of union voice was positively related to the proportion of the total plant force engaged in maintenance and construction. Fourteen establishments having influence scores ranging from 1 to 3 were assigned to a "high influence" category. These cases proved to be located in plants with a higher than average proportion of maintenance and construction workers, 11.8 as compared with 8.4 for the sample as a whole. Moreover, the absolute figures for plant and department size revealed a bias toward the high side. Average plant employment size was 9,010 as compared with an average of 4,240 for the entire sample, and average department size was 1,070 in contrast to a sample mean of 355.

The twenty-five no influence cases, establishments with a score of 6, presented a striking contrast. The proportion of maintenance and construction workers in the total force was lower than average, 6.9 per cent. The average plant size was 2,500, a figure considerably lower than the sample mean. The average department size of 175 also was substantially lower than the sample mean.

An intermediate influence group included thirty-five firms scoring 4 and 5. With regard to the questions of proportion and size, this group also placed in a position intermediate to the high and no influence groups—fairly close to the sample average. The proportion of the total force engaged in maintenance and construction was 7.7, mean plant size was 3,400, and mean department size was 260. The positive relationship of union influence to factors of plant size and the proportion of maintenance and construction group to the total force persisted for all categories of influence.

Union influence and technology

The relationship between union influence and differences in technology presented a more diverse and less clear-cut picture. As one might have anticipated, process firms constituted a somewhat higher proportion of the no influence cases, 39 per cent as compared with 30 per cent for fabrication. On the other hand, fabrication had a higher proportion in the moderate influence category, 54 per cent in contrast to 38 per cent for process. Finally, the high influence group included 23 per cent of the process and 16 per cent of the fabrication companies.

These differences in proportion were not large enough to be statistically significant, although the differences in the moderate category approached this condition. However, it was of interest to speculate on the reason for the direction of these differences in proportion—the tendency of the process plants to hold the higher proportion of no and high influence cases and for fabrication to be stronger in the middle ground.

From the standpoint of a potential invader of the management right to contract-out, the structure of the process plant had both favorable and unfavorable aspects (see also Chapters 4 and 15). Process plants typically had a substantial proportion of the total force engaged in maintenance and construction. In the sample used, process plants had an average proportion of 10.8 in maintenance and construction, while fabrication had a lower mean proportion, 6.5. Moreover, in process industries, where the ratio of labor cost to total cost was typically lower than in fabrication, the size of these forces was not so sensitive a matter. Then, too, process technology involved a higher degree of commitment to the use of inside forces. In a period of change the potential pressures to preserve the inside function were great.

On the other hand, process industries tended to have a tighter, more centralized management structure, with a higher degree of consensus among the members (see Chapter 15). Our data also indicated that, in contrast to fabrication, process management was more rights-conscious, especially in light of the need to adjust to new economic and technological pressures. Thus, one found a combination of strong latent pressures from the inside forces and a firm managerial resolve to resist, backed up by a pressure-resistant management structure. Under these conditions, one would tend to anticipate vigorous struggles, with either one side or the other emerging victorious. The potential rights invader may have had a more difficult time getting his foot in the door. But if he succeeded, developing cracks in the organizational armor simplified his task, for he then could benefit from the ability to exert strong internal pressures.

Historically, fabrication industries, with the exception of some large plants, have had less commitment to the inside forces. On the other hand, their management structure has been less resistant to invasion, and thus the stage was set for a more moderate kind of union "penetration."

In explaining the extent of union influence within these major groups simple factors of size and proportion dominated the picture once more.

Within the process industry group, differences in plant employment size and proportion in the maintenance and construction force were associated with differing influence ratings. For instance, the process firms in which the union had high influence averaged 11.1 per cent of the total force in maintenance and construction, in contrast to an average of 7.9 per cent for the process firms in which the union had no voice. The corresponding figures for the fabrication group were 13.2 per cent in high influence companies and 6.5 per cent where the union had low influence. The average size of the high influence process firms was 11,420, in comparison with 1,720 where no influence was found. Parallel figures for fabrication were 6,900 for high influence and 3,160 for low influence.

The relationship of union influence to factors of size and proportion remained clear, but the findings regarding the relationship to technology were only suggestive and require further research.

Union influence and union structure

However, the relationship between union influence and simple aspects of organizational structure, such as size and the proportional relation of a part to the whole, was confounded by the factor of gross union structure. For one type of union organization had preponderant weight in the larger plants, where union influence was stronger, and other types of union structures tended to be concentrated in the smaller establishments. Seventy per cent of the plants (fifty-one) were organized by industrial unions or industrial branches of craft unions that included both production and maintenance and construction workers in a single bargaining unit. The presence of the industrial union structure in the larger plants was reflected in the industrial group's higher than average employment size of 4,970 and mean of 435 employees in the maintenance and construction departments. Twelve of the fourteen high influence establishments, scoring from 1 to 3, were members of this group, and almost three-fifths of these had an employment size of over 5,000. For the entire sample of seventy-four plants, the average union influence score was 4.7, but for those with the single industrial union bargaining unit the lower score of 4.3 reflected a somewhat higher influence.

A small number of plants were organized entirely on a craft basis. These seven companies had a mean employment size of 3,510 and an average of 240 workers in maintenance and construction. In the majority of these establishments, the union either had no influence (four cases) or was very weak (two cases). The average influence score of 5 was affected considerably by a group of crafts that had achieved a high score of 1.

From the standpoint of union structure, the weakest situation involved a combination of both industrial and craft unions in one plant. These companies were concentrated at the lower end of the size range, with employment averaging 2,230 and maintenance and construction forces 150. In the sixteen plants where this structure prevailed, union voice was weak, with a mean score of 5.4. In seven of these plants, some maintenance workers also were included in the industrial union, and in one of these cases the single high score of 3 was found. However, in nine plants there were no craft workers in the industrial union, and small numbers of these men were organized in separate craft locals, which were by and large indifferent to the problem. In these cases, union voice was almost nonexistent, with an average score of 5.8.

In an effort to distinguish between the effects of union and company organization structure, we investigated the success of these differing forms of union organization in plants considerably above or below the mean sizes for each group. How effective were the craft and mixed types in larger plants and the industrial union type in smaller plants? The craft and mixed forms of organization did not fare better in the few large plants where they were located. In fact, the scores hinted that these structures may have been less efficient in larger organizations.

On the other hand, the industrial union had slightly more influence when size factors favored its position. When the proportion of construction and maintenance workers in the industrial union exceeded 10, some union voice was assured. Establishments with a no influence score of 6 vanished from the scene. In addition, the industrial union score averaged 4.0 in plants with an employment size of over 2,500 and 4.5 in those under this figure. Where the proportion of maintenance and construction workers in the total force was over 10, the union scored a mean of 4.1 in contrast to 4.4 in cases where the proportion was under 10.

From these data one could conclude that union influence on contracting-out found a more congenial environment in an organizational base that was strong in the numerical sense—ideally in a large plant with a maintenance and construction crew that constituted a sizable proportion of the total work group. In addition, there was an indication that this numerical base was more easily translated into an impressive force when maintenance and construction was included in a single, undivided union organization.

Management defenses and union influence

It has been indicated that defenses were geared to the current situation with regard to pressures on management. Thus, union influence may have served better as a predictor of type of defense than as a measure of its effectiveness. As a matter of fact, there were significant differences in the average influence scores associated with the various defenses. In firms employing the management-controlled defense, the average influence score was low, 5.04. The score for plants employing a mixed management-controlled and barter defense was 4.04, a figure higher than the overall average of 4.7. In the purely barter defense firms, a mean score of 2.4 indicated high union influence.

While ostensibly directed at the inside union and tuned to the extent of its activities, these defenses clearly affected other groups at interest as well. One was prompted to inquire, "Defenses against what?" Certainly the union was not unique as a source of pressure on contracting-out. The union's concern about maintaining the size of a department often was no greater than that of the manager who ran it. A policy of permitting a department to decrease in size through a process of attrition affected this company official as well as the union and its members. Our research indicated that other pressure groups existed in abundance, but to what extent did awareness of the total complex of pressures potentially or actually add new dimensions to management's measures of defense?

GROUP PRESSURES AND MANAGEMENT RIGHTS

The interview data revealed a substantial managerial awareness of multiple pressures on contracting-out. Nearly one-half of the members of the sample reported persistent pressures from the following sources: twenty listed the industrial plant union; three, the craft union in the plant; twenty, management groups in the company; six, informal worker groups in the plant; and six, craft union and contractor groups in the community.

With the exception of the outside craftsmen, these groups tended to be cited not alone but as one of several sources of pressures. There were only four cases in which the inside industrial union was mentioned as a single source of pressure. Management groups held this position as a single source in seven cases, the inside craft union in one, and the informal worker groups in none. The outside contractors and craft unions were named singly in five out of the six cases reported. The sole exception involved a potent alliance between outside forces and inside craft unions that had jurisdiction over the entire plant. The results of this combined pressure were noted previously—all nonproduction work was contracted-out.

One-half of those reporting pressures named more than one source.

The largest number described in any one company was five. In this firm, construction and maintenance management, the inside union, and some informal work groups were pressuring to keep work inside, and other managers and outside contractors and craft unions were exerting efforts in the direction of contracting-out.

The most frequent source of combined pressure involved internal management groups, such as construction and maintenance, and the inside union. The average union influence score for the thirteen plants reporting this combination was high, 3.2. This finding supported our field observations that multiple-pressure situations could offer potent support for union efforts.

The organizational meaning of loss of rights

This chapter has considered management rights and their defense and union influence as functions of structural and technological forces. In our study it was evident that contracting-out offered a considerable challenge to the potential inside union invader of rights. Therefore, we were interested in studying cases in which the union gained substantial headway, proceeding to the point where it might be described as being in the driver's seat. Four plants in the sample fell in this class. What did they have in common? They were divided evenly with regard to technology, two being process and two fabrication firms. There was no uniformity with regard to plant employment size. Two establishments were large and two were small, by the standards of our sample. In three plants, both production and maintenance workers were organized in a single industrial union. The other was the previously described craft-organized plant in which union pressures encouraged contracting-out. In all the industrial union organized companies the construction and maintenance crew constituted over 12 per cent of the total force, a high proportion. Thus some of the structural factors favorable to high union influence were present. One would anticipate uniformly strong contract clauses, but two of these unions had none. A clause on contracting-out was traded off for other bargaining gains because these unions saw no need for one in view of their actual achievements.

But all these cases had one very important characteristic in common. The union had achieved what might be described as a very thorough penetration of the organizational relationships associated with contracting-out. For instance, the unions called on contractors in the area and developed understandings with them. In all these companies, the union's pressures were supported by those from inside management and workers or outside groups in the community. Thus, success was not simply a matter of union prowess as a singlehanded operator. Rather, it was a matter of combining efforts with similarly oriented groups and controlling those with a different orientation.

Informal union-management agreements often have been cited to explain research findings that formal contracts fail to tell the whole story of a union-management relationship. But in these situations one found a different and more complex source of control. The union has invaded the world of internal and external management relations with regard to contracting-out. In other words, the union had become part of the very processes by which management usually controlled the union's ability to gain a voice in this decision.

SUMMARY

Developing a coherent picture of a management defense is no simple task, for one is confronted with a certain amount of order amid considerable confusion.

In our study the data gave no indication that the management rights theme was either extinct or submerged by more "modern" approaches. In fact, the defenses observed in action were a curious blend of the legalistic and personnel approaches recommended in the literature and lessons learned in everyday organizational life. The compromise seemed to take the form observed in the two patterns for the management-controlled defense. In the legalistic mood there were short-run devices to meet piecemeal challenges from the inside forces. And there were organizational measures involving drastic changes in structure. Middle-range solutions oriented toward smoothing and regulating organizational process were largely missing.

Even though in actual practice defenses moved away from a literal interpretation of the wins-losses management rights erosion model, they were affected by it. The legalistic influence on management actions was reflected in an emphasis on form rather than substance, as evidenced in the stress placed on retaining the appearance of unilateral control. Moreover, the anticipated consequences of a defense tended to be viewed in narrow, legalistic terms.

Only a small number of the firms had managements that were strict legalists in action as well as in theory. The exclusive use of the no discussion defense was limited to the few—as was substantial submission to inside union control. However, the majority had reached the stage of bartering something in return for their "rights." On the whole, the executors of management defenses were not happy with their lot when the tactics they used moved out of the management-controlled area. Cooperative union-management relations regarding contracting-out proved to be a rare bird indeed.

Although the defenses were management-initiated actions, changes in their composition and character arose largely in response to new external pressures. Long-range managerial master plans did not abound in this field, nor did rigidly and consistently applied patterns of defense. Moreover, a "hard-nosed" position on management rights did not necessarily mean that management would be able to limit itself to a management-controlled defense. This particular defense seemed to be restricted to situations where it was feasible, largely by reason of favorable structural conditions.

Barter defenses had a self-defeating quality. The items traded made the area accessible to the opposition and became the basis for union demands and recalculations of "fair shares" in light of management's newly acquired freedom to act. There was a constant effort to preserve a noncontractual flavor in these defenses, a casual, uncommitted look. The search for an unchallengeable trading item of unchanging value continued, but to no avail. In defending the area of contracting-out rights, management encountered the same types of problems that the union faced when it tried to invade it.

Defenses in this area entailed complications because they frequently affected more than one party at interest. In turn, allied pressures from various interest groups were generated, and real losses of management "rights" seemed to take place when potent combinations of these groups went into action.

The other side of the management defense coin was union influence. In common with management defenses, union influence proved to be a function of organizational structure. Union influence was positively related to plant employment size and proportion of the total force in maintenance and construction. A less definite relationship between union influence and technology raised some interesting questions about differences in process and fabrication industries as objects of penetration by potential invaders of management rights. Another factor, differences in the structure of union organization, indicated that a base for organization that was numerically and proportionately favorable in the maintenance and construction field also was more easily translated into an impressive force when these workers were included in a single plant-wide union organization.

Finally, upon looking into the future, it was evident that some of the old stand-by defenses were obsolete, especially those geared to handle piecemeal challenges. As the failure of these defenses becomes increasingly apparent, they may be abandoned and neglected systems of defense, focusing on control of organizational process, may in time take their place.

part iv

The Inside and Outside Forces

chapter 7

The Outside Forces

THE GROUP STRUCTURE OF BARGAINING ISSUES

In the field of industrial relations there is a widely accepted proposition that labor and management have basically and inevitably different orientations. Formerly, the only answer to this proposition was the "human relations" approach, which advocated incorporating workers, who were physically inside but psychologically outside, into a plant community of management and employees, with common goals in a common enterprise. Supporters of the first point of view denied the validity of the human relations position and advanced the counter-argument that the labor-management relationship is fundamentally a power struggle. However, both these models have missed some aspects of the real nature of the process being investigated.

119

Each issue in labor-management relations has its own particular interest group structure and structure of bargaining relations. Failure to exploit this fact further has been due partially to the prominence of wage negotiations as a subject for study and of the tendency to assume that nonwage disputes follow the patterns of the union-management relationship for the wage issue. According to this view, the bargaining table is the central arena for the relationship, for it is here that the gap between two strongly held positions—management's first "offer" and the union's first "demand"—is narrowed as these two groups proceed to test one another's negotiating skills and strength.

However, the resolution of the great variety of nonwage issues in labor-management relations has not necessarily followed this pattern. For instance, prowess in the field of nonwage issues, such as contracting-out, may have been less a function of the single factor, union strength, and more a function of elements such as the combined supportive pressures that were marshaled behind the particular problem. Economic power may have been of little avail if the "organization" was lacking, and conversely, given the organization, economic power could be unnecessary. Developing a good organization meant that the group first had to recognize that a variety of interests could furnish potential support for its efforts. Therefore, the group's leaders needed to develop structures that would facilitate and not block the goal realization of other groups with complementary interests. Moreover, these officials had to learn to work with existing structures within their own and other organizations—and to respond appropriately to changes within these structures.

In Chapter 6 it was observed that the extent of the inside union's voice in the contracting-out area was related positively to simple structural factors such as the proportion of the total plant force engaged in maintenance and construction. And it was indicated that the few cases of real inside union penetration of this area were dependent upon the union's possessing a strong inplant organization with the appropriate external bonds. It is obvious that these prescriptions for building a good organization apply to other parties at interest in addition to the inside union, especially to the outside contractors and craft unions. Ultimately, the competitive effectiveness of both the inside and outside organizations was to be tested by their continuing ability to adapt to new needs—to proceed in a fashion that facilitated rather than hampered the making of advances, especially in new fields.

This chapter (Chapter 7) will focus on the structural adjustments of the outside forces, and Chapter 8 will examine the inside organization. Chapter 9 will assess the potential results of the inside-outside competition.

Before proceeding with the above analysis, it may be helpful to set forth the general structure of group relationships for the contract-ing-out problem. Labor and management clearly were not the mono-lithic forces of interest for our organizational analysis of contracting-out. Treatment of the rights issue definitely focused on the relationship between two forces, the inside union and industrial management, and discussions of organizational problems tended to follow suit. But the only monolithic forces involved in either the management rights or the organizational problems never identified themselves as such and rarely were thus identified by others. The shifting nature of alliances pre-cluded any firm specification of membership, but in general one could note two broad groupings, the inside and the outside interests. The inside interests, who opposed contracting-out, included in the hard core the industrial plant maintenance and construction workers and management and the union representing these workers. The outside interests, who favored contracting-out, included in the hard core the craft workers in the community, their unions, and their contractor-employers. These were the groups that we have designated the inside and outside forces. Beyond this hard core were many other groups that might become involved, such as associations representing specialty, general, and integrated contractors, national craft union organizations, community officials, general industrial management, and various de-partments in the industrial firm such as engineering, purchasing, and industrial relations. Any one of these elements may have supported actively the inside or outside cause, and at times two or three may have joined forces, but in many cases they constituted loose aggrega-tions, taking their several routes to an identical goal—either to con-tract-out or to assign work to inside crews.

The particular parties at interest and the constellation of relation-ships observed at a given time and place were a function of relevant technological and structural factors. Thus, plans to bring an outside maintenance contractor with a nation-wide operation into a modern-ized process plant may have been opposed by a coalition of the indus-trial plant union, the head of the plant maintenance department, as well as community officials and general and specialty contractors and craft unions who wanted the work assigned to a local construction company. Pressures to facilitate the move may have been exerted by top management in the company, the plant engineer, and a contractor's association, representing the national group.

Thus, we found that the external labels were deceiving. Within common organizational housings there were diverse property claims, and across the boundaries there were common interests. Contractors, unions, and members of industrial management were aligned on both sides. At the same time there was the paradox of rights and organiza-tional issues that were viewed as a struggle between two united forces, labor and management. In reality, there was not just one rights or organizational dimension to contracting-out: rather, there were several. Failure to recognize this point has endlessly complicated the solution of problems.

THE STRUCTURE OF THE OUTSIDE FORCES

Interestingly, the outside dimension in problems such as contracting-out generally has been conceived in narrow terms. In part, this phenomenon may have been a function of bias resulting from the tendency of research studies to concentrate on the inside organization, e.g., the industrial plant. And for the neglected contractor-industrial firm relationship, a legal document, the contract, often was regarded as the essence of the bond. Thus, one was confronted with stereotyped views that disregarded the existence of close and continuing working relations.

As a member of the industrial scene, the contractor supplied jobs for workers, many of whom were members of craft unions, markets for the sellers of materials and equipment, and services for industrial management. In return, he received varying degrees of support from these groups. Traditionally, contractors have had a close alliance with their unionized craft workers—much closer than that between industrial management and the inside employees and their unions. In this chapter we shall discuss new trends in the outside organization. These trends involved changes in structure, e.g., moves away from specialization and toward integration. We also shall note a trend away from contractor reliance on certain aspects of the relationship with the craft unions and toward the development of structures to exploit some emerging common interests of industrial management and the outside contractor.

The contractor-craft complex

The close alliance between the contractor and the craft union has had both favorable and unfavorable aspects from the standpoint of developing the industrial work market. In part, this bond could be explained by the fact that the contractor was likely to have an early background as a member of the craft labor force. This fact, in turn, apparently had a significant effect on the contractor's view of the contracting-out problem. For many years—often until the late fifties—he considered contracting-out a labor problem, a matter determined largely by jurisdiction. His approach to industrial management often reflected this line of thought. On some occasions he exerted direct pressures and tried to assert the claim that certain work was, in fact, his property. When licensing requirements reinforced this stand, industrial management complied but this approach met with managerial resistance in other cases. On the whole, these actions undoubtedly slowed the entrance of contract services into the industrial field.

While these cases were far from universal occurrences, they had a symbolic value far beyond their actual incidence, for in effect the outside forces were threatening management's right to accomplish work with inside forces! A few managers asserted that outside pressure activities had lessened their resistance to inside department demands for work and even to inside union demands for contract clauses restricting contracting-out.

In one metropolitan area included in the sample, industrial management noted that the secretary of the local building trades group had for years made the rounds periodically, encouraging companies to contract their work. Moreover, these managers reported that, when industrial work was to be contracted, the secretary would call on them and indicate which contractor should get the job. This building trades official was oriented toward the goal of getting work for union men and for contractors who were thought to treat their employees fairly. Probably very little consideration was given to the effect of this behavior on the attitudes of industrial management toward the outside forces. The outside craft unions that conducted these activities were in effect the contractors' salesmen. However, as they used their own group as a prime source of information, they worked with limited data and tended to acquire little sophistication in the ways of the industrial organization. Therefore, they were likely to rely on direct pressures rather than on more subtle techniques. A metals-processing management reported that the building trades unions threatened to refuse to perform work that was governed by licensing requirements if other assignments were not forthcoming. But the craft organizations tended to feel that, if these pressures were not exerted, they would receive no work at all. As one union leader commented, "The big companies won't talk to us unless they feel they have to."

Moreover, after contract forces entered the plant, the labor problem orientation often persisted. In one case outside electricians refused to handle panels wired in an industrial-union-organized factory, saying that the work had to be sent to a "blue label" (craft-organized) shop for assembly. On the other hand, no such difficulties were incurred when the panels were installed by the company's own maintenance crew. When outside craftsmen observed the inside forces at work, they had the opportunity to note many more infractions of their jurisdiction and these, too, were the subject of actions ranging from simple harassment of the inside workers to indignant walkouts. Needless to say, in the infrequent cases in which the labor problem focus manifested itself in persistent pressuring, the contractor and his men often were more a hindrance than a help to industrial management. Traditionally, managers have insisted that the contractor be responsible for all aspects of his men's behavior and settle all the disputes that may arise. While contractors had a reputation for controlling the quality of their men's work by discharging those who did not meet standards, their control of the quality of their employees' interactions with plant personnel was much weaker. The lack of emphasis on the latter point may have reflected the fact that in some cases the matter of jurisdiction was just as vital to the contractor as it was to his men.

The contractor had his own "jurisdictional" battles with members of inside management. In part, these were the inevitable clashes of two managers of separate organizations engaged in a common enterprise. Each manager tended to feel fully responsible for the entire project and fully entitled to all the benefits that flowed from his activities. At times credit for a task well done was difficult to share, but even more problematical were points of economic overlap—for instance, who should serve the purchasing function? Each side accused the other of hampering efficiency in an effort to reap profits through materials purchases. The company that insisted on purchasing its own materials was not popular with the contractor, and vice versa. Of course, some companies actually solicited purchasing services from contractors. Problems usually arose in cases in which the firm operated a similar facility for which it purchased the materials in question. Thus, the manager of an electric utility stated, "We have better buying facilities than the average contractor. We ask them to bid only on the labor and equipment involved." A contractor in the same area complained that the materials furnished often were inappropriate for the job but that nevertheless he had to guarantee the work. Moreover, he maintained that he could not afford to stay in business under these conditions.

The purchasing issue was encountered a number of times during the course of our research. In the long run it might be resolved by basic forces such as technological developments. In the short run, both sides relied on a variety of pressures to maintain or achieve their chosen position. There was little evidence of moves to compromise. For some companies in certain industries the use of contracting was contingent upon the contractor's acceptance of inside purchasing. A plant management journal supported inside control over purchasing by noting that the "contractor's interests are incompatible with those of the plant engineer. The job of the plant engineer is to protect the owners' interests in all matters relating to the physical plant."[1]

[1] *Plant Engineering*, 1963, 17(1):22.

Thus, while the contractor's men were struggling for jurisdiction over specific inside jobs, the contractor may have been fighting with inside management in another battle for control over his total function, as he conceived it.

Asserting jurisdiction was the outside forces' counterpart of the legalism of the staunch management rights advocate. To many observers, jurisdiction symbolized the "way of life" of the outside craftsman. But, as in the case of management rights doctrine, the symbolic value may have exceeded the extent of strict adherence to the concept. For instance, the extent to which jurisdictional lines were followed apparently varied with the state of the outside labor market. Industrial managers reported that, if craftsmen in the area had been unemployed for a while, they were much more sensitive to the inside forces' infringement of their jurisdiction than if conditions of full employment prevailed.

Historically, in cases of long-standing contractor relationships with the industrial establishment, the question of defending jurisdiction tended to become academic. Jurisdiction, then, became synonymous with the work the contractor customarily performed, and rigid craft practices often were modified, in part to ensure a continuance of the relationship. In the style of the inside department, the contractor developed an accepted "monopoly" over a particular function. The contractor actually might have become a member of the firm. In a utility company, we encountered an instance in which the inside department had its origin in a steady relationship with one contractor. In time, the outside organization was taken into the firm. The bond that had developed appeared to consist primarily in the contractors' growing dependency on this firm rather than in real, mutual acceptance. The former contract group complained that it was accorded no better than second-class citizenship. For instance, the company continued to pay the workers on an outside craft basis, and thus they received no fringe benefits. Going full cycle, the management finally returned to contracting-out and drastically reduced the functions of this department. The former contractor reestablished his own business.

Another case of this type was found in the food industry. A plumbing contractor who had served this firm exclusively became very dependent upon the economic welfare of the food processor. During periods of economic distress when the company reduced its out-of-pocket expenses, the plumbing concern faltered. Finally, its financial position became so unsound that its only customer took it over as a wholly owned subsidiary. This relationship had persisted for fifty years and seemed to be extremely stable. It was apparent that independence and dependence were the two sides of the coin of the traditional industrial management-contractor relationship.

Traditional craft organization

The question of jurisdiction was not an isolated issue. Rather, it was manifested in some traditionally inflexible aspects of the structure of the outside craft organization—an organization that in many ways was becoming increasingly ill suited to the industrial needs of the 1960s. In this organization, contractors were divided into general and specialty groups, work was allocated via the bid system, and the work force was organized according to craft skill groups rather than functional units. With regard to the latter characteristic, it is interesting to note that one-fourth of the industrial plants in our sample had inside departments organized on the same basis!

From the standpoint of industrial management, the prospect of writing detailed specifications prior to putting out for bids tended to discourage contracting-out. General contractors were hired for large undertakings, but in other cases managers reported that their enthusiasm was dampened by the need first to negotiate with a series of separate specialty contractors and then to manage the relationship with each one.

The red tape that served to maintain craft identity and distinctions may have been mildly annoying in the past, but it developed into a first-class "headache" in the era of automated process work. Sending out a whole crew consisting of a series of narrow specialists became inefficient and costly, and with this type of arrangement the downtime expense could be exorbitant. A functionally sound system involved the use of individuals competent in a broad range of skills and specialized in several. To conform to these requirements, the industrial contractor needed to have command of a wide variety of managerial talents, and his workmen had to meet the same standards in terms of skill. Needless to say, a contractor could compete more effectively for industrial work if his organization represented a net gain over the internal operation in terms of flexibility and efficiency. The traditional contract system functioned adequately for industrial construction projects and other one-shot jobs. However, it became apparent that this system failed to serve the needs of lines of activity that were organized on a continuous or integrated basis, e.g., modern maintenance functions.

However, as one examined the potential for adapting to new requirements, it was obvious that traditional contract work organization had certain features that constituted distinct advantages. With regard to flexibility in size of work force, the outside organizations were well tooled to meet the needs of industrial management in times of uncertainty. This description aptly applies to periods of economic adjustment and technological change, for these tend to generate managerial hesitancy regarding the acquisition of inside personnel.

In contrast to the inside force, outside craft workers were less dependent on the employing organization. They were accustomed to shifting from place to place and area to area. Their allegiance was directed toward their craft rather than the workplace. They opposed seniority and accepted layoffs as a normal part of work life. Thus, their traditional behavior was well suited to periods of changing employment relationships. Then, too, contractors could play their historic role of supplier of labor and absorber of risks. The notion of the durable, protected relationship between inside supervisor and subordinate in industry has been particularly relevant in stable periods and in periods of expansion in staff. As requirements in terms of personnel began to change in the late 1950s, at times it became more appropriate to allow the continuing source of employment to come from an outside agent who supplied the needs of a series of establishments.

The above discussion indicates that the traditional organization of the outside forces had both a positive and a negative side as far as meeting the needs of the changing industrial scene was concerned. The prospects for effective adaptation were heightened by the fact that, historically, the technical conditions of construction work have placed great emphasis on the swift evolution of an organization, and therefore such talents were plentifully present in the outside management group. However, this adaptation did not prove to be an easy process, for it necessitated changes in the very structure of outside management organization and thus hit at the core of strong vested interests.

From labor problem to marketing problem

It was clear that the outside forces had to turn their attention away from combative channels regarding matters of jurisdiction and toward a constructive approach to the industrial work market. Certain leaders in the contract construction industry began to move in that direction in the late 1950s. In addition, the separation of construction labor and management that was required by the Taft-Hartley Act forced construction management to adopt a new approach to the marketing function. Before this requirement was instituted, local unions were active participants in this activity and, as indicated above, a strong labor problem emphasis existed.

However, the new approach still involved joint contractor and craft union efforts. A move toward cooperation to obtain new industrial work markets was evidenced in a 1958 agreement between the National Constructors Association, comprising twenty-four major contractors who performed 90 per cent of the country's heavy industrial building, and the building trades unions. The initial accord covered heavy construction projects in oil refineries, public utilities, steel mills, and chemical plants. It was designed to cut mounting construction costs by encouraging the full use of laborsaving machinery and wiping out wasteful practices such as early quitting time and manpower padding that had arisen in the peak years of prosperity during and after World War II.[2]

A variety of growing needs stimulated the development of a new organization. In 1959, the Construction Industry Joint Conference was formed to "preserve and promote the contract system."[3] The group included members of both labor and management eight representatives of national unions, four from basic and four from specialty trades, and eight representatives of national contractors associations, four from general and four from specialty units. The group met regularly to discuss, among other things, the need to present to industry the advantages of the contract system.

The decision to move to a marketing approach was underlined by the publication in September, 1959, of a brochure entitled, *Maintaining Production for America* (Construction Industry Joint Conference, 1959). The brochure emphasized the advantages of the contract system, especially stressing the benefits that would accrue to company management as a result of applying the contract system to modernization and continuing maintenance in industrial plants. The following points were listed: savings in costs, better quality, convenience to the owner, and speed—in essence, a flexible, buyer-seller relationship.

Interestingly, the issuance of the brochure also proved how difficult it was to abandon the era of the labor problem approach. While this document was directed at and circulated to members of industrial management, it inevitably came to the attention of the inside forces, especially the inside unions. The booklet's role as an advertising medium soon became secondary to its role as a prize bone of contention between the inside and outside unions. Although to an impartial observer the presentation might have seemed mild and restrained in tone, it quickly drew blasts from industrial union leaders. David McDonald, president of the United Steelworkers, called it a "reprehensible document," and Walter Reuther, president of the United Auto Workers, accused the construction trades of "unethical collusion with the anti-union employer."[4] Controversial sections of the booklet pointed to savings on inside labor costs that could be realized through the use of contract maintenance.

Thus, the initial venture in the marketing approach took on the hues of a full-blown labor problem. Translating this effort into labor problem terms, the craft groups were, in effect, urging industrial manage-

[2] *New York Times*, Feb. 6, 1958, p. 1.
[3] Construction Industry Joint Conference (mimeographed document), 1959.
[4] *New York Times*, Feb. 12, 1960.

ment to exercise its "right" to contract-out. An unanticipated consequence of this appeal was the near dissolution of the AFL-CIO. A second brochure issued the following year carefully avoided all reference to the controversial benefits of contracting. It was spared the labor problem status so clearly earned by its predecessor.

Despite the notoriety achieved by the advertising matter, some of the other activities of the conference probably were more effective in achieving the goal of expansion into the industrial work market. Of prime interest were programs that also could fulfill the basic need of the contractor to obtain a year-round source of employment and thus introduce a stabilizing element into the construction industry. One obvious solution involved the continued use of the forces that built a structure to maintain and repair it. Along this line, a number of programs were initiated to encourage contractor exploration of the maintenance field.

In addition, means were sought for solving some of the contractors' organizational problems that constituted road blocks to the extension of service to industry. Various types of joint ventures were recommended to solve the managerial problems created when the industrial firm had to conduct relations with diverse groups of outside specialists. Later in this chapter, we shall discuss the operations of a newly formed effort of this type. The conference also strongly promoted the notion of continuing maintenance by contract and worked to adapt traditional craft programs to this end. It cooperated with the General President's Committee on Continuing Maintenance, a group representing the building trades unions. This group negotiated and administered a standard form of agreement developed to meet the needs and special problems of functions such as modernization and continuing maintenance. These agreements could be obtained by any contractor who had a commitment to perform work of this type for an industrial firm.

The project agreements for maintenance by contract attempted to adjust traditional conditions geared to one-shot jobs to the new set of expectations that accompanied continuous inside employment. In order to move inside, the outside craft worker was asked to forgo some of his independence and allegiance to craft. Rather than walk off the job in the case of a jurisdictional dispute, he agreed to an on-the-spot temporary settlement in order to permit the continuance of work. If a settlement was not satisfactory, disputes could be referred to the international office of the unions concerned. The agreements also contained "no strike" clauses.

To compensate for the benefits of steady employment, certain fringe wage items were reduced. For instance, overtime work was rated at time and one-half instead of double time. Provision was made for multiple rather than single shifts, and there was to be no payment for subsistence, travel allowance, mileage, or travel time. There was no effort to lower craft rates in order to bring them into line with inside pay, partly because of possible conflict with "real" outside workers who might be brought in on a temporary basis. However, the total cost of an operation potentially was reduced through provisions relinquishing strict adherence to craft jurisdiction and permitting instead the use of mixed crews whenever this step became necessary.

Curiously enough, the spirit of compromise evident in this example of the marketing approach did not serve to obliterate the labor problem treatment of contracting-out. In another arena, these same outside craft unions were signing pacts with inplant industrial unions, guaranteeing to the latter all the routine maintenance work of the industrial firm (see Chapter 11). And in still another arena, the outside forces were fighting for jurisdiction over work at missile bases where manufacturers were being used as contractors and plant employees as construction mechanics. In this case, pressures were exerted on the Federal government to halt the "extension of manufacturing" (also see Chapter 11).

In some ways, the continued use of the labor problem approach served to hold together rival craft union and contractor groups, for this approach focused on outer jurisdictional battles with the inside unions and manufacturers. On the other hand, contract maintenance and other programs designed to keep pace with technological developments inevitably introduced new sources of intergroup dissension. These programs had understandably little appeal to organizations such as specialty contractors who had invested their time and energies in other procedures.

On occasion, organizations have been formed to promote activities that fail to materialize. The real test of the new marketing approach was its realization in actual practice, and in many ways this outcome was dependent on the ability of construction management to make changes within its own organizations that would permit the wide exploitation of new opportunities in industry. In the following section we shall examine some of these changes.

TRENDS IN THE OUTSIDE MANAGEMENT ORGANIZATION

Management as well as labor organization in the construction industry traditionally has had its base in craft distinctions, and the organization of work has been determined by the craft structure. A specialty organization, e.g., that of an electrical contractor, that receives a prime contract can subcontract parts of the job to other contractors whose craft may be involved. For example, the electrical contractor may subcontract duct work to a mechanical contractor. On the other hand, a general contractor may receive a prime contract and then subcontract to a variety of specialty contractors.

The relationship between the distributor and recipients of subcontracted work frequently has been less than cordial. Like the labor contractors of past centuries, the "general" has been thought to be prone to pass on to the subcontractors his real or imaginary misfortunes. Thus, rather than representing the subcontractors' interests, the general might have accepted a poorer deal, knowing that he could "share" it with the others via bid-shopping. The suspicion always was present that the general contractor fared no worse than before, while the specialty subcontractor suffered a considerable disadvantage.

These were old problems, and the specialty group engaged in repeated moves to reform the system. However, the lines were clearly drawn, and considerable accommodation had been made to historic forms of inequity. But, conflict within the context of a familiar structure was threatened with at least some replacement by a new prospect —integrated contract organizations that did not subcontract their work. The specialty group was faced with another problem, the need to develop organizations that could compete with these new structures.

The construction industry was encountering new versions of centuries-old problems engendered by the familiar combination of technological dependence and organizational independence (see also Higgin, 1963). New structures were created in recognition of the increasing significance of the former factor and to overcome the increasingly difficult problems caused by the latter.

Contract maintenance

The new integrated contractors provided package maintenance services to industry and were especially active in seeking opportunities in new and renovated continuous process plants. In contrast to the narrower view of the specialty contractor, these organizations proposed moving the entire maintenance function into the fringe category (see Chapter 3). However, the size of the package could be tailored to fit the needs of the firm. If inside management so desired, it could abdicate almost all its functions by purchasing a full maintenance management contract. According to this agreement, the contractor would furnish a complete staff, including general management, planners, engineers, estimators, draftsmen, field supervisory and office personnel, and hourly personnel such as timekeepers and clerks, but no matter how extensive the service, contract maintenance basically tended to be a contract for maintenance craft labor.

In many cases, the supplier of contract maintenance services was a construction contractor who was attempting to stabilize his work load. In comparison with the small size of the run-of-the-mine contractor, some of these operations were mammoth in size and international in scope. Rather than placing all their eggs in one basket, these large firms were able to increase their survival potential by diversifying their operations and the number and kind of risks they assumed.

Contract maintenance was typical of a large number of operations of this type that developed in the late 1950s. While these new contractors were similar to one another with respect to their large size, beyond this point there were substantial differences. For instance, we found a definite variation in the concept of the proper role of the outside force.

The construction philosophy

Contractors who entered the maintenance field from a construction base approached this task in a different fashion from those whose basic commitment was to maintenance. The construction contractors were in much the same position as industrial management—maintenance was not the prime concern of either. Nevertheless, firms that built new industrial structures such as oil refineries, chemical plants, paper and steel mills, and electric power plants entered this field. In some cases, the maintenance work did not prove to be a large profit item—a situation that must have been agreeable to industrial management. The goal for a strongly construction-oriented firm often was the development of a relationship with a good growth company, with the hope that this relationship would lead to further construction contracts. The manager of a construction-oriented firm noted:

> Having been established with a growth company increases our chances of doing their next big construction job. We wouldn't break our necks getting a contract all by itself. With the horizontal and vertical unions, the labor problem is not too easy. But if we construct a plant, then we attempt to negotiate maintenance contracts with them. Because we built it, we are already on the job, and of course we hope there will be more expansion. It costs $25,000 to move into a plant, and this gives us an edge on our competitors. We figure we make about 5 per cent on our time and effort.

In some cases, a permanent relationship evolved from one based on expediency. Industrial management would seek maintenance services from the construction contractor in the period before plant operations moved into full swing. If the temporary arrangements proved to be satisfactory, they simply were continued.

When the contract maintenance agreements with national craft unions became available, construction firms that had done some maintenance work over the years entered the new field. In accordance with tradition, the construction companies relied on the international unions to make arrangements for personnel at the local level. In the case of trouble at this level, the international was expected to iron out the difficulty. To obtain cooperation, these firms relied on the influence they could wield through their major line of activity, construction. As one manager explained, "If we have trouble with a local union, we call the international. They move in and settle it. After all, we give them 10,000 dues-paying members. They don't want to lose that."

But while the outside unions played a leading role in the contractor's relations with his own men, the conduct of relationships inside the employing firm generally was placed in the hands of a contractors' representative. The construction contractors recognized that moving inside on a continuing basis involved much more than merely supplying labor. In fact, any inference that they were serving as labor brokers or labor contractors was resented in the extreme. In one case the contractor maintained a permanent staff of about fifty supervisors and workers in the client's plant. When the need arose, this force was supplemented with men hired from the local labor market, at times as many as two hundred. The contractor's district superintendent supervised the entire operation. This man was chosen for his ability to deal with a variety of groups. He needed political as well as technical skills, for he had to get along with both industrial management and inside workers—persons over whom he had no authority. If he required assistance, he could call on the services of the contractor's labor relations staff, a group which covered the entire region, traveling from one site to another.

Sensitivity to the difference between inside and outside work was reflected in the way in which this contractor selected his inside staff. He noted that the permanent force had to be chosen with discretion to ensure proper performance as an inside worker. As the building was being constructed, "maintenance types" were spotted in the construction crews. The contractor summed up his approach as follows:

> You have to be careful. Construction and maintenance people are entirely different. The construction worker gains great satisfaction from seeing a building go up. It's something tangible. He is an extrovert. He travels all over the country. He either picks up his family and takes them along or he moves out of the family quarters and comes home weekends. After a year has passed and the building is finished, he is ready to leave and go on to the next. He may stick to one region of the country, but that's all. The maintenance worker is more of an introvert. That work requires patience. It takes different skills to repair a chair than it does to put it together. It's not as rewarding. People don't notice it. We try to

pick men we think would be good for maintenance. It's a problem. We spot them and let them know that permanent work is in the offing.

As we shall see, the theme of "fitting in" was symptomatic of the construction group's view of adjusting to the inside organization. It was clear that, among firms offering contract maintenance services, there was variation in the type of commitment to maintenance work— or to put it another way, the maintenance work served differing organizational purposes. At one extreme there were those for whom it served as a wedge for obtaining future major construction work. At the other, there were construction firms that concentrated on the contract maintenance field. In common with most "specialists," members of the latter group emphasized their greater *expertise*, stressing that they really knew the difference between plant operations and construction.

However, whether the contractor had both feet—or only one— firmly planted in the maintenance field, the great majority of those of construction origin underlined the fact that inside management was the "boss." One of these contractors commented to us, "We are not interested in running an independent show. A prima donna can't last in this business. The plant engineer is boss over our entire operation. We do what he wants. We do what top management wants. We have found that this arrangement works out best for all concerned."

A manager of a contract maintenance group who was being interviewed by a management journal expressed much the same sentiment when he noted, "Our philosophy is not, 'We'll take care of your plant the way we decide.' We submit to whatever degree of controls the company wants. We go over requirements with company management and recommend procedures. But the company decides how little or how much."[5]

Thus, in return for costs plus a negotiated percentage for overhead and profits, industrial management was offered a substitute for or a supplement to the internal department. Moreover, the candidate offered to play a submissive, compliant role. Contractors pointed to the fact that the inside functionaries' traditional devotion to duty came at a high price in the form of overstaffing, featherbedding, and make work. Alternatively, the outsiders stressed that their relationship to industrial management was strictly a buyer-vendor arrangement. If management was not satisfied, cancellation was a simple matter.

Thus, one witnessed a rather remarkable transformation of the independent contract construction management and union member, as both attempted to model themselves according to what might be described as an idealized image of the inside force. This model for

[5] *Factory,* 1959, 117(7):186.

behavior fits almost perfectly the accepted model for the inside relationship presented in Chapter 1. The contractor holds objectives in common with industrial management, is submissive to authority, fits into a scheme of rational decision-making, and extends the boundaries of the firm in a completely predictable and controllable fashion. The accepted image of the outsider as an unpredictable party with separate objectives, negotiating and challenging authority, was absent. It also should be noted that the idealized image of the inside forces was found only rarely in the real-life inside operation.

During our research, industrial management's evaluation of contract maintenance was still tentative and conditional. However, the assessments that were made had little bearing on the elements of the submissive model. Judgments were formulated in terms of the traditional inside-outside rivalries and some aspects of the competitive model presented in Part II. For instance, a chemical process firm's management reported general satisfaction with a contractor's work but noted troubles with the familiar coercive comparison between inside and outside wage rates and differences in union status. Not surprisingly, the quality of inside management tended to be rated higher than that of its counterparts on the contractor's staff.

There also seemed to be a desire to keep a foothold in both the inside and the outside camps. In a new refinery, management reported, "Our permanent crews are deliberately kept down in size, but we don't want to go all the way on contracting. The contractors want our business now, but the honeymoon may be over. Our men are a small carefully selected group. If we decide to do more ourselves, we can fall back on them for a start. And besides, they keep the contractor on his toes. If he sees his competition staring him in the face, he will do a better job."

The maintenance philosophy

Firms entering the modern industrial maintenance field from a maintenance rather than a construction base tended to develop a more subtle and skill-requiring relationship with the inside organization. In part, this behavior undoubtedly was the result of long experience at working as an "inside" outsider. Thus, in contrast to the maintenance contractor rooted in the construction tradition, the contractor with a maintenance background did not place so much emphasis on matters such as willingness to accept industrial management's authority. In some cases, these two groups competed for the same work; in others, they branched into different activities. The differences between them were far from the traditional distinction between black and white, but these differences did serve as the basis for still another intercontractor competition. As anticipated, those with a maintenance point of view tended to be critical of the construction group. The latter were characterized as "One-shot operators. They don't care if something falls down after they're gone." Naturally, this rivalry was accentuated whenever these two groups found themselves competing for the same contract.

Industrial maintenance contracting is an old field. Many of the original enterprises were small family-operated concerns, specializing in janitorial services. The unique aspect of the situation in the early 1960s was the trend toward very large concerns that diversified their activities into seemingly endless fields, including construction work, the home base of their rivals, and integrated backward into the engineering, planning, and designing stages of their work.

Management in one of these "integrated" maintenance firms had a philosophy of neutrality and anonymity, of being neither a part of industrial management nor under its thumb but rather a separate entity. This organization viewed the retention of its status as an outsider as a positive contribution to its relationship with the industrial client. Of course, the position on neutrality was shared to some degree by all other "independents" in the field, for this stand also constituted a defense against fellow outsiders who actually were a part of inside organizations, for example, industrial firms that had diversified into contract operations.

Anonymity was a subtler concept than neutrality and required that the separateness that existed was never to be a conspicuous quality. Thus, there were no identifying signs or garments that would serve to distinguish the contract forces from other inside workers. (On the other hand, industrial management reported that construction contractors were less sensitive to this point.) Obviously, to retain an inconspicuous separateness, additional measures were needed. Therefore, members of the contractor's staff were moved from one place to another to prevent their developing the traits of an inside retainer, the very type of employee that contracting was supposed to eliminate. As the contractor noted, "If I don't move my key men around, they become pets. In one case I wanted to transfer a supervisor and the company refused. I tell them they will become just as attached to his replacement. You have to do this for their good and for your own. If you don't, your people will be no better than the old retainers they had on their staffs before."

However, beyond this point, the construction and maintenance groups shared similar problems. Both were extremely dependent on the quality of their on-site supervisors. To quote one maintenance contractor, "You can't rely on the kind of labor you hire to maintain

standards of workmanship. Quality is a product of good supervision."
Interestingly, some of this contractor's best supervisors were the former
employees of his industrial clients!

Like the construction men, the maintenance contractors viewed
industrial management as a "specialist," concerned with the central
purpose of the firm's business, for example, manufacturing automobiles. They proposed relieving management of activities that fell in the
"periphery." And the notion of what properly belonged in the periphery seemed to be expanding continually. One of these contractors
noted, "We walk where angels fear to tread. We say we take over
other people's headaches."

Paradoxically, although dedicated to the principle of specialization
for others, many of these new organizations were unable to practice
what they preached. They were extremely reluctant to contract-out
their own work. Like the new industrial organization that operates on
a do-it-yourself basis for lack of proper supporting groups,[6] the new
"integrated" contractors felt the need to "run the entire show." In
response to a query about the possibility of his firm's subcontracting
some of its tasks, one manager remarked, "Certainly not. We don't
believe in it. We want the experience ourselves."

In general, this remark provided a good clue to the approach of
these organizations. They expanded vertically into all aspects of the
total maintenance operation, following a pattern of behavior that has
led us to characterize them as a new breed of integrated contractors.
However, one of the most difficult of the "headaches" assumed by the
integrated contractor was a familiar and historic burden of this group,
the labor problem. One contractor explained, "We take over the labor
problems. Management stays out entirely. It's a big order." The great
majority seemed to feel that even intermittent labor troubles would
end their usefulness to industry.

Contractors starting from a construction base generally relied on
agreements with the national building trades unions and the intervention of national union officers to smooth out grievances at the work site.
Others preferred to deal only with local unions, using a case-by-case
strategy. It was agreed generally that the local strategy required
greater managerial skill and the services of an adept labor relations
staff, a group that seemed to be a prominent part of every integrated
contractor's force.

As the range of the contractor's activities broadened, inevitably
more and more unions became involved. Even if the use of shortcuts
such as the national building trades agreements were desired, these
arrangements would not suffice. Unions such as the Machinists, Build-

6 See Chap. 3.

ing Service Employees, Transport Workers, and others entered the picture. To complicate matters further, in some cases inside unions such as the Oil and Chemical Workers organized the outside contractors. One contractor had dealings with over sixty unions. The quality of contractors' labor relations was variable. Some had remarkably good records. These men attributed some of their success to competition between the inside and outside forces. The outside workers felt called upon to prove their worth, and this sentiment was reinforced by reminders from their contractor-employer that labor troubles would lead to their replacement by inside crews.

Like their industrial counterparts of another era, the integrated contractors took pride in their growing organizations. Some pointed to a shift away from the former low status of this field. The higher status enjoyed by these contractors undoubtedly was due in part to the scope of the services offered, including management, research, planning, and equipment design as well as the conduct of the routine day-to-day activity. Moreover, the offerings penetrated into a number of fields so that industrial management might be only one of a number of recipients of a given contractor's services. A firm that came to our attention because it supplied fueling, baggage, and repair service to the air-line industry proved to have a variety of other activities. Among these were maintenance and service activities in relation to the Berlin air lift, world fairs, sports stadia, commercial buildings, and shopping centers. The scope of this operation was international, and integration backward was a key concept. Thus, in the case of the consolidated airport fueling systems, the company financed, designed, installed, and operated these facilities. In operations at distant air bases, it conducted classes in mechanical training for local personnel.

Like the industrial empires whose work load these contractors were sharing, the outsiders were, in the words of one manager, "beginning to feel the pressure and strain of a large organization." The economic effect of the efforts of these groups was reflected in one estimate made in 1962, which placed the total value of industrial and commercial maintenance contracts at 700 million dollars.[7]

The labor contractor

In contrast to the broad scope of the integrated maintenance contractor, there was a growing group that furnished labor services primarily. The package contractors deplored the lack of quality controls in the work of these specialized labor brokers. Nevertheless, the integrated group was faced with competition from these suppliers of manpower in areas where the work of the two groups overlapped, for

[7] *Business Week*, Apr. 28, 1962, no. 1704, p. 72.

instance, in routine maintenance services. In appealing to industrial management, these groups emphasized the potential savings in labor costs that could be realized through their services. One such firm pointed to "three big areas of cost erosion—insufficient use of existing personnel, overstaffing and inadequate utilization of space."[8] Through what was described as a "controlled overhead" plan, the client could reap benefits by maintaining his full-time staff at the level justified by the minimum work load and then using the agency to meet peak load, seasonal, and emergency problems.

Thus, an industrial firm in need of maintenance crews could contact the industrial division of one of these agencies and acquire the needed workers at an hourly rate higher than the one paid to the inside force, but one that was described as being free of incidental overhead costs. It was noted that "The usual costs such as social security, taxes, workmen's compensation, the many fringe benefits, and unemployment compensation are eliminated for the customer." Bringing the relationship with the contractor to an end was described as being "as simple as turning water on and off at the tap."[9]

In general, those who supplied this type of service did not have contracts with unions and did not engage in the large-scale labor relations programs found among the integrated contractors. In the clerical field, a main source of business, competition from unionized inside forces, was largely absent. However, in unionized industrial situations, the leased labor contractor tended to tread the ground lightly. In most cases, leased maintenance labor worked directly under plant management, using the lessee's equipment on the lessee's premises. In order to minimize competitive sentiments on the part of the inside forces, the contractors emphasized the peak-load, temporary nature of their relationship to the firm. However, the contractor who was selling only labor services could not afford to add to his overhead through the extensive use of labor relations techniques. Thus, the effort expended was simple and direct. The contractor might check with the inside union, and if it failed to object, he accepted the assignment. His interest in overcoming obstacles at a particular plant was understandably limited.

It should be noted that the difference between the leased labor and integrated contractors was becoming one of degree rather than kind. The leasing arrangement inevitably moved into the package field, supplying management, supervision, and facilities for special projects. And the integrated maintenance contractors moved into other work fields, where their function became essentially that of a labor contractor, e.g., furnishing regular hourly production workers to process plants.

[8] *The Controlled Overhead Plan.* Manpower, Inc., Milwaukee, Wis., 1960, p. 3.
[9] *Ibid.*

The manufacturer-contractor

Contractors have been accustomed to competition from manufacturers
who have preferred the inside operation to contracting-out. Disputes
between contractors and air-frame manufacturers at the missile sites in
the early 1960s centered in this familiar kind of difficulty. The manufacturers were seeking to expand into a new and developing field in
much the same way as were the construction contractors who performed contract maintenance in order to gain new construction contracts in high-growth industries. Thus, the manufacturers engaged in
missile research and development work in order to obtain the experience and preferred position that would increase their chances of
winning production contracts. They maintained that, in the interests of
secrecy and of furthering research and development work, it was
necessary to use inside forces for connecting basic equipment and
other operations preparatory to actual launching. Outside contractors
presented a counterclaim that their jurisdiction was being infringed
and that the manufacturers were primarily interested in reaping the
profits involved in this operation. (Details of the struggle between the
two groups will be presented in Chapter 11.)

The competition between outside contractors and manufacturers
serving as government contractors primarily represented a variation on
the old theme of integration versus specialization, but other developments asserted more of a claim to novelty. These were instances in
which manufacturers diversified into contracting. As noted in Chapter
3, some of this diversification represented the marketing of a former
integration activity. Moreover, this endeavor represented a threat to
members of both the inside and outside forces. When a manufacturer-
contractor entered a client's plant, the inside forces in that plant shared
the misfortune of competing elements in the outside forces who might
otherwise have obtained the work. However, while there were some
notable areas of overlap with the contract maintenance operations in
the process field, the manufacturer-contractor tended to be more active
in fabrication industries—in repairing and servicing production and
transportation equipment. Electrical machinery manufacturers offered
contract services in part to overcome the sales resistance of potential
customers who might have shied away from purchasing new equipment if this action entailed the installation of expensive repair facilities
which could have become obsolete rather rapidly. Equipment sales
that included service contracts and the introduction of sealed units in
guaranteed equipment were other developments that served to move
repair work back to the manufacturer's premises or into the hands of
members of his staff.

In some cases, the manufacturer's repair and maintenance staff entered the customer's plant and performed the work on the site, in the fashion of the outside maintenance and construction contractor. In other cases, equipment was removed and sent to the manufacturer's central repair facility.

Two developments were of special interest. One was the introduction of package service programs similar to those offered by the integrated contractors. As in the case of contract maintenance, the customer could choose the type of service that best fitted his needs, and if desired, a comprehensive maintenance service was available for all the equipment in a complete manufacturing facility. Technical staff and engineering directed the efforts of those stationed in the customer's plant. Another development was the introduction of the large, highly mechanized service shop, operated on an assembly-line basis. In describing a new facility of this type, one journal indicated that inplant maintenance departments would have to plan to compete with these manufacturer-operated commercial service organizations if they expected to continue to do their own overhaul work.[10]

Inevitably, some manufacturers who performed service contract work found themselves in the difficult position of competing with their own customers. A chemical firm that operated an industrial contract cleaning service discovered that competing cleaning contractors were boycotting its products. Eventually, the sales division pressured for and obtained abandonment of the contract operation.

Old interests and new developments in the outside forces

One would assume that specialty contractors, whose livelihood was based on traditional craft jurisdiction, would evince little enthusiasm for the developments described in this chapter. A minority of these contractors headed very substantial operations, but, as a group, their place in industrial society at least, psychologically, was that of the small operator, the small businessman who was against big business, big unions, and big government. The position of such a contractor was made increasingly insecure by each new large rival who appeared on the scene—the general contractor, the integrated industrial firm, the inside industrial union, the integrated contractor, and the manufacturer-contractor. Each one posed a new threat and, in the specialty contractor's eyes, apparently had the backing of powerful forces.

Estimates of the extent to which specialty contractors had lost business to the new groups varied. For instance, one of their representatives estimated that the integrated contractors had absorbed about 5 per cent of former specialty business, but he stressed that the real specialty losses were the failure to move ahead into the growing fields.

10 *Factory*, 1963, 121(1):76.

In view of the ever-extending activities of the new contractor groups it was difficult to pacify the specialty men with the argument sometimes advanced, that these operations were only special-purpose tools. Moreover, the specialty officials felt that the newcomers violated the principles of traditional craft work. To them, the lack of a firm bid appeared to be a major defect. One specialty manager noted, "The contract maintenance people say they do all that planning, but as far as I can see, it is mainly a way to cut out firm bids. It encourages poor management." The specialty man's other point concerned quality of work. One of them felt that the new contractors created problems for the others. He remarked, "The trouble is, they ruin an area for us. They gather all the troublemakers on those projects—the coffee break guys. Our men work on the projects because of the high wages. Then they are no good for regular work. When we get them back, they don't care about cost any more."

These competitive sentiments were hardly surprising. More surprising was the lack of universal concern about such matters. While there was no question that the specialty group faced serious problems in relation to developing new markets, the *status quo* was pleasing to many of them. Those who envision new fields sometimes make the mistake of assuming that all those who might potentially enter are eager for the opportunity. However, the numbers in this "eager" group often represent a small proportion of the total.

For instance, the average specialty contractor was not oriented toward continuing assignments with industrial firms. In this sense, he did not feel threatened by those who undertook such projects, for he thought in terms of one-shot jobs, obtained on a bid basis. To him, working for an industrial firm involved bringing one's equipment to the plant, performing the assigned task, and then clearing out. The notion of coming back to the plant to build further on the relationship seemed out of line. One returned only if the customer requested further adjustments in the work. Developing a continuous relationship was a foreign concept to many of them. One contractor remarked, "By the time you're finished, they're sick of seeing you around."

Thus, of the specialty contractors in a given area only a small proportion would be interested in seeking a continuous relationship with industrial management. Of five hundred contractors of a certain type in a given region, probably only a fraction, say seventy-five of the larger ones, would belong to the contractor's association. Of course, among the nonmembers there would be many who, in response to the market opportunities available, shifted between the roles of worker and entrepreneur. But even among the association members only a small group—perhaps one-fourth of the total—would be interested in seeking industrial contract work.

For the others, the industrial contract market would present endless problems. The lack of skills in the local labor market might be a crucial factor. For instance, the union might be able to supply great numbers of electricians who could lay conduit and pull wires but very few who could install and maintain modern automated equipment. In some cases the local craftsmen actively resisted assignments to industrial plants (see Chapter 12).

Those who were willing to qualify for certain work by training their men in the needed skills still would be baffled by certain major problems, such as the marketing of their talents. The contractors generally were not salesmen by training, and some found the task of selling their services an overwhelming one. To them the industrial firm often appeared to be an alien world dominated by members of the inside forces. The notion of the firm as an entity seeking their assistance was regarded as sheer folly by some. Those who approached industrial management usually added to the folklore regarding the difficulty of gaining entry. Thus, in one case a contractor reported, "The plant engineer said he would like to give us the work, but he pointed to a bunch of men sitting around the coffee machine. He said, 'We don't have enough for them as it is. What am I going to do with these guys?' "

Another of their problems was characteristic of the outsider attempting to break into a given decision structure. Who made the decisions? Who was the right person to see? One contractor remarked, "How can you look for a job when you can't find out who signs the work orders?"

The long history of working on bid jobs and obtaining contracts through the unions accentuated this block over the matter of contacting managers and selling industrial work. In addition, there seemed to be in many areas certain plants that developed the reputation for contracting-out only "dirty-end-of-the-stick" work, and these cases acquired a negative symbolic value. A process plant in one community was known for its lack of interest in using contractors' services. Some of the company's specialty craft crews included over one hundred members of a single craft. However, occasionally, the firm did put out for bids on work, and when it did, the contractors viewed these "opportunities" through smoke-colored glasses. One of them commented, "They want you to install a whole data-processing system in two weeks. Their men would be given six months, if they could do the job. You can take it, but you can't make any money on it. They don't want to pay anything. They never do."

While these negative attitudes undoubtedly had an effect on contractor behavior, some of the deeper problems involved the ability to organize to meet the current needs of industrial management. In some cases, fulfilling these needs meant combining various crafts in order to provide effective service, but this was a step not easily undertaken. Work on automatic equipment requires a combination of skills, and thus a joint enterprise of contractors with electronic, electrical, and mechanical skills might have made good organizational sense. However, the high values placed on the independent operation were difficult to abandon. The old problem of dividing up the contract—getting a fair share—remained a key issue. These case materials illustrate the problems encountered in bringing the traditional craft structure into the industrial organization without first making adaptations appropriate to that purpose.

Contractors frequently were told by those who had studied their potential market that they had captured only a small fraction, perhaps 2 per cent, of the total work available. However, the average contractor would express disbelief at statements of this type. Like the farmer, he saw little that was favorable in his situation. The large contractor who had obtained industrial work on a continuing basis was regarded as exceptional and atypical.

However, some specialty contractors, usually the larger ones, obtained contracts for performing industrial work on a continuing basis. In one case a specialty contractor had a contingent of seventy persons in a fabrication plant. This operation constituted a package deal wherein the contractor furnished nine staff members who engaged in planning and design and sixty-one craftsmen who performed the actual installation and repair work. The contractor's firm specialized in the automated equipment field, and while officially only one craft seemed to be involved, some of the key men had been given additional training in fields such as electronics.

In assessing this experience, the contractor stated that "This work is hard to get, but once you do, it is very satisfying." Of course, some of his assignments developed in a relatively uncomplicated fashion. Like the integrated contractor, in some cases this specialty contractor moved inside after completing his share of the construction of a new plant. In other cases, he had the more difficult assignment of replacing an existing inside force. Initially, his men worked with the insiders, but as the members of the inside crew retired or were transferred, the contract force simply took their place.

For this contractor, continuing industrial jobs provided a steady flow of work and served to iron out the peaks and valleys of the work load in the construction field. In addition, he began to place tremendous value on his role in the industrial firm. He participated in management meetings, made some recommendations, and even had the satisfaction of seeing a firm adopt a long-range program that he had outlined. Abandonment of the traditional independence of the outside craftsman evidently brought rewards to those for whom the role was at all congenial.

Clearly, specialty contractors did not rise as a group to enter new fields or to meet the challenge of new competition. But in addition to single-handed enterprises such as the one described above, at least one organization was established in an effort to compete with the integrated contractor. Using the familiar philosophy, "If you can't beat them, join them," a general, piping, electrical, and equipment installation contractor formed a group called Construction Associates. This group sought work in utility power plants and large industrial projects in oil, chemical, paper-mill, and nuclear installations. Its process plant market was markedly similar to that of the integrated contractor.

Talk of a union of craft specialists immediately brings to mind the term "jurisdictional conflict." Informants in the field who had attempted these arrangements sometimes shook their heads and remarked, "Never again." However, this group developed an organizational structure that solved some of the common problems. The general contractor was selected as project manager for the first contract at a utility substation. This choice seemed to be logical, but it was difficult to move away from the old general contractor-subcontractor relationship and successfully introduce the notion of equal partnership. When an outsider was brought in as head of the project, the problem was solved. Differences at the work level could not be handled in this fashion, of course, and the workers' unwillingness to share tools with other crafts blocked some anticipated savings in this area for a considerable period of time. Jurisdictional disputes flared up at the usual rate but reportedly were easier to settle as the job progressed and a feeling of teamwork developed.[11]

Joint ventures of this type permitted the specialists to bid on big contracts for which competition was less intense and the opportunities for profit greater. From the standpoint of the industrial customer, one of the main objections to dealing with specialty contractors was eliminated because the contractors' group was given single responsibility for the entire package. Therefore, the firm's management did not have to integrate and coordinate the activities of separate specialty groups and devote time and energy to continual interpretation of the scope of each one's obligations. This case represented another instance of changes in contractors' organizations that involved a trend away from specialization and jurisdiction as a factor dictating their basic structure.

As indicated above, efforts of this type may continue to be confined to a select few in the specialty crafts, but the developments illustrate

[11] *Qualified Contractor*, 1962, 27(10):78–83.

the dynamic nature of the field of industrial contracting as well as the fallacy of writing off any one of the competing forces as "obsolete" or declining.

SUMMARY

In this chapter we have examined the structure of group relationships for the contracting-out problem and noted the multiplicity of parties at interest both inside and outside the firm. External labels, such as contractor or industrial manager, would not have been good clues to position regarding contracting-out, for across the boundaries of the groups to which such persons belonged there were common interests and within them were conflicting property claims to work. Moreover, the competition between the inside and outside forces for the industrial work market had little to do with establishing legalistic claims. Rather, one of the key elements in this competition involved the building of an effective organization—an organization that would not block the goal realization of others with complementary interests.

Most research efforts have focused on the structure of the inside organization, for example, the industrial firm. By way of contrast, the outside organization has been conceived in narrow terms, and little attention has been devoted to its structural problems. Contracting-out often is viewed almost exclusively from the standpoint of the industrial firm. Our study revealed two major developments regarding the structure of the outside forces. Both were designed to meet more effectively the problems of adapting to the industrial work market. Firmly rooted in the concept of jurisdiction, the traditional crafts had the wrong organization for this market as industry entered the era of automated equipment and integrated process plants. A demand was created for greater flexibility and simpler structures for intergroup relations. The outside forces were faced with the problem of capitalizing on their strengths, such as the ability to evolve an organization swiftly; and of minimizing the effect of rigid elements in their traditional structures. However, it was found that concern about change and capturing new markets was far from universal among members of the outside forces. Rather, new developments interested only select elements within the total group.

The first major development, it was found, represented a trend away from specialization and toward integration. Formerly, craft specialization dictated the character of the outside organization. New integrated contractors and joint ventures of specialists developed more flexible organizational structures and in addition began to offer services that were larger in scope—package deals in which they integrated backward into managerial, planning, engineering, and design phases of the work. In fact, if a customer desired this, these contractors would assume the entire function. Paradoxically, although dedicated to the principle of specialization for others, some of the new contractor organizations were extremely reluctant to contract-out some of their own work.

A second development involved a trend away from contractor reliance on certain aspects of the relationship with the craft unions. In the process, the concept of contracting-out as a labor problem was replaced to some extent by a new marketing approach. In reality, the two approaches continued to coexist, simply operating in different arenas.

For the contractor, moving inside inevitably involved a compromise between satisfying his own organizational goals and those of industrial management. Some contractors sought continuing maintenance contracts as a means of developing a relationship with a high-growth company, others sought primarily to even out the peaks and valleys in their work loads, and finally some sought the satisfactions of a new business relationship. Insiders, such as manufacturers, diversified into the contracting of services, in part to solve marketing problems.

Members of the diverse groups offering their services perceived the goals of industrial management with varying degrees of accuracy. We distinguished two basic approaches to this problem—one the maintenance, the other the construction philosophy. Adjusting the one-shot, new construction philosophy to a continuing inside operation presented the most difficult problems. Those in this category tended to conceive of the adjustment in terms of an idealized and unrealistic model for the inside relationship. Despite a persistent tendency to see the inside-outside relationship as one of either complete organizational independence or complete organizational dependence, there also appeared to be an increasingly widespread sophistication about the problems of moving inside and a consciousness that smooth, "no trouble" relationships were an important criterion for continued success. However, in making the adjustments necessary for moving inside the contractor probably never could answer fully the question: Adjustment to what? As the discussion in Chapter 8 will indicate, problems of the internal organization that were beyond the contractor's control may have been a determining factor in his success or failure.

The continued entrance of new elements into the contracting field indicated that the traditional members of the inside and outside forces may have had difficulty in keeping track of all the emerging threats to their position. In reality, the possibility of any one of these competing groups completely replacing the others was slight, to say the least. The inside forces in old manufacturing plants, the specialty and general contractors, the integrated contractors, the labor contractors, and the manufacturer-contractors served specific functions that were not shared by the others. However, competitive sentiments were strong because the traditional forces were losing in the new and growing fields. And those contractors who were assuming a major role in the developing areas were far from modest in either size or scope of operations. Traditionally risk-takers for industry, the large maintenance and construction firms of this new period were able to increase their survival potential by diversifying their assumed risks.

Historically, the contractor has been regarded as the competitor of the inside forces, but the increased intercontractor competition for markets came closer to home and served to stimulate moves for changes in the traditional organizational structures of the contractors —a result that years of competition with the inside forces failed to achieve.

chapter 8

The Inside Forces

The inside counterpart of the outside forces is the maintenance and construction department, its management and workers, and the associated inside union. In our study, we were interested in the similarities and differences in the relationships of these two forces to the industrial firm. In many ways, the similarities were more striking than the differences. Buyer-vendor and superior-subordinate, the ideal models for outside and inside relations, respectively, were seldom found in reality. Rather than two distinctive styles of relationship, it was found, for instance, that both groups were involved in a variety of reciprocal relations with others in the firm. Both were concerned about the matter of jurisdiction. In part, the inside department's interest in jurisdiction seemed to be a reflection of the outside craft origins of a number of the members of this group, but this behavior has been observed in other managerial circles, whose members did not share this background. Thus, defense of jurisdiction may also be a general product of intergroup competition for the resources of the organization. Like the outside contractor, the inside department had independent organizational goals and in some cases possessed a structure which effectively blocked the goal realization of its internal clients.

However, there also were significant differences between the two forces. Even though both might perform the same function, the outside forces could not establish the same kind of relationships with client departments as the inside group. The inside department was included in the internal (intrafirm) system of rewards, and the contractor was not. (However, the contractor's success or failure sometimes hinged on the fate of persons who were a part of this system.) For general industrial management, relationships with both inside and outside forces involved negotiations, adjustments among distinct interests, and the lack of clear lines of authority. The inside maintenance and construction department controlled and was controlled by internal client departments; the same was true for the contractor, but the systems of control available and applicable to each were different.

Historically, in contrast to the inside forces, the outside forces have tended toward a much closer worker-management alliance in relations with other groups. However, it was noted in Chapter 7 that, for the outside forces, moving inside on a continuing basis involved the abandonment of some aspects of this bond. Despite this example of convergence in the structure of the two forces, another structural factor served to differentiate them. Within the firm, the outside forces generally tended to have somewhat better-placed supporters. Industrial management has not proved to be an unfailing backer of the inside forces. The inside group may have been sustained by certain elements at the middle and lower levels of management, but top management and others at the middle level have taken the opposite side and have favored a policy of contracting-out as an appropriate response to current trends. Thus, to obtain support for their position in the plant, the inside forces, in conjunction specifically with the in-plant union, have had to turn outside, for instance, to arbitrators who have proved to be uncertain allies at best.

THE SERVICE DEPARTMENT

We found that the internal maintenance and construction department shared with the outside contractor the need to change in response to changes in the requirements of the industrial organization. For instance, developments such as automation and its companion, integrated management, have had definite implications for the role of this department. Integrated management constitutes an effort to undo the organizational monstrosities created by compartmentalizing specialties and expecting cooperation to flow from moralizing job descriptions and organization charts. As an alternative, companies have been speeding attempts to tie together staff and service groups with their line colleagues. The potential effect of other forces on both the internal service department and the contractor will be explored further in Chapter 9.

No matter what future developments hold in store, it should be noted that the internal service department has had both loyal supporters and durable characteristics. The head of a maintenance department in a large, self-sufficient fabrication firm remarked, "A contractor's staff will never have the loyalty and devotion to duty that ours has. Our men are here for life and they feel a sense of responsibility for their work that is hard to match."

Proposed changes

Still, one of the notable findings of our research was the indication that 40 per cent of the companies wanted to make some kind of change in the service departments that performed maintenance and construction work. This high percentage was the result of reactions to economic and technological trends as well as to internal organizational problems. Slightly under one-fourth of the companies planned to reduce the size of the service department in response to factors ranging from major technological change to specific complaints about poor performance and lack of cooperation. We found cases in which in a period of three or four years service forces of as many as 2,500 men were reduced by more than half through a combined process of attrition, attractive severance pay, and early retirement programs. Slightly over 10 per cent had highly tentative plans to increase the size of the department. The majority of these were planning to hire skilled persons to work on automatic equipment. In one company the increase in department size at the plant in question represented a decrease for the firm as a whole, for a central facility was being inaugurated that would serve all the various branches from this single location.

A small group of five firms were planning to change the organizational structure by centralizing maintenance in four cases and decentralizing in one. A manager in a firm that was introducing a centralized structure commented, "We need better control over this work. Things get done eventually, but we often wonder how. Costs are another problem. A central department will give us better cost control and cut out paper work at the same time." In another case centralization was designed to solve a variety of organizational problems. The industrial relations manager at company headquarters explained, "The works manager often hears about the matter for the first time when the union files a grievance. No one tells the industrial relations manager in the plant, and yet it is his responsibility to handle relations with the union. Then, it may seem like a small thing to an outsider, but we have been plagued with certain deals that have grown up over the years. This will give us a chance to wash all that out."

Interestingly, of the total of thirty plants devising overall structural changes, eighteen also were considering specific moves that were directed at solving and controlling organizational problems. An example of these moves would be the introduction of methods to ensure that each department received equal treatment and a "fair share" of the total services being rendered. Some of those proposing changes had a fatalistic attitude toward the possibility of success.

In one case, most routine jobs were ordered by department heads who went directly to the shops, bypassing the plant engineer, who had official responsibility for this function. His attempts to introduce control devices such as work orders were resisted by some department heads and service managers. He explained his predicament as follows:

> Most routine jobs get done through private arrangements. I never hear anything about them. Department heads go directly to the shops. That way I don't know what is wrong with the machinery and I have no way of exercising control over our maintenance dollar. Last year I was able to replace the old fossil who headed the stationary engineers and I have a new young fellow in as head machinist. They will go along with me.
>
> For instance, there is no such thing as a work order in this plant. I have designed one. It is simple—a request for the job, the amount it might cost, and then the action taken. I don't see how I can get it accepted. Our electrician is a good man. He works harder than anyone around here, but he wouldn't use these forms. He would complain about the time, the red tape, but it is more than that. It is a matter of saving face. He likes to feel that his men can do the job. He doesn't want to admit an outsider might be better. If I tried to contract-out a small wiring job, I would certainly run into trouble with him. It can cause problems. They can't fix a machine, but they don't want to admit it, so the work sits. It doesn't get done until we need the machine in working order desperately. Then some action can be taken.

Proposed changes of the type mentioned above have an obvious effect on managers and workers in the firm. For example, with centralization, the service function in individual departments loses to a combined facility, and new work orders or new priority systems upset stable reciprocal relations between certain service managers and department heads.

As noted in Chapter 7, one-fourth of the plants surveyed had service departments that were organized along fairly rigid craft lines. In some cases there were separate supervisors for each craft and job descriptions that emphasized craft skills rather than functions. A few of these companies planned programs to bring the craft structure in line with changing technological requirements.

Our research as well as that of others who have worked in this field (Dalton, 1959) indicated that many of the plans for altering the present inside organization were destined to fall short of their mark because they were based on an ideal model of the situation in the firm and not on the actual system of relationships that existed.

Relations with client departments

Ideally, of course, the internal service department was supposed to be well equipped and staffed to efficiently dispatch assignments at the request of the various operating divisions. Moreover, the insiders' intimate knowledge of internal operations should have provided the ultimate in intelligent solutions to problems. Certainly, these points constituted the rationale for the establishment of an inside force.

Moreover, the service function was described as being supportive and peripheral to the major purpose of the firm. But close examination of our data revealed that the terms "peripheral" and "supportive" were not the key to the inside service department's position in the firm. On the contrary, this department sometimes played an important role in the organizational struggle for position. Certain aspects of its own position in the firm tended to facilitate its assumption of this role.

Apparently, the majority of service departments were not subject to as much control from the upper levels of management as were their counterparts in production. As an auxiliary function, divorced from the main flow of work, these service groups often were allowed to shift for themselves, while operating functions received the major share of attention. Their role as an organizational stepchild afforded a kind of freedom obtained by default and undoubtedly provided a permissive environment for the development of the relationships that will be described presently.

Interestingly, what might be characterized as the "political" role of the service department was far from being either a secret or a little-known matter. The management literature has cited many instances wherein the initial purpose of these groups went astray. Part of the picture was empire-building. Koontz and O'Donnell (1959, p. 186) noted, "It is here [the service department] that the empire builder is seen at his best. The heads of these departments are quite free to propose further services from time to time . . . and the lack of adequate service standards create a no man's land wherein he who asserts that a service is needed is rarely opposed."

While expanding, via minute accretions of function, into an impressive overhead burden, the service department also develops a unique organizational subculture. The above writers (1959, p. 191) describe this syndrome as "poor communication, delays, failures to act and simple arrogance. . . . It is unfortunate but true that personnel in service departments occasionally develop an overbearing attitude toward other activities. . . . Lordly attitudes breed suspicion and opposition, which disrupt the basic activity of service to the line." In extreme cases, ignored or avoided by members of the line as much as possible, these functionaries may have to fight for their prerogatives in a largely hostile environment.

Of course, general pictures of this type tended to gloss over the fact that service department patterns of behavior were not uniform for all industries and plants, nor did they affect all parties in the firm in the same fashion. For instance, technological factors provided one significant source of variation. In general, the more fractionated the technology, the greater the service group's ability to remain separate and to conduct shrewd bartering relations with others in the firm. Thus, in fabrication industries, both parties, operating and service, could change the scheduling of operations or interrupt the normal flow of work without immediate repercussions. Actions of this type were much less possible in process industries, where adverse effects might have been felt almost instantaneously.

With regard to the service department's relations with client departments within the firm, it should be noted that the "delays and failures" of the service subculture were in the picture, but they were only part of a total network of relationships, some of which were running smoothly. The latter constituted the bonds through which the service departments controlled its client departments. Some units in the firm have a poor stock in trade, possessing little that they can give or receive when it comes to the question of reciprocal relations. Basically, it was found that the service department was well fixed in this respect. Service work was a favorite source of organizational slack or leeway, and thus it tended to be used by operating divisions as an avenue for bolstering a sagging cost position. Good service and favorable job cost treatment could place a department ahead of its less fortunate competitors. Thus, service work was obtained at favorable rates, one department's time was charged to another's account, and the maintenance department's budget served as a source of funds through which department heads could extend their own appropriations for equipment. In Chapter 2, it was indicated that maintenance account-poaching also was practiced in the Soviet Union.

Reciprocity was involved in these relationships, for, in return, favored departments provided support for maintenance and construction projects and interests.

Managers widely recognized the existence of these practices, but enthusiasm for them was not equally widespread. It was obvious that not everyone could be a recipient of maintenance's largesse. Nor were all the disfavored the victims of calculated reciprocities. Poor planning and scheduling and limited resources in relation to total claims took an equal or greater toll. No matter what the reason, the work and interests of some groups in the firm suffered, and as the backlog of their orders grew larger and larger, pressures for change began to build up. However, the commodities being distributed continued to exist in short supply, and often the best that could be hoped for was a shift in the prevailing pattern of inequitable treatment.

Moreover, the systems that companies in our sample used to control the process were similar in some respects to the legalistic approach in preserving management rights. There was overconcern that procedures should produce a good formal record of each case and not sufficient concern with the nature of organizational process.

Thus, in the above-mentioned case of the engineer who attempted to introduce work orders, the ongoing system had persisted for years. Despite the fact that the plant was large, activities traditionally were conducted on a personal basis. This company enjoyed a better than average standing in its process-type industry, and thus there was no evidence that these practices were doing irreparable harm. Managers who had failed to ingratiate themselves with maintenance may have benefited from the work orders. But on the other hand their use by the maintenance newcomers who were hired by the engineer could have had unforeseen consequences. The newcomers still had to compete for position with others in the service group and had to establish satisfactory relationships with client departments in the terms of the old system. The accepted procedures for determining executive rewards and punishments were not changed or controlled by the introduction of the work orders. During the course of our study, the meaning and use of the orders were adapted to suit the "requirements" of the old system.

If the work orders were strictly administered, the beneficiaries of the old system would become the new dissidents. As long as "getting things done" and competing successfully within the organization required resources beyond those officially assigned to a department, the best that could be hoped for was a redistribution of benefits and the creation of pressures for new reforms.

In a fabricated-metal plant we encountered a reform "first come, first serve" priority system for work scheduling that had been operating for about a year. In some cases it was enforced strictly, but jobs that fell into the emergency category doubled in number that year, indicating again the durability of the system that the new procedures had attempted to replace.

The work of other researchers tended to confirm the fact that the above were not just isolated or unusual cases. The reader is referred to Dalton's (1959) extremely interesting account of what happened in a company in which the maintenance function was centralized in order to cut costs, increase efficiency, and check politics. The "political" maneuvering and cost-data manipulations that finally destroyed this central "field work" department exceeded the bounds of any encountered in our research, but the case illustrated well the fact that severing old relations via a formal structural change did not ensure the quality of the new structures that replaced the old ones. The struggle for survival in the organization continued, with new faces playing the old familiar roles.

Old problems in new forms

This presentation may seem to be designed to prove that the internal maintenance department had inherent venalities, but actually our real intent was to indicate the kinds of organizational processes in which it could become involved. As the structure was changed, the familiar problems were recast into new shapes and forms, but even complete decentralization did not serve to eliminate the basic problems connected with priorities and job costs. Although an arrangement in which each department had its own maintenance facility would seem to eliminate the intergroup competition that characterized the use of a common service department, our most extreme case from the standpoint of backlogged orders occurred in a plant using this system. With this structure, the potential for heightened local conflict was greatly accentuated.

One also could obtain from these data an understanding of the reasons for the rather high percentage of companies planning changes in their service function. The service department had a number of prime commodities to trade—"efficiency," controlled by a work priority system, and "economy," controlled by a system of charging and allocating job costs. While those who were currently benefiting from the ongoing system applauded it, the disadvantaged constituted an ever-present source of pressures for change.

It also was apparent that effective plans for change were not easily formulated. The real issues were sensitive points and therefore seldom brought forward. In fact, this aspect of inside relations suggested an organizational explanation for contracting-out. One of the motives may have been the need to make changes that the organization could not cope with internally. Unable to attack an internal problem effectively, one could always side-step it. Contracting-out avoided the issue. Sources of cost leeway that could not be controlled simply were eliminated.

By the same token, opposition to contracting-out may be interpreted as having broader dimensions, as actually being a part of a general opposition to changing the prevailing internal system of rewards. Currently favored groups would lose their advantages either under an internal reorganization or under contracting-out. On the other hand, the disadvantaged might favor either a reorganization or contracting-out as a means of bettering their position. Thus, although contracting-out usually has been posed as a threat to the internal maintenance and construction department, the loss suffered generally has been viewed in a limited sense in terms of a decline in number of persons supervised and dollars controlled in the budget. Less frequently considered were losses in terms of the service department's relation to other groups in the firm and in terms of its claims to future support from them.

One also might conclude that if the appropriate internal organizational changes could be made, in some cases, contracting-out would lose its attractiveness. As one of our management informants noted, "A vigorous, far-seeing, dynamic maintenance man is the equal of a contractor any day." However, achieving this condition was not simply a matter of good leadership or managerial skills. It meant making sensitive adjustments in organizational structures and systems of reward. Internal bartering to obtain a favorable cost position will persist as long as this position is used as a basis for judging performance in the process of making salary adjustments. The "symbolic" and stop-gap changes that took the place of the required adjustments in the system of rewards merely created other unstable structures.

Changes directed toward greater tolerance of contracting-out also were contingent upon revisions of the commonly found systems of reward. The attitudes of the inside maintenance chief often might have changed if his organizational value was not judged on the basis of the criteria cited above, the number of persons supervised, and the dollars controlled in the budget.

The service department's jurisdiction

The inside service department certainly was not a passive unit, waiting for others to reorganize it according to their wishes. Obviously, the trading relations described above represented one significant device for gaining support that served to promote this department's defense of its jurisdiction (see also Strauss, 1962). This elaborate mechanism was not available to the contractor, who generally had to rely on relationships of a more limited nature.

However, the inside department also became involved in defenses of its jurisdiction that were reminiscent of the old-style behavioral model for the contractor. Moreover, the inside jurisdictional defense was not limited to protection against threats from the outside contractor. For instance, we encountered several cases in which the inside department actively opposed the attempts of others in the firm to reproduce its functions locally. In one case the central maintenance department learned that a separate unit was slowly being developed in an operating department. The maintenance manager frowned on this do-it-yourself program and told his men to "observe" the local unit, much as outside craftsmen would heckle inside workers when the insiders were doing work the outsiders claimed as their own. The maintenance manager also pressured to have the stock room "run out" of supplies requested by the maverick group. Finally, an emergency arose, and the "disloyal" department desperately needed the services of the central group. At this point, the maintenance manager moved in to bargain for a cessation of the offensive activities that menaced his jurisdiction, promising in return to furnish "equal or better" service.

Another threat from within the firm was posed by construction and maintenance divisions that performed "contract" services for other units within the same general region. The local client sometimes treated the regional service group in a fashion generally thought to be reserved for outsiders. This eventuality may not have occurred to members of top management, who conceived the plan as a means for avoiding duplication of facilities and for ironing out the peaks and valleys of the single operation's work load.

In one case, a steel company brought in a work force from another division to erect structures at a site in its headquarters area. However, the local construction manager regarded this move as part of a program to minimize his function. He suddenly became very busy and refused to assist the "outside" group in any way. His men belonged to the same union as did those from the other division, but they were extremely resentful because layoffs were increasing in the local group. The entry of the men from the other division was quiet and uneventful, and officers at headquarters reported that "things were going well." But when the "outsiders" began to perform the work they had been assigned, the members of the local group reacted much as they might have to the entry of outside contractors. They walked out in protest.

Instances in which headquarters staff was rejected by a local unit were probably more in line with general expectations. The local man rarely engaged in full-fledged jurisdictional disputes with headquarters members of the construction and engineering divisions, but the inside service department employed a wide battery of avoidance techniques that served to protect its jurisdiction from headquarters interference. For instance, to avoid the "assistance" of this division, jobs were broken down into smaller units that permitted their remaining strictly local matters.

The inside union generally was somewhat sensitive to the way in which the jurisdictional winds blew at the local level. At times, the union used this information as the basis for reinforcing the efforts of local management, as in the steel-mill case described above. In other instances, the local union attempted to achieve its goals by threatening to "bring in headquarters," knowing full well that the local man would be inclined to yield rather than face questioning from central staff personnel. Some union officials collected elaborate dossiers of items of potential interest at headquarters—managerial short cuts, failure to observe safety regulations, to conduct sufficient inspections, to charge work to the proper accounts, etc.

In Chapter 7, we noted that the outside forces were experiencing a loosening of the close bond between management and union interests. One might have anticipated that the growing insecurity of the inside forces would produce the reverse reaction—a defensive drawing together of management and labor. Certainly, the inside union's strongest managerial allies were those directly associated with the maintenance and construction function. The structure of the inside industrial union paralleled that of the integrated firm. Thus, moves to contract-out had an adverse effect on both management and the union, but the notion of hand-in-glove cooperation between these two groups was not accurate.

In one case, a maintenance manager had reclassified some work in order to bring it within the range of his standing appropriation. At about the same time, the inside union "traded off" work in this category to the local building trades group in return for other concessions with regard to jurisdiction. The actions of both management and union reflected their increasing feelings of insecurity, but at the same time each was attempting to solve its own organizational problems. While the two groups shared the same general problem, the inside manager's jurisdiction was shaped by company rules and he was attempting to use means within his control to expand his territory. On the other hand, the inside union's jurisdiction appeared to depend in part on agreements with the outside unions. In reality, none of these activities were successful. An equipment manufacturer finally obtained the work in question.

The above data pointed to another way in which the outside forces

failed to be a unique element. Managers who were insiders in the
sense that they all were employed by the same firm still actively competed for work, and this statement also applied to workers who shared
a common employer. Competition with other insiders even tended to
be expressed in patterns of behavior commonly used in relation to
outsiders. Unquestionably, the fact that the competition was an outsider and not an insider provided a convenient hook on which to hang
one's negative arguments, but at the same time it was apparent that
the manager who contemplated establishing or introducing a competing inside function faced many of the same problems as the one
who was considering contracting-out.

INSIDE PROBLEMS AND OUTSIDE CONTRACTING

It seemed clear that contracting-out, substituting outside for inside
forces, sometimes represented a managerial attempt to solve certain
organizational problems, problems not necessarily generated by ob-
streperous inside unions. Some of the results of the move toward
contracting-out generally were anticipated correctly. Other results fell
in the class of unintended consequences, much like those that flowed
from internal changes in structure. In our case studies, we found that
in the same firm some members of management found advantages in
the contract arrangement and others objected to it. The competitive
situation within the firm improved for some and worsened for others.
Thus, contractors who replaced the inside forces inevitably were held
accountable by some for harming their competitive relations within
the company. On the other hand, some operating departments expected an improvement in their position as a result of contracting, and
they attempted to establish relations with the contractor that would
ensure this eventuality. As one examined the role of the inside force
in the establishment, one also was constructing the matrix into which
the outside force that replaced or supplemented it would have to fit.
In general, one could anticipate that the more "political" the matrix
into which the contract relationship was plunged, the greater the
expectations that contracting would provide the solution to a variety of
"human relations" problems that had little or nothing to do with the
contractor's technical skills.

As noted in Chapter 7, in order to move inside, some contractors
decided to abandon their traditional independence in favor of con-
forming and submitting to authority. Others selected a strategy of
strict neutrality. However, as the different interests in management had
differing expectations, it was impossible to fulfill some without dis-
appointing others. Neutrality was an equally difficult strategy under

these circumstances. The contractor simply was not moving into a neutral environment. Outsiders almost unavoidably became involved in internal jockeying for position. In this light, it appeared that the contractors' notions of effective methods for adjustment to the inside organization were somewhat unrealistic.

While inside management in some cases issued an edict to the contractor that "we will not stand for any trouble," the contractor was not free to take the same position. He could not devote endless time and energy to the inside organization's political problems. Nor could he afford to ignore them. At times, they became part and parcel of his working conditions. Some managers reported that they preferred dealing with a contractor because outsiders were easier to pressure than the inside service department. Thus, the contractor sometimes found himself involved in internal situations that manifested both tight control and strict supervision. Anxious to make a good showing, an insecure inside manager in one case was willing to leave absolutely nothing to chance. On the other hand, in our research we did not encounter any situations in which the contractor was able to exercise the full-blown range of controls available to the internal service department. In order to achieve this position, the contractor would have had to be a part of the system of internal budgetary appropriations and would have needed discretionary control over a part of these funds. Lacking this requirement, the contractor rarely became part of the larger system of internal relations, in the sense that this phenomenon was observed in the case of the inside department.

Instead, the contractor's "inside" relationships often were confined to a few select members of management, but in these instances the bond often assumed significant proportions. In fact, the fate of the contractor tended to be tied closely to the fate of the management personnel who were instrumental in selecting and hiring him. The contractor inevitably was affected by the success or failure of these parties. To those anxious to succeed, the contractor sometimes represented a private resource, an extension of the manager's communication nets beyond the boundaries of the firm. This resource tended to be guarded jealously. Other members of management who might have regarded the relationship with a particular contractor as a diffuse entity—the common property of all—were surprised at the vigor with which the plant engineer thwarted their attempts to contact directly one of "his" maintenance contractors. The inside manager who enjoyed a "most-favored nation" status with the inside service department had his counterpart in the manager who sought the same kind of benefits in a relationship with a contractor.

Within the firm there was a conviction that the contractor-manager relationship must offer something different and better from the resources available internally. As has been indicated, contracting-out was just one of a series of possible structural changes designed to cope with internal problems. Some managers condemned its serving this function. One of them remarked, "It's just another 'head in the sand' solution. The engineers like it because it's easy. They don't have to face up to the problems we've got."

Yet, the effect of the contract relationship on the inside organization often was judged largely in terms of deviation from the official norms for this "connection," namely, that this bond should be an impersonal matter, with terms set and scrutinized in the market place. Thus members of management not directly involved were critical of continuing, long-time relationships with the same contractor. There was a persistent feeling that contractors should be changed. One manager noted, "If we are so concerned about costs, why do we have the same contractors year after year? They couldn't be checking too closely. I don't mean that anyone is being bribed outright, but someone may be getting a case of whiskey at Christmastime." However, in a continuing relation with a contractor, the inside manager bypassed time-consuming official channels in favor of personal contacts that facilitated the conduct of business. The formal agreement also was circumvented in give-and-take relationships between contractors and managers aimed at smoothing both major crises and minor difficulties. Others in the firm who noted these incidents tended to frown on deviations from the buyer-vendor model, but in the process of decrying departures from a nonexistent ideal situation, the real effect of the contract relationship often went unnoticed.

Contracting also was viewed as another form of account-poaching. For instance, in one company contract work was attractive to department heads because it could be charged against the plant manager's budget, whereas work performed by the inside maintenance group was charged against departmental accounts. In another firm a manager attempted to balance his budget by keeping the inside men on a five-day week and then bringing in a contractor on Saturdays and Sundays. The contract work was charged to another account. This particular case became a *cause célèbre* and resulted in a transfer for the manager in question.

The above incidents illustrate clearly that the manager was seeking in the contract relationship solutions to old, familiar internal problems. Despite the feeling that contracting somehow should be different and should not resemble the inside relationship, the extent of difference was limited by the nature of the solutions that were sought. Our research indicated that the economic and technological reasons for contracting were of tremendous importance, but in addition there were organizational explanations for this action. Many of these could be summed up as the desire for greater freedom and greater control. While these factors may have constituted part of the actual justification for contracting, they rarely were officially stated. The same was true of internal structural changes. Official statements rarely reflected the struggles that preceded the action in question.

Thus, contracting permitted changes in procedures that would have been difficult to execute internally, for a request for a new method tended to imply a criticism of the old. And contracting permitted escape from unpleasant or time-consuming duties. A prime element among these was the employment relationship. The construction and maintenance contractor not only performed certain functions for the firm: he also recruited, selected, trained, supervised, disciplined, and compensated the workers who were involved. The real points of control in terms of responsibility for initial conceptualization and satisfactory completion of the work remained with industrial management, but the in-between area, which contained many potential challenges to "rights," was farmed out to others. A superintendent of industrial engineering in a machinery plant described his version of the differences in the character of the employment relationship that would be obtained through contracting. He noted, "Those contractors pay their boys high wages, and they tell them to jump to it or get out. We would never treat our employees in this fashion. We have to keep up good relations."

Optimistically, the relationship with the "entrenched" inside forces would be traded for a contract with an insecure outsider, who passed along his insecurity to his employees. If the contractor's employees showed too much spirit, their employment opportunities went down the drain as their employer lost his contract either through cancellation or through failure to renew. It was easy to extrapolate to a situation in which the manager regained all his old "rights" in the employment relationship while the worker moved back to the days before the Wagner Act.

However, as the materials of Chapter 7 indicated, the members of the inside crew frequently were replaced by members of the outside forces who were far more vocal than docile. Thus, the unofficial reasons for contracting often were modified or doomed to failure as the contract relationship became a part of the total complex of relationships within the firm. A combination of the problems the contractor brought with him plus those introjected by the inside forces and competing managers in the firm served this function quite adequately. The achievement of real freedom and control often would have been contingent upon the ability of both the contractor and the client managers to sever all their other organizational relations!

In the not too distant future, industrial processes may be rationalized to the point where account-poaching and other organizational "malpractices" noted here will be nonextant, but internal improvements of this type will not provide a complete answer to contracting-out problems. There is a real need to study further the effect of the contract relationship on the inside organization. The role of the inside manager as a contract administrator implies the need for new systems of incentives and rewards. Some such systems have developed of their own accord, but these are not necessarily adequate for the purpose. Some managers in industry have served primarily as contract administrators. In some governmental agencies the same situation has prevailed. Our information showed that an interesting phenomenon was occurring with regard to the relationship among the various contract administrators of our sample. The structure of competition tended to shift from the now unimportant number of men supervised and size of the departmental budget to the number and size of the contracts administered. Moreover, there seemed to be some indication that the inside administrator's sense of accomplishment was somewhat diminished because others were conducting the actual operations. It is possible that, if contracting were carried to its ultimate extreme, the role of the industrial manager might become so emasculated that the argument about using contracting to free time for essential activities would have no meaning.

Clearly, a satisfactory structure for manager-contractor relationships was not easily achieved. In general, these relationships have been allowed to grow like Topsy, to decline or flourish of their own accord. Again, this is a problem that requires further study. Past emphasis on the structure of inside relationships has led to neglect of relationships involving both insiders and outsiders.

SUMMARY

In this chapter we have examined the relationship of the inside service department to the rest of the firm, as well as the organizational processes in which this group tended to become involved. We have also investigated the similarities and differences in the relationships of the inside and outside forces to the industrial firm. With regard to the similarities, in our sample both groups were involved in a variety of relationships with others in the firm, were concerned about the matter of jurisdiction, had independent organizational goals, and in some cases possessed a structure which effectively blocked satisfactory performance in terms of the needs of its internal clients.

With regard to differences between the two groups, the inside maintenance and construction department controlled and was controlled by client departments; the same was true of the contractor, but the systems of control available and applicable to each were different. The outside forces had better-placed supporters within the organization, but the inside department was a part of the internal system of rewards and sanctions and as a matter of fact was often in a position to offer some fairly valuable commodities to others in return for support of its organizational goals. Thus, the service department was a part of the structure of intergroup competition and trading relations within the firm, and it was affected by the instability characteristic of any competitive system. Some members of management benefited from the ongoing system, while others did not. Inevitably some agitated for change.

One of the notable findings of our research was the indication that 40 per cent of the companies wanted to make some kind of alteration in these service departments. In this sense, contracting-out was placed in a new perspective. For those seeking change, it was one of an array of alternative strategies that included a variety of internal measures, such as centralization, new priority systems, etc. New internal programs often have served to redistribute benefits within the firm. Contracting-out also has served this function. Therefore, antagonism toward contracting-out may have been part of a general opposition to change, which included the changing of the internal system as well. Moreover, if the appropriate internal changes were realized, in some cases contracting-out might have lost some of its attractiveness as an alternative.

However, certain parallels between the inside and outside forces made seeking internal reforms almost as complex as contracting-out, the step usually associated with potential trouble. The inside department often defended its internal jurisidiction with vigor—not only against outsiders but also against invasion by other members of the inside group. Clearly, competition for the work of the firm was not a phenomenon reserved for insiders and outsiders, although when the competitor was an outsider, his membership in this category constituted a convenient hook upon which to hang a negative argument.

As one examined the role of the inside department and the organizational processes in which it tended to become involved, one also was constructing the matrix into which a prospective contractor would have to fit. This organizational matrix sometimes had its political as well as its economic and technological problems. The complexities of some internal situations militated against the success of simple contractor strategies for moving inside. Inside managers often were seeking in the contract relationship solutions to old and familiar internal problems. Many of the organizational reasons for contracting-out could be summed up as the desire for greater freedom and greater control.

In general, the firm paid little systematic attention to the manager-contractor relationship, which tended to develop on an *ad hoc* basis. Possibly, as technological advances increasingly serve to rationalize internal managerial systems, these also will contribute to a rationalization of the contractor's functioning in them.

chapter 9

Inside Versus Outside:

Trends and Developments

THE CONCEPTS INSIDE AND OUTSIDE

In our research the definition of the concepts inside and outside was based on the source of the employment relationship, the industrial firm and the contractor, respectively. It is also possible to suggest distinctions of a sociological or psychological nature, based on interaction patterns or identification. Thus, members of a contract force long employed in a particular industrial firm may come to identify with their place of employment rather than with their contractor-employer. For research on questions of rights and jurisdiction in the

167

United States the employment relationship bond has had great significance because of the multiplicity of conflicting union and management structures built around it. However, future developments in the field of industrial and union organization may lead to different uses of these concepts and to the development of organizational contexts that will serve to alter their commonly accepted meanings.

For instance, in our study it seemed that the distinction between the two groups was, in practice, more meaningful in fabrication than in process industries. In fabrication, the outside forces were institutionalized more fully as a separate entity. The nature of process work, especially in the modern integrated plants, was such that outsiders had a tendency to become insiders, or at least the two groups tended to develop remarkable behavioral similarities. Eventually, the source of the pay check may be the sole distinction worth noting. This seems to indicate, in turn, that inside-outside conflict in process industries may be a temporary phenomenon. It may, in fact, be a vanishing phenomenon as manufacturing in general becomes less a fabrication and more a process operation.

THE CHANGING EMPLOYMENT RELATIONSHIP

Thus, although some critics were still bemoaning the deleterious effect of the large organization on the individual, we found often unnoticed trends toward greater flexibility in the employment relationship. These trends have largely been ignored by those who continue to envision salvation in a close-knit supervisor-subordinate group in which the ultraskilled leader converts anomie and industrial discontent into productivity by his insightful human relations techniques. On the other hand, there have been those who are concerned about the consequences of inordinate coddling, high wages, proliferating fringe benefits, seniority guarantees, and charitable personnel policies. The total result of these practices has been conceived as excessively and destructively close ties between the firm and the employee, and more particularly between the boss and his subordinates. In the process, the desire for mobility is reduced, along with the incentive to progress, to incur risks, and to think creatively. These, of course, are legitimate problems, but the prescriptions of the theorists, whether they have tended toward Spartanism or hedonism, invariably embed the individual in the matrix of a continuing relationship with one firm and attempt to find there the means for social salvation and a better way of life.

This single-minded focus on the problems of the long-term, one-establishment employment relationship may diminish as the need for greater flexibility becomes more widely recognized. Extrapolating to the future, one can anticipate a decline in the significance of the durable, shielded relationship between industrial supervisor and subordinate. Part of this decline will be attributable to situations in which the supervisor shifts to the role of contract administrator and continuity of employment, traditionally furnished by the integrated industrial firm, becomes the product of a series of agreements held by an outside bureaucrat, the contractor. Or, in line with greater flexibility in the employment relationship, the industrial worker's primary attachment may be his association with a given technology or industrial process. Thus, he may work interchangeably for an industrial firm, for a contractor, or in the contract division of one firm performing a service function in another. Obviously, for substantial growth of this new type of employment relationship, structural changes would have to be made to adapt industrial and union organizations to the realities of technological developments. Moves in this direction have taken place. Some of these will be discussed in the following sections of this chapter.

INSIDE AND OUTSIDE: ORGANIZATIONAL DEVELOPMENTS

On the organizational front we have noted the rise and fall of various elements in response to economic and technological changes. Formerly fractionated units have been joining forces, and once united groups have been splitting apart. With regard to the contracting-out issue, we found that labor and management apparently were as likely to be allies as enemies. Nor did the allies of the inside and outside forces constitute everyone in industry versus everyone in the contracting field, as these labels might tend to indicate. Rather, both sides had "old" and "new" elements. Inside, one found management and workers who had direct interests in the maintenance of the traditional internal function. On the other hand, there were those who favored contracting as the appropriate move to meet new organizational needs. Outside, there were new groups, such as those offering contract maintenance services, as well as the traditionally organized general and specialty contractors. When one included the competing old and new union organizations on both sides, possible alliances in rights and jurisdictional battles became almost endless. Even the most unlikely combinations seemed to have been formed in a particular case. Thus, on the union side, the rival "old" inside (industrial) and outside (craft) groups have combined against the new outside forces when the latter threatened to deprive both these old rivals of work.

The fluidity of the lines between inside and outside was illustrated further by the emergence of organizations that encompassed both sides of the fence. The manufacturer-contractor described in Chapter 7 was one example of this trend. A firm of this type battled the inside unions both as an employer and as a contractor-competitor vying for the same work. In the latter role, the manufacturer also was opposed by the traditional outside forces. The contract operation usually was a unit in a single manufacturing company, but in the future these contract divisions may represent pooled facilities, jointly owned by a number of manufacturers in a given industry or in allied fields.

Moreover, industrial unions, based in the structure of the integrated firm and loyal defenders of the interests of the inside forces, have moved in some cases to organize the outside forces that have replaced their members. One such union is the Oil, Chemical and Atomic Workers; another is the International Association of Machinists. In explaining the position of his union the president of the Chemical Workers noted:

> In OCAW we will continue to attempt to persuade our industrial employers to minimize the amount of maintenance work they turn over to outside contractors, but we have come to recognize that in certain situations, whether we like it or not, there will be maintenance contracts let. We have come to the conclusion that it will be necessary for us to organize the employees of maintenance contractors (Knight, 1961).

This union had some success in organizing maintenance contractors. The 1960 contract covering the outside forces provided base wages identical with those of permanent inside employees. An additional 39 cents an hour was included in lieu of fringe benefits. Needless to say, the international building trades unions who claimed this jurisdiction for their own were not enthusiastic about this "inside" invasion of outside territory. In an interview a leader of an inside union that had been organizing contract forces noted that members employed by industrial firms complained about the organizing of their outside competitors. He commented, "They say, 'You don't care about us,' but we tell them we can't stop progress and if we don't organize them, things will be worse."

RIGHTS, JURISDICTION, AND TECHNOLOGICAL CHANGE

In analyzing management rights problems, there has been a tendency to identify one party with the *status quo* and the other with change, as though each one were engaged in active and independent pursuit of these objectives. In the late 1950s and early 1960s the inside forces found themselves defending the *status quo*, while the outside forces were benefiting from the changes taking place during that period. However, the real determinants of the parties' positions were external to both of them. While their rights and interests were affected vitally, by and large, the significant factors were beyond their realm of control. Existing interest groups were either harmed or helped by the developments, and new interest groups were created as a result. All struggled for position within the limited context of the variables they controlled, but the factors that ultimately determined their success often stood apart from these activities.

The case of the airline industry illustrates the above points as they refer to the struggles of the inside and outside forces over contracting-out and management rights. During the piston plane era, some of the unions representing repair and maintenance workers had succeeded in "nailing down" rights to work on the equipment owned or operated by the airlines. Some of these rules were airtight. Others provided that no reduction in employment opportunities should result from contracting work. On paper at least, the rights of some managements were largely past history. However, the shift from piston planes to jets opened a new era for management rights in the repair field.

Engines in the piston planes often were interchangeable, and when an advanced model was introduced or a change was made from one model to another, only minor retooling was required. A single shop could handle many kinds of engines, and thus it was feasible for the airlines to perform much of this work. Moreover, in comparison with other industries, the airlines were advanced technologically. As there were few outside sources of facilities, these companies tended to do all their own maintenance and repair, including air-frame overhaul. As the employers were oriented toward doing work inside, forgoing the right to contract-out seemed to be largely an academic question.

But with the advent of the jets the inside operation faced serious problems. The jets required technical skills that the inside men lacked, as well as repair facilities that the airlines could not afford to build and equip. Moreover, the work load developed peaks and valleys due to longer engine life and a reduction in the number of aircraft. Shorter flying times permitted some airlines to consolidate their facilities. All in all, there was less work, a less steady flow of work, and more need to farm it out to specialists.

To add to the woes of the inside forces, the manufacturer-contractor appeared on the scene. Engine manufacturers began to lease power to the airlines. These companies overhauled their own engines and replaced them, taking this aspect of the repair work entirely out of the airline facility. In a parallel development, manufacturers of warrantied instruments came to the airline shops to repair their products with their own crews.

Taking advantage of the newly created market for their services, repair and maintenance contractors established organizations to handle the air-transport companies' work. Engine overhauling was offered by "fixed-base operators," who sometimes purchased surplus facilities formerly used for the overhaul of military planes. These new contractors were able to maintain a steady flow of work and to specialize in a large variety of engine types. Their services were especially valuable to the smaller airlines.

Other developments made the contracting of routine maintenance activities attractive. New airport commission requirements called for the use of a single fueling contractor, and the vast size of the new jet ports created problems in the organization of cleaning and the handling of baggage. Interestingly, the fueling, baggage, and cleaning activities were undertaken by a mammoth, nationwide contract operation.

On the economic side, the prosperous days of the airlines had come to an end, and spending to furnish these new facilities internally was out of the question for some of them. The inside repair and maintenance workers were in poor shape because their job property claims and rights were based on an obsolete piston plane technology. If airline management "rights" to contract-out were lost in the prosperous days of the postwar period when technology was relatively stable and economic factors undemanding, these rights were somewhat regained in the era of competition and technological change that began in the late fifties.

As for at least one of the unions involved, it was not content to fight a losing battle to keep all the work inside. Rather, the Machinists followed the airline work wherever it went and proceeded to organize the fixed-base operators and the maintenance and fueling contractors.

INSIDE–OUTSIDE COMPETITION

Through this research, we have developed a picture of the inside and outside forces vying for the maintenance and construction work of the industrial firm. While each side made strong property claims to this work, we found that they were not as free to compete effectively as one might have anticipated. The two groups were placed in the position of responding to economic and technological factors, taking action that they hoped would serve their best interests. Only some aspects of the cost picture and of organizational structure were under these groups' control to a significant extent. In Part II we examined the dollars-and-cents aspects of the competition. In this section, Part IV, we have investigated some of the relevant aspects of organizational structure.

Clearly, one of the greatest organizational assets was flexibility. The inside organization was moving in directions that made the assimilation of outsiders much simpler than in the past. In terms of taking advantage of this development, the outside forces had both liabilities and assets. Both outside management and workers were flexible in their treatment of the employment relationship, but both groups needed to make further efforts to break down narrow jurisdictional boundaries. In general, inside management was less plagued with this particular difficulty, but it was hampered by other problems involving vested interests. On either side, flexibility was a valuable but hard-won property. Its achievement was resisted by those who did not wish to compete on these terms. For instance, the outside forces were flexible with regard to the size and rapid evolution of an organization, but when inside management attempted to obtain an equivalent situation by reducing the size of the inside forces, the action met with opposition from those directly involved.

Competitive sentiments arise when one party leaves its traditional preserve and invades the stronghold of its rivals. This event occurred during the course of our research when the outside forces entered the large process plants, en masse. In terms of our findings, one could formulate a compound picture of the situations that each group customarily had found maximally favorable. The stronghold of the outside group was a middle-sized fabricating concern with a small internal force that had membership in a craft union. The plant in question was located in an area where craft rates were not high. On the other hand, the stronghold of the inside forces was a large process establishment with a large maintenance and construction force that had membership in an industrial union. High outside craft rates prevailed in the area (see Chapter 4). However, in plants that typified the latter situation forces were acting to alter traditional patterns for performing work.

The technological changes which serve the cause of the outside forces appear not to have run their course. Yet it is possible that future developments will make contracting less attractive in certain fields. For instance, in work on fully automated equipment the boundaries between machine operation and repair and maintenance may disappear (Davis, 1962). Thus, the internal maintenance function may be closely integrated with others in the plant. While service work still could be contracted-out, the outside forces may have to be on guard against the day when the transitional phase ends, for industrial management may decide to pull back functions farmed out during the adjustment to automation. When operations become stabilized, the appeal of a closely controlled inside force again may assume dominant proportions. Disillusionment with the old, independent maintenance empire may have been forgotten and may be considered irrelevant in

any case. The outside forces may have to put up a real struggle to
retain their industrial work market. In any case, for both the inside
and the outside forces, a premium will continue to be placed on the
ability to adapt to new situations.

Emerging union structures

The fact that the work force is organized into two competing groups,
outside (usually craft) and inside (usually industrial) unions, is a
structural liability that compounds problems in periods of adjustment.
The efforts of each group to defend its particular job territory against
the invasion of the other tends to constitute a pathetic side show rather
than a problem-solving contribution to the main event, the reorganization of the work of the industrial firm and its impact on the labor
force as a whole.

Management probably has benefited when competition between
the inside and outside forces has stimulated either group to improve
its operating efficiency. In fact, managers have encouraged this type
of competition. Thus, we found cases in which company officials,
spurred on by new technological developments, threatened the inside
forces with a move to adopt contract maintenance. But when competition represented an extension of the old labor problem approach
and focused largely on the exclusion of one or the other group from a
given area, the emphasis shifted from improving efficiency to improving political strategy. In Part V we shall present details of the inside-outside competition in relation to a wide range of divisions of the
industrial work territory, but at this point we are interested in the
larger implications of this rivalry for the structure of union organization.

If we agree that war between the inside and outside forces has
done little to advance the interests of either group and that, as we
shall see in Part V, truces and pacts between them have served as
largely symbolic arrangements, other, alternative solutions must be
considered. In our society, the possibility of either the inside or the
outside workers' accepting the role of a Japanese-style buffer group
is remote, to say the least. But, in the past, conflicts over jurisdiction
have led to the eventual merger of contesting organizations. It is possible that the hard-to-resolve inside-outside conflict may be the seed-
bed for eventual mergers, although this does not necessarily imply a
firmer consolidation of the existing craft and industrial branches of
the AFL-CIO. A more logical alternative would be the grouping of all
inside and outside units related to a particular production process. New
union structures, "superunions," including all those working on a given
technology or process, might lead to the end of jurisdictional battles

for the work of the industrial firm. Unquestionably, management, as well as the unions, would benefit from this development.

Thus, union actions that serve to bolster management "rights" in our problem area, contracting-out, need not take place at the bargaining table. Rather, these rights may be augmented by union programs relating to structural changes, possibly in the creation of superunions of insiders and outsiders, that would permit maximum flexibility in coping with the problem of who shall perform industrial work. As noted earlier in this chapter, some unions have moved in this direction, but, by and large, these have been piecemeal activities, designed to protect a particular inside or outside jurisdiction, rather than concerted efforts to rationalize the system.

Future developments

What is the future of the competing inside and outside forces who were the subject of this research? It was apparent that much of the day-to-day sparring involving inplant or outside unions and industrial management or craft and industrial unions on the local or national scene could be regarded as a holding operation in the face of change. But one should not make the mistake of assuming that the parties will remain as they were at the time of our study. While functions such as maintenance and construction certainly will persist, they may be structured differently. Because of technologically determined changes in the internal organization, the inside crew may be abandoned in favor of workers who are employees of large contractors. Some industrial supervisors may become primarily contract administrators, and the long-term relationship of some managers with plant employees may be shifted to a contractual relationship with a firm that not only performs a technical function but also assumes responsibility for the employment relationship.

After the transitional period of adjustment to automation has passed, some contracted work may be reclaimed for the inside forces. Moreover, future developments may cause at least some aspects of the inside-outside distinction to lose their significance. For instance, contractors may lose some of their independent free-market characteristics and become integral parts of one or several industrial establishments. New superunions or new offshoots of old unions—not the traditional craft and industrial groups that dominated the scene in the thirties, forties, and fifties—may organize the industrial contractors and plants associated with a given process and in this manner become a new and powerful factor on the labor-management scene. Technological and organizational problems, such as contracting-out, have assumed prime importance in labor-management relations, and this observation may provide a clue to potential directions for restructuring the interests of the labor movement. Old job-oriented unions may be supplanted to some extent by those with a broader orientation—unions that will seek as a foremost goal a direct influence on technological and organizational matters. Again, this changed focus would serve to reduce distinctions between inside and outside forces that are based on such factors as the historic jurisdictions of each group.

In reality, the competition between the inside and outside forces is a struggle for a new industrial work market—a venture that can be accomplished successfully through skillful adaptation to changing economic and organizational structures. It seems clear that the battle over contracting-out will not be settled by the superior strength of one union in contrast to that of another. With many important factors lying outside the realm of control of these groups, the resolution of the problems they faced depends on the ability of the groups involved to adapt, either singly or jointly, to the needs of new situations. Even struggles fought on old battlegrounds, over traditional jurisdictions, are primarily a reflection of the gains that rivals are making in new fields. Thus, the battlegrounds may lie in the areas of *status quo*, but the actual victories involve no battles and lie in the areas of change and with the parties who are willing to sacrifice some of the trappings of their present identity.

part V

Concepts of Equity

chapter 10

Rights and Equities

Questions of conflicting rights and principles may seem to have no answer. One authority pointed out that, in the case of contracting-out, "negotiations from principle are, of course, irreconcilable" (Crawford, 1960, p. 5). However, in practice, agreements have been reached, and these generally have been formulated on the basis of what one might designate as "equities," or in common parlance "fair shares." Thus, while two parties publicly declare their inalienable rights, their privately conducted settlements reflect a kind of compromise between two sets of equities. While neither side may have experienced a change of heart, both have moved away from an all-or-none position. If rights in contracting-out questions are absolute, equities, in the sense in which we are using the term, are not. They define a fair share, a division made in recognition of the interests of others—and of the extent to which they potentially could assert their counterdemands.

EQUITY IN WHAT?

In our study, with regard to the problem of splitting the industrial work pie there were three questions that required answers: what, who, and how. The definition of "what" was determined partially by cultural values. A comparison of our culture with the Japanese pointed up a significant contrast. In Japan, the obligation to provide work for the permanent employees of the firm was recognized as a worker equity that was *independent* of the amount of productive work available (see Chapter 2). In other words, work was a flexible quantity and in true Parkinsonian fashion expanded to fit the force available. Thus, a maintenance worker who had no duties to perform might be given tasks that were remote from his specialty and nonessential in a strictly utilitarian sense, for instance, tending the tea service. American managers, on the other hand, reported real worker resistance when attempts were made to assign unneeded maintenance mechanics to jobs that had a largely aesthetic effect on the surroundings: for instance, trimming the shrubbery around the factory. Surplus maintenance workers sometimes requested "any kind of work," but the range of acceptable tasks was not as broad as this statement implied.

But these self-imposed limits were far from being the most significant ones faced by the worker in answering the question: Equity in what? In the United States, utilitarian criteria have predominated, and these criteria have involved the assumption that work must be productive and available before a worker's equity in it generally is recognized. The distasteful label featherbedding has been used to designate payment for units of work not needed. Thus, railroad workers and others who have defended alleged featherbedding activities have not based their case on the need for the income or on the existence of a general management obligation. Rather, they have tried to argue that the work in question was needed in the interests of safety and efficiency. Available productive work has been much preferred by both managers and workers who are part of a cultural system that disdains featherbed activities (see also Jacobs, 1962).

In 1963, a generally "liberal" United States Secretary of Labor upheld the criterion that the work a man performs should be needed by noting:

When a union representative meets that same problem [layoffs due to technological change] by insisting that permanent sinecures be arranged for men who are no longer actually needed in the plant, he weakens collective bargaining by using it to produce a wrong answer, which won't stand up—for an economy that must achieve its full growth to survive cannot afford a manpower waste (Wirtz, 1963, p. 49).

An economist describing projects organized to keep the inside forces busy indicated the dubious values of these efforts by designating them as "make work" (Oxenfeldt, 1956, p. 78). The popular literature has offered more vigorous affirmation of the position that work being performed should be needed work. In denouncing the union's opposition to the elimination of telegraphers employed by the Chicago and Northwestern Railroad, one newspaper described the union's stand as "a belief founded on the notion that an enterprise exists primarily for the purpose of furnishing jobs and not to provide services at fair prices to the public and profits for its owners."[1]

Differences between the employment relationship in the United States and in countries like Japan have not always been equally evident. The Japanese culture has dictated a firm managerial commitment to the permanent worker. In the United States, this commitment has been qualified in nature, but in stable and prosperous times the situation has tended to be quiescent. Under these circumstances, practitioners and scholars alike have made plans and analyses in terms of a long-enduring employment relationship. But in times of technological and economic change the employment situation becomes turbulent, and the worker's real lack of tenure stands out clearly. The pool of available productive work diminishes, and at this point pressures rise for additional sources of this commodity. Activities that industrial management contracts-out apparently are deemed essential to the functioning of the firm, for industry rarely has hired contractors to perform featherbedding work. Thus, the cultural demand that work be needed explains in part why the pressures of the inside forces have focused on contract operations within the plant.

At its maximum size, the pie to be divided among the various inside and outside claimants generally has consisted of all the available work of the firm. Additions in the form of make work or specially constituted projects have been the exception and not the rule. The criteria for determining availability simply have been those which govern the everyday running of the business. Our research showed that, as far as the inside forces were concerned, the operational definition of available work was simply their current work plus whatever work was contracted-out.

[1] *Chicago Sun-Times,* Oct. 10, 1962, p. 31.

WHO DIVIDES THE WORK?

In our sample the contracting-out problem could have reached the ultimate point in complexity if each of the parties at interest had made separate deals with every other party regarding fair shares of the work of the industrial firm. However, this structural horror was averted, on the formal level, at least. Yet, if one included the divisions made by third parties, such as arbitrators, there were conflicting patterns sufficient to satisfy the most morbid expectations.

One must not lose sight of the fact that the prime actor—the initial divider of the pie—was industrial management. All other divisions represented attempts either to reinforce or to change this basic action. But the potential influence of those who proposed change was limited severely by the fact that the actual determination of the size of the pie to be divided rested largely in the hands of industrial management.

Not all the parties at interest had an equally passionate concern about the matter of equity in the work of the industrial firm. In part, the intensity of this concern seemed to be greatest among those closest to the receiving end of a given plan for dividing work. At the top levels of management and unions, notions of equity were most contaminated with questions of rights. For those nearer to the day-to-day problems, fair shares often appeared to be the real issue, while questions of rights may have seemed to be largely academic. The contractor, aside from industrial management the other main actor in the contracting-out problem, was one of those on the receiving end of a given division of work. In this capacity, he occupied a position similar to that of the manager of the inside maintenance and construction force. Members of both these groups attempted to expand their fair share of the work. Some of their activities have been described in Chapters 7 and 8, and they will be discussed further in Chapter 12.

But the real dividers of territory and students of fair shares were the unions. They focused their attention on special agreements and formulas designed primarily to reform the present and project the past into the future. Both the inside and the outside unions have attempted to define their respective equities in industrial work through formal and informal agreements with industrial management, although, as one might have anticipated, the inside union has engaged in the bulk of these activities. In addition, the two rival union groups have made agreements with one another at both the national and the local level. These pacts, in effect, have divided the industrial maintenance and construction work market between them. Although they may have regretted it since, both industrial management and the contractors formerly had encouraged this type of activity. The captains of industry did not want to be troubled with what appeared to be interunion affairs of slight importance, and the contractors felt that the whole matter was basically a labor problem (see Chapter 7).

It should be noted that interunion agreements need not be the inevitable result of jurisdictional disputes. For instance, when the airline pilots and the flight engineers struggled for occupancy of the third seat in the cockpit of the new jet planes, the pilots were not interested in making a division with the engineers. On the contrary, in the early 1960s the pilots crossed the picket lines of the engineers and proceeded to attempt to demolish the weaker union. In some cases, one rival may "swallow" the other. But in the contracting-out problem the rival union interests were fairly evenly balanced in strength, and this situation was conducive to the development of pacts dividing the work between them. In fact, organizing jurisdictions and contracting-out have been the two major battlefields wherein the merged branches of the AFL-CIO have expressed their divided institutional interests and struggled over fair shares of the total job territory.

The manager was the initial divider of the industrial work pie, and the inside and outside unions constituted the second force of real consequence. However, members of a third group also appeared on the scene to attempt to reconcile the divisions made by the first two groups as well as to make some original contributions of their own. Appropriately, these individuals and groups usually are designated as third parties—the arbitrators, the courts, and the government. All are customarily involved in labor-management questions, although, for the contracting-out problem, arbitrators were the most significant group.

In the process of reviewing cases, both arbitrators and the courts have devised standards for dividing industrial work between the inside and outside forces. In the key Warrior-Gulf decision of 1960 (see Chapter 11) the United States Supreme Court effectively turned the job of tertiary pie-divider back to the arbitrators, although in the early 1960s the National Labor Relations Board moved in as another active force.

The role of the United States government in relation to contracting-out has reflected the ambivalence of its position, for it has served as both arbiter of disputes and letter of contracts. At times, its policies in these two roles have contradicted one another. Moreover, the general tenor of government predisposition toward inside or outside interests has appeared to alter in response to changes in the socioeconomic climate surrounding the general issue.

HOW IS THE WORK TO BE SHARED?

Our research indicated that the final question, "how," was crucial for the successful sharing of work. Recognition of a right or an equity is the beginning and not the end of the route toward its realization in fact. The opposition can throw up numerous road blocks, but focusing upon these often obscures a rather simple prerequisite for achieving a workable answer to our question, namely, that a satisfactory basis for measurement must be established. Many an agreement to "divide the work" has met its Waterloo at this point. In the case of the typographers' equity in work preset by outsiders, measurement presented no serious problems. Members of the typographers' union simply have hung on the reproduction hook all relevant work brought in from the outside. Their "fair share" has included all this typographical work, even though some of it actually was performed by others. An examination of the newspaper could provide a simple measure of each day's claim. Moreover, typically there has been no question that the work could have been done inside. Bogus work may seldom be performed in practice, but it has been so clearly defined that it has served as a negotiable item. In this capacity, bogus work has been traded for other benefits.

Unfortunately, contracting-out has provided no such golden opportunities for measuring worker equity. The president of the New York Typographical Union 6, Bertram A. Powers, has likened reproduction or bogus work to restrictions on contracting-out.[2] But, with regard to the quality of measurability, reproduction has been a far superior performer. We failed to locate any cases of the inside forces ticking up the numbers of hours of contract work as a pool or reserve against potential unemployment. Although some such cases may have existed, they would have been the exception and not the rule. Granted that the contracted work was both available and needed, there was always the question of the ability of the inside forces to perform the job, and new and troublesome potential measurables were introduced regarding the matters of scheduling and qualifications.

In some cases the inside forces have been able to take unusual benefits enjoyed by the outside forces and isolate these from the operation of criteria specifying contingent factors. Thus, the relevant number of overtime hours worked by the outside forces have been "hung on the hook" for future matching by inside management. As will be noted in Chapter 11, some fairly successful ways of measuring the inside forces' equity have been devised in the case of production subcontracting in the garment industry. But in general, equivocal criteria such as "past practice" have plagued this field, as have vague condi-

2 *New York Times,* Apr. 18, 1963, p. 26.

tional criteria and claims that specified ambiguous and easily manipulable categories of work. Settling for an equity that included less than "everything" clearly created knotty problems.

Measurement has been complicated further by the lack of regularity and predictability in some types of maintenance and construction work. Trains run daily; newspapers are published on the same schedule. Thus, the oversize crew and the bogus claim could be attached to each unit. But maintenance and construction work may be sporadic in nature, may be postponed, reorganized, changed in form and content. The inside forces were faced with the problem of claiming work as it appeared. Maintenance and construction crews were not sufficiently close to the end product of the firm to exact real tribute or royalties.

Those who have predicted a possible widespread trend toward featherbedding have failed to recognize that only certain tasks can be controlled in this fashion (see Jacobs, 1962). Those who performed auxiliary services as members of the inside force not only had problems due to their inability to measure their universe adequately: in addition, it obviously was essential to have at least some remnant of a group present to make the assessments. For instance, in new plants when an entire service function was contracted-out or monitored by automatic controls, the question of the inside forces' equity in the work never arose. Actual, as compared with paper, rights and equities were a function of the nature of the process the workers were attempting to control. When measurement difficulties were encountered, rights and equities had a heightened tendency to remain the "property" of industrial management, the original designer and divider of the industrial work pie.

INTERRELATED SYSTEMS OF EQUITY

Two long-standing parties at interest may never reach an agreement on an equitable division of a given territory that both have claimed, but, over time, each learns to take the other into account in planning his actions. Thus, the relationship develops both stability and predictability. However, in times of change, energy expended in formulating agreements that govern the old, stable patterns of opposition may essentially be wasted because these agreements either are about the wrong thing or are made with the wrong party. For instance, certain specialty contractors reluctantly made an "equitable" division with a local industrial union only to find that both were being replaced in new work by an integrated contractor (see Chapter 7). Or an industrial union may have obtained an arrangement with an independent integrated contractor regarding limits on appropriate fields for the latter's activities only to find that both are being replaced by a pooled facility owned in common by several manufacturers. In fact, the very threats that finally brought the other party around to the point of agreement may have been the same factors that served to render his "Cross my heart" relatively valueless.

It was found that those claiming a share of the work were no longer confined within the boundaries of a particular country. Jobs literally could be flown out to foreign bases. This statement applied especially to the repair and maintenance of high-speed mobile equipment such as jet planes. As national boundaries lose their significance, the prospect and problems of making agreements with groups such as foreign repair crews loom in the future.

In the next chapter, we shall examine the various systems of equity that applied to the contracting-out problem as we studied it. The most important of these systems involved either the ultimate holder of the property in question, industrial management, and a property claimant or two counterclaimants. Interestingly, comparisons of the position of a given interest group in two or more systems sometimes revealed contradictory claims regarding a fair share of the work. This was especially true in respect to a party's position on fair shares in relation to another claimant and that same party's position in relation to the prime property-holder.

Unquestionably, in some cases the parties to a given arrangement hoped that it would serve to pressure another uninvolved party into recognizing the legitimacy of the agreed-upon division. In this sense, it was possible to shop for a fair share in more than one market and then attempt to enforce universally the best deal obtainable. Unfortunately, commodities (shares of the work) obtained in one of these markets often did not have an equivalent value in another.

In studying the contracting-out issue, it was much easier to analyze the separate pieces than to determine how they fitted together. In a variety of bargaining relationships designed to determine fair shares of work, one does not expect the closely interrelated network of relationships that would characterize a chain of command. Rather, the picture that emerged involved a given group (or groups) attempting to solve diverse problems in different relationships without trying to reconcile the inconsistencies that arose among these solutions.

Did pressures from others serve to induce consistency—possibly to bring a party's best deal in line with the worst? Or did a strong gain in one market for fair shares serve as a red flag, stiffening the opposition and at the same time stimulating attempts by others to duplicate this achievement? For example, one strong gain might have heightened conflict in the entire system.

On the other hand, if a loosely hinged chain of relationships of parties at interest had a weak link, all the others could use this party to take the brunt of the various settlements. In true pecking order form, the share of the weakest party could be decreased to the point where it almost ceased to exist. For instance, in the early 1960s disputes over the number of seats in the cockpit of a jet plane involved designers, plane manufacturers, the airlines, the Federal government, and two rival unions (see also Jacobs, 1962). While, in 1962, the weak link, the Flight Engineers, appeared to lose out primarily to the Pilots, the Engineers actually bore the brunt of all the settlements made at that time. Thus, the existence of a weak link may facilitate the total process of arriving at a solution. With regard to contracting-out, the inside union in some cases played a role similar to that of the Engineers. But, on the whole, the inside union was not sufficiently weak. The absence of a convenient "soft spot" may have been a major factor contributing to the "no settlement" status of issues regarding contracting-out and equities in the work of the industrial firm.

Unquestionably, some elements in the structure of agreements on contracting-out were more potent than others. In the eyes of the various parties at interest, the disputes between inside management and union tended to be critical in this respect. Certainly, the various parties were sensitive to the possibility of losing their share as these two key parties redivided the industrial work pie during the course of negotiations. The contractor's equity was not even mentioned in a formal statement that described contracting-out as a conflict between the right to manage and job and union security (Crawford, 1960). Were other equities effectively ignored, or was the inside management –inside union battle a convenient shorthand for the entire complex of interests?

As we shall see in Chapter 11, none of the parties, individually or jointly, succeeded in making a definitive division of the industrial work pie. Rather, one finds diverse and conflicting solutions, but the efforts to devise satisfactory rules for the equitable division of work between the inside and outside forces never ceases.

chapter 11

Rules for the Equitable Division of Work

In this chapter, we shall examine the rules for the equitable division of work that were developed through interunion pacts, arbitration, collective bargaining, and the activities of the Federal government and its agencies.

INTERUNION PACTS

The 1958 craft–industrial union pacts regarding the division of maintenance and construction work between the inside and outside forces represented a departure from the usual schemes for settling jurisdictional disputes. Although to the outside observer these pacts may appear to be rooted in traditional practice, at the 1957 Building and Construction Trades Convention, George Meany, president of the AFL-CIO, noted that the covenants constituted a departure from jurisdiction.[1] Thus, from the standpoint of the outside unions the pacts represented an innovation, for all the work of a particular craft was not assigned to its members. Instead, equities or fair shares were measured according to a rule that crosscut jurisdictions in order to freeze historical relationships. In effect, the past was cast forward into the future and secured against further change. The agreements established property claims to gross segments of work, specifying that all industrial maintenance work belonged to the industrial (inside) unions and all new industrial construction work to the craft (outside) unions. Assignment of jobs in the in-between area was to be governed by past practice. As this document also contained an implicit formula for industrial management's decision regarding contracting-out, its publication stimulated much excitement among management rights advocates.

Historical background

These federation-level pacts cannot be understood without reference to the historic relationship between the inside and outside forces. The very concept of inside and outside jurisdiction was in part the product of the craft unions' long-standing refusal to admit into their ranks skilled workers in industrial plants. The craft unions had little concern for industrial workers and were interested in industrial jobs only on their own terms. An apt description of the situation in the middle 1930s was given by Meany:

> When we [the craft unions] had industrial work crop up that we felt we should do, we made an effort, if we had any weight, any pressure, to get that work for our contractors. We would not work directly. We wouldn't work for anyone but our own contractors. We didn't want the people that were on the work; we merely wanted the work. So far as the people that were on the work were concerned, for our part they could drop dead.[2]

For the industrial unions that began organizing in the middle 1930s, the appropriate jurisdiction included all the production and maintenance work of the firm. Craft union jurisdictions clearly were infringed upon by this claim, but, for many years, the craft unions regarded this infringement as a matter of minimal importance. Moreover, in return,

---

[1] *Report of Proceedings of the Fiftieth Anniversary Convention of the Building and Construction Trades, AFL-CIO.* Washington, D.C., 1958, p. 183.
[2] *Ibid.*

some craft unions invaded the industrial field. Both groups were expanding on an *ad hoc* basis. Finally, the technological and economic developments that came to a head in the late 1950s produced the conflict that potentially was built into the structure of the craft and industrial union system. Industrial unions, shrinking in size, clashed head on with construction contractors and unions seeking new and stabilizing industrial markets for their work (see Chapter 7).

The Peace Pacts and the principle of minimum surrender

Devising a formula for sharing the industrial work market proved to be a step almost as difficult as the 1955 merger of the AFL-CIO. In 1957, the head of that organization, George Meany, warned that renewed labor warfare would not solve the problem of dividing responsibility for work on major repairs in factories. In making his point, he inquired of the building trades convention, "Is anyone here going to turn over members that they have organized for twenty years at the point of a gun? You fellows know that isn't going to happen. . . . The only ones who gain are the enemies of labor." [3]

The first version of the pact was formulated in June, 1957, and the following four years were occupied with attempts to gain acceptance of it, with renewed warfare and with revisions of the original document (see Figure 11-1). A division of the industrial work pie that successfully resolved the conflicting institutional interests of these unions would have been nothing less than a miracle. It was not surprising that the pacts that did result fell considerably short of this mark. In solving this problem a complex formula probably would have served the purpose no better than a simple one, for the prescription had to be accepted by two parties who agreed upon very little with regard to the matter in question. In fact, the principle underlying the pacts seemed to be rather simple. One might describe it as the principle of minimum surrender. Although the division was specified in terms of categories of work, an ancillary aim appeared to be the freezing of union membership rolls.

If one asked the question: Was this an ephemeral struggle born of changing employment conditions or a basic contest for control? the pacts reflected the fact that the answer clearly was the latter. Each major union group had a basic problem of loss of strength due to loss of members, and the very existence of the pacts indicated the intensity of this problem. Thus, a truly flexible arrangement or one that recognized the opening of new work opportunities for either group was not feasible. In a period of change, the agreements failed to take cogni-

[3] *Ibid.*

Black, white, and gray formula

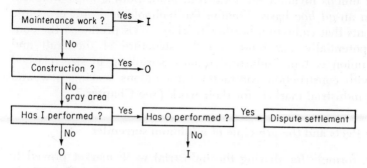

Established work relationship formula

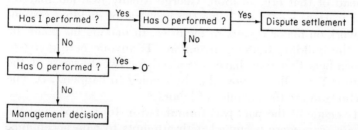

Fig. 11-1 *Division of work between the inside and outside forces: The interunion pacts.*

zance of the trends of the times. Rather, the pacts constituted benign affirmations of an idealized version of the historic *status quo.*

The following section from the basic agreement, the Miami Pact of February, 1958, illustrates this point:

> There are two areas in which the jurisdictional lines between the building trades craft unions and the industrial unions are clear. New building construction, on the one hand, should be the work of the workers represented by the building trades craft unions; production and running maintenance work, on the other hand, should be the work of the workers represented by industrial unions. Between the two clear areas set forth above there is a doubtful area. In this doubtful area, decisions should be made on the basis of established past practices on a plant, area or industry basis.[4]

The formulators of the Miami Pact anticipated disagreements in the "doubtful" area, with its ambiguous past-practice criteria. Peace machinery was established to cope with disputes. In the first step, two-man teams consisting of a craft and an industrial union representative would attempt on-the-spot settlements, if possible. If they did not

[4] The reader is also referred to the *New York Times*, Feb. 6, 1958, p. 1.

succeed, top representatives of both groups would meet with an officer designated by the president of the AFL-CIO. The last step involved intervention by a joint committee of federation vice-presidents from craft and industrial unions. There was no real terminal point to the procedure.

Later agreements that attempted to build upon the Miami Pact attacked the problem of spelling out the contents of the doubtful area. The Detroit Pact of January, 1959, tried to clarify the doubtful area by breaking it down into a confusing array of categories. These categories were: work on new buildings on new plant sites, work on new buildings on existing plant sites, complete remodeling of existing buildings on unrelated existing plant sites, complete remodeling of existing buildings on existing plant sites, complete remodeling of buildings under production, and plant rearrangement.[5] The general tenor of this agreement gave the outside unions priority in all categories except the last one, plant rearrangement. In order to justify a claim to this work, the inside forces would have had to establish a basis in past practice.

High hopes were held for the Miami Pact when it was approved by the AFL-CIO Executive Council in February, 1958. But the building trades unions continued to balk at signing the agreement, as did inside unions such as the Steelworkers. Some steel mills have construction divisions numbering well over one thousand men, and, for their employees, agreements that new construction belonged to the outside crafts were inconceivable. Initially described as an uneasy settlement among the top leaders, the pacts also proved to be largely unacceptable to the individual unions. Moreover, the anticipated signing of local agreements proceeded slowly.

The local pacts

Local pacts seemed to be confined primarily to areas that constituted special cases, for instance, situations in which the inside and outside forces were fairly evenly matched in strength and both had substantial claims to work in industrial plants. In general, the outside union's acceptance seemed to hinge on the inside union's affirmation of limited aims as far as its fair share of work was concerned. Thus, the first of these local agreements, the Detroit Pact, contained what the outside unions regarded as a key concession:

> Whenever past practices permit the owner of a plant to use his employees for the work indicated, it is not the intent of this agreement to permit the owner to hire new employees for the specific purpose of denying employment to members of the Detroit Building Trades.[6]

[5] *Mechanical Contractor*, 1959, 66(2):44–45.
[6] *Ibid.*

The wording of this clause clearly indicates that it was not designed as a public relations document aimed at industrial management.

However, this particular agreement on contracting-out clearly was designed to solve numerous problems internal to the labor movement. The document was signed early in 1959, just prior to the annual meeting of the AFL-CIO Building Trades Department. This action appeared to be timed to head off moves to secede from the federation —a step that was being discussed freely by leaders of the outside unions. Both the contracting-out issue and battles over organizing jurisdictions served as key stimuli in this movement. The Carpenters, Plumbers, and Hod Carriers–Common Laborers announced their intention of pulling out of the merged labor organization, and the reactions of the industrial unions were hardly conciliatory in nature. A top official of the Steelworkers was quoted as saying, "If they (the building trades unions) get the right to organize industrial plants, that gives us the green light to build buildings—and we can do it. We'll knock their ears down around their shoe tops." [7]

At the local level in Detroit, the inside unions were disturbed by another type of secessionist move. Inside craftsmen who were members of the United Auto Workers expressed discontent regarding their wage rates, and an organization called the Skilled Trades Society proposed to solve the craft workers' problems by taking them into their group. The failure of many Detroit building trades unions to join the state AFL-CIO further reflected the strain in the relationship between the inside and outside unions. Instead, the building trades group tended to be closely allied with the Teamsters. The prospect of a craft union–Teamsters alliance conducting organizing campaigns in industrial plants caused much uneasiness among the inside unions, both nationally and locally in cities such as Detroit. This challenge certainly served as a stimulus to the inside union's willingness to subscribe to the peace pacts.

For the inside forces, these agreements represented an official move away from a structure based on that of the integrated industrial firm— an official recognition of the equity of the outside unions in certain segments of the available work of the firm. In essence the outsiders were saying to the insiders, "If you don't agree to a formal sharing of your territory, we will organize parts of it and make it our territory." Moreover, to substantial segments of the outside group the pacts represented a sharing of something that was unsharable, namely, the sacred matter of jurisdiction, and "insiders" experienced similar reservations. The inside unions tended to feel somewhat like an industrial manager who has just agreed to a formal union "invasion" of one of his traditional functions. In fact, one inside union leader commented

[7] *Wall Street Journal*, Jan. 15, 1959, p. 1.

to us, "We're like the boss now. We're making concessions where I can't see that they [the outside unions] have any right to them at all."

Some top national union leaders viewed the Detroit Pact as the beginning of an overall craft–industrial union armistice. Hopes soared even higher when in September, 1959, the Steelworkers made a local agreement with the craft groups in Youngstown, Ohio. As noted above, the Steelworkers were considered to be arch-opponents of concessions to the building trades unions. Therefore, this conciliatory action, taken in the middle of the 116-day steel strike of that year, was hailed as a landmark in relations between craft and industrial unions.[8] Other pacts were signed, for instance, in Bridgeport and Indianapolis, but the hope that they might become part of a universal peace movement was not realized.

Renewed conflict

Even while the pacts were being negotiated, there was evidence of strong resistance that easily could have served to turn the tide of conciliatory action. The outside forces contained important elements that wanted to fight for full victory on the jurisdictional issue. Some contractors continued to feel that the industrial unions were their prime antagonists. One contractor's journal described the problem as "the erosion of our business in the industrial fields by antagonistic labor that has bluffed a docile management into surrendering important prerogatives."[9] These contractors rejected the notion that the peace pacts represented a feasible solution to their difficulties. Instead, they threatened to take legal action in the courts and to seek congressional legislation "to outlaw the restrictive provisions of certain labor agreements which prevent owners from doing their construction through the efficient and time-honored contract method."[10] In testimony before the Senate Labor Subcommittee in February, 1959, a representative of a leading contractors' association charged that inside union efforts to gain restrictive clauses constituted "a burden on commerce and a restraint of trade."[11]

Moreover, the post-Miami Pact period was marked by some notable physical struggles between the inside and outside forces—struggles in areas in which the pact averred that the "jurisdictional lines were clear." A few of these battles were recorded as news items of national interest. One involved a situation at a steel mill in which the inside union members ousted building trades craftsmen who were to have

[8] *New York Times*, Sept. 4, 1959, p. 22.
[9] *Mechanical Contractor*, 1959, 66(2):45.
[10] *Engineering News-Record*, 1959, 162(6):89.
[11] *Ibid.*

performed a 12-million-dollar construction job. After a one-day strike by the steel union, the company decided to keep the building tradesmen off the project. In retaliation, the contractors and the local (Birmingham, Ala.) building trades council filed a series of damage suits in the courts. They also asked the National Labor Relations Board to find the inside union guilty of an illegal secondary boycott.[12]

It is clear that, when the outside forces issued the famous brochure *Maintaining Production for America* at the end of 1959, this bid for industrial maintenance work did not serve to disrupt a new-found peace. (For a full discussion of this event, see Chapter 7.) Rather, the document seemed to provide a hook upon which potential dissidents could hang their hats. The Steelworkers, who had hailed the Youngstown Pact as a significant step in craft-industrial union relations, now accused the craft unions of scabbing on the industrial unions and of furthering the same ends that were sought by the employers in the steel strike of 1959.[13]

Top leaders of the AFL-CIO also expressed reservations about future prospects for peaceful settlement.[14] In some cases, relations between the inside and outside unions became strained to the point where members of the outside group felt that they no longer could function as representatives to inside organizations. Thus, in March, 1960, the Plumbers and Pipefitters pulled out of the Industrial Union Department (IUD) of the AFL-CIO.[15] Finally, in January, 1962, the International Brotherhood of Electrical Workers became the last IUD construction crafts affiliate to withdraw from the department.[16]

Black, white, and gray in review

According to the Miami Pact and its immediate offshoots, the jurisdictional distinction between construction and maintenance work was as clear as the difference between black and white. In-between jobs admittedly constituted a problematical gray area. The interesting point about the conception of these categories was their contradiction in the actual behavior of all the parties concerned. Moreover, the contradictions became increasingly marked during the years immediately following the original formulation.

Contractors and their craft workers actively sought and performed industrial maintenance work. Industrial union members worked on major and minor construction jobs and clearly were not willing to content themselves with maintenance work. For them, the relevant

[12] *New York Times,* Feb. 9, 1959, p. 18.
[13] *New York Times,* Feb. 12, 1960, p. 1.
[14] *Ibid.*
[15] *Business Week,* Mar. 26, 1960, p. 58.
[16] *IUD (Industrial Union Department) Bulletin,* 1962, 7(1):3.

universe was the available work of the firm and not just the tasks falling within one category. With regard to the gray area, the past-practice criterion would have been more successful if the original management decisions also had been governed by it. As a matter of fact our research did reveal a certain amount of consistency among management decisions within a given period, but delving further into the past yielded only one resource, a plenitude of inconsistent data (see Chapter 14).

If unions had held to the jurisdictions assumed by the pacts, then industrial unions should have consistently challenged management's right to contract-out maintenance work and should never have responded in this manner to the contracting-out of new construction. However, our data indicated that, while the proportion of challenges was somewhat higher in the gray area, the union had a notable degree of interest in work in all categories, as measured by the grievance rate for our series of management decisions on contracting-out (see Chapter 14). There certainly was no evidence of inside union consensus that maintenance work was the prime category of concern. In fact, the big jobs, which frequently involved construction activities, appealed to both internal maintenance and construction management and workers because of the large project's substantial contribution to the "health and welfare" of the entire group.

The history of interunion attempts to make an equitable division of the work of the industrial firm began with one problem, the gray area, but it quickly appeared that this designation fitted the black and white areas as well. The gray area receded in prominence as the main controversy began to center in whether the inside or outside forces should be awarded job rights in new maintenance fields. While the divisions of work in the Miami Pact were being specified, the outside forces were making new "inroads" into the industrial maintenance function via contract maintenance agreements. During the 1960–1961 recession, the controversy over this work intensified as job opportunities became increasingly scarce.

Moreover, by the end of 1961, the missile-site issue had become a prime center of dispute. While the inside unions decried losses of industrial maintenance work to the outside unions, the latter accused the inside unions of "taking away missile site jobs from building trades workers and giving them to industrial union members at lower wages which prevail in manufacturer's plants." [17] This controversy focused on the question of control over certain new construction and installation work at missile sites. With the great expansion anticipated in the missile program, the potential employment stakes were high. The outside forces estimated that 75,000 jobs were involved. In the light of

[17] *New York Times,* Nov. 30, 1961, p. 30.

these developments, it seemed that whatever appeal the Miami Pact possessed may have lain in its reaffirming for each side control over areas currently under invasion by the other.

Established work relationships

From jurisdiction to past practice

As problems mounted rather than receded, more than one leader of the inside unions noted that, if solutions were not found, the AFL-CIO might break asunder. The Miami Pact represented an interesting mixture of outside (jurisdictional) and inside (past-practice) criteria. While neither criterion provided a realistic basis for dispute settlement, the specification of an incontrovertible standard such as exclusive jurisdiction proved to be a major stumbling block. The question of equity or fair shares was converted, in effect, into a matter of principle or of rights.

Finally, a new agreement was formulated at the end of 1961. Abandoning the notion of jurisdiction, this plan spoke of "established work relationships," a concept more in line with the thinking of the inside unions. Building trades leaders quickly sensed this fact and charged that the terms were "rigged to favor the industrial unions over the craft unions." [18] According to the new principle, even the most sacred of jurisdictions could be invaded via past practice. Moreover, while the neat categories found in the Miami Pact gave the appearance of some order, allegations regarding established work relationships clearly were untidy matters whose settlement required the services of third parties.

The inside unions, who were concerned primarily about retaining rather than gaining work via these claims, favored binding arbitration, with recourse to the courts in case of failure to comply with the award. As one would have anticipated, the outside craft unions opposed these measures. Finally, a compromise provided for mediation and then arbitration, but arbitration was not to be the final step. The arbitrator's decision could be appealed to the AFL-CIO Executive Council. Sanctions were provided for failure to comply with the final decision, but, in essence, the individual unions remained free to comply or not, as they wished.

The new pact

The new pact assumed the stature of an amendment to the constitution of the AFL-CIO. This amendment provided a general plan for the settlement of internal disputes. Key concepts were established collective bargaining relationships and established work relationships (see

[18] *Ibid.*

Figure 11-1). The following clause specified the plan for resolving disputes over maintenance and construction work:

> Each affiliate shall respect the established work relationship of every other affiliate. For purposes of this article, an "established work relationship" shall be deemed to exist as to any work of the kind which the members of an organization have customarily performed at a particular plant or work site, whether their employer is the plant operator, a contractor, or other employer. No affiliate shall by agreement or collusion with any employer or by the exercise of economic pressure seek to obtain work for its members as to which an established work relationship exists with any other affiliate, except with the consent of such affiliate.[19]

The new agreement clearly eliminated all sacred territory. Claims to a given share of the work presumably hinged on a past record of consistent performance in that specific field. However, as in the case of the Miami Pact, the question of enforcement was left up in the air, not only because arbitration was not final, but also because some crucial parties, such as industrial management, were not included in the agreement. Thus, an outside union may have claimed an established work relationship regarding tasks that had been transferred to the inside forces. Or an inside union may have challenged contracting on the same basis. The aggrieved party finally may have obtained a favorable decision from, say, an arbitrator called in as the next to last step. In effect, the disputing craft and industrial unions would have obtained from an arbitrator an opinion prescribing a course of action for two other parties, industrial management and the contractor, neither of whom were included in the agreement. The two groups of unionized employees would have had to rely on standard pressure tactics to gain compliance with their "peace pact." For this system of equity to function properly, all four groups—unions and managements on both sides—would have had to agree to be bound by its operation. Needless to say, the possibility of such a development was nil.

The "no agreements or collusion" clause in the new pact obviously was a product of negative outside union reactions to "anti-contracting-out" provisions in "inside" collective bargaining contracts and negative inside union reactions to joint contractor-craft marketing campaigns. Apparently, agreements and collusion were permissible if the other party did not possess an "established work relationship" in an area. Ascertaining whether or not such a relationship existed would have required much checking back and forth between the two sets of union officials, who surely could have established some claims in the case of old work. In the case of new fields, which were the center of greatest competitive activity, neither party could have claimed an established

---

[19] *New York Times,* Dec. 14, 1961, p. 39.

work relationship, and presumably then, in the really crucial areas, "agreement and collusion" could have proceeded freely. As far as competition for work in the old, established areas was concerned, the two union groups appeared to be proposing to use as their yardstick the former decisions of industrial management.

Dispute settlement

The postamendment era did not mark a sharp break with the past. As cases arose, some refinements were introduced into measurements, and some situations were declared immeasurable. The past-practice criterion tended to place new situations in the immeasurable class. In one case a manufacturer, the Western Electric Company, was installing a telephone central office exchange in a new building. Members of an outside craft union, the International Brotherhood of Electrical Workers, challenged the right of the manufacturer's employees to perform this work. In protest, the electricians cut off the power to the building. The "inside" workers were serving as a contract force in this case so that actually this was a dispute between the employees of two contractors. Nevertheless, for new situations it illustrated the difficulties inherent in departure from the concept of jurisdiction. In returning the case to the parties, the arbitrator noted that neither set of claims to an established work relationship could be substantiated. As the work was new—a new building under construction—there was no basis for determining who customarily engaged in these tasks.[20] The effect of the decision was to leave the work with the Communications Workers, the manufacturer's employees, who were making the installation at the time of the dispute.[21] Thus, in a period of change when new rather than established situations become the rule, even the satisfaction of a nonenforceable decision may be denied to the contending unions.

Of course, not all disagreements concern work in a new or dynamic area. Geared to the application of certain criteria, disputes machinery inevitably "selects" its cases, for instance, in this situation, those stable enough to develop a history. The permanent arbitrator then inherits the unenviable task of applying the rather limited logic of the past-practice concept. The more consistent the practices, the simpler the process of dispute resolution. As will be indicated in Chapter 14, some degree of consistency was provided by the very nature of the organizational processes involved. That is, management decision patterns, rather than fluctuating back and forth between decisions to go outside or to do work with inside forces, tended to favor one or the other alternative for at least limited periods of time. However, as one pushed

[20] *New York Times*, Apr. 5, 1962, p. 21.
[21] The NLRB later confirmed this decision.

further into the past, the history of a challenged operation generally revealed some variability in this regard. In practice, time limits were implicitly attached to most job property claims.

In deciding in favor of the inside union at a chemical plant an arbitrator ruled in a manner that tacitly recognized the facts developed in our research. The inside union maintained that its established work relationship prevented the building trades unions from seeking major alteration work at the plant. Apparently, the inside union had handled this work during the preceding six to eight years, of necessity a much longer "run" than any included in our data. The arbitrator pointed out that, although building trades members normally might have performed the work in dispute, the established work relationship must be "viewed as of the time of the complaint, and the customary work assignment must be primarily that in force in the years immediately preceding." [22]

When one considered that dispute-causing changes in assignment of work often were preceded by a consistent block of decisions in the other direction, it was obvious that, in applying the above rule, the arbitrator's decision would tend to be biased in favor of the plaintiff. It was also obvious that, if the plaintiff won, he would attempt to elevate the case-by-case past-practice decision to a matter of principle, essentially an assertion of jurisdiction. In the above case, the victorious side asserted that "The Cole decision means that the Building and Construction Trades Department unions can no longer seek the type of alteration work involved in the Lederle dispute without violating Article XXI, Section 3, of the AFL-CIO constitution." [23] In this sense, one was witnessing not a "departure from jurisdiction" but rather the substitution of one basis for determining it for another.

On the whole, the notion of jurisdiction based on the past-practice criterion tended to militate against the outside forces, for it was difficult for them to establish ownership of inside work. Under these conditions, the situation was favorable to the outsiders largely when the inside forces also had no basis for a claim. In seeking legalistic affirmation of their position, the building trades unions were likely to run into the problems experienced by electricians who challenged the inside forces' "right" to lay conduit. The National Labor Relations Board heard the case and decided that the work in question was not new but rather belonged in the gray area within the terms of the Miami Pact. However, the gray area's past-practice criterion did not favor the outside craftsmen who had wanted to extend their assignment beyond the installation of central wiring, for "past local practice revealed no consistent pattern in awarding such work to outside electricians as

[22] *IUD Bulletin*, 1962, 7(11):16.
[23] *Ibid.*

opposed to the electricians employed in the company's maintenance department." [24]

As one might have anticipated, the interunion pacts did not lead to a cessation of former "solutions" to contracting-out problems. In collective bargaining with management, the inside unions persevered in their efforts to obtain clauses restricting contracting-out and sometimes were successful, as in the case of the 1963 contract between Lockheed Aircraft and the Machinists Union.[25] Moreover, the contracting-out issue continued to be the focus of long and bitter strikes. In one case the inside workers at an oil refinery struck over contracting-out and related issues almost nine months after the signing of the national "established work relationship" agreement. When the strike was eight months old, the inside workers noted with some bitterness that the refinery was being operated by supervisors and employees of outside contractors who were crossing the picket lines.[26] Despite the pacts, interunion competition continued to assume varied forms and to take place in a variety of arenas.

Interunion agreements at the local level

During the course of the research, we discovered a few interunion plant-level agreements that apparently had some effect on management decisions. As is often the case, the nature of the influence was not correctly anticipated by the formulators of these compacts. For instance, in one process plant, the inside forces agreed to normally refuse to perform work that belonged in the building trades jurisdiction, and in return the outside crafts in the community were to yield this work if inside men with the appropriate skills were on layoff. Management was to be informed that it could continue to enjoy the services of the outside forces only if the relevant inside workers were called back for the period of the contract. In practice, the inside men usually were given other work, or if no work was available, the employees on layoff were compensated for the equivalent of the time lost.

Management stated that initially this "featherbedding" arrangement caused it to do more work with inside forces, for contracting involved checking back and forth, with subsequent inconveniences and costs. As a result of the decrease in available work, the craft unions became disenchanted with the agreement and failed to comply with their end of the bargain. They declined to give information to the inside union or to support its efforts in a united front against management. The success of a "collusive" pact generally was contingent upon a fairly

[24] *Qualified Contractor,* 1963, 28(4):15.
[25] *The Machinist,* Feb. 7, 1963, 17(49):2.
[26] *IUD Bulletin,* 1963, 8(4):6.

equal sharing of the benefits to be derived. However, the agreement's impact on a vitally concerned party, such as industrial management, may have resulted in situations that favored one, rather than both, of the pact members. Thus, as in the above case, arrangements of this type have had within them the seeds of instability and eventual failure.

Static criteria and dynamic situations

From the language of the national interunion pacts, a student of management rights might well have assumed that as a result of these agreements the rights had become largely past history. Phrases from the Detroit Pact, such as "It is not the intent of this agreement to permit the owner," certainly pointed to this conclusion. One could readily envisage a "cartel-like" arrangement in which the two union groups divided up and mutually controlled all the maintenance and construction work of the industrial firm. In essence, work orders would be processed at union headquarters. At the time of the Miami Pact, one manager commented to us, "We are just waiting to see what the unions will tell us to do."

However, the pacts proved to be shotgun weddings rather than true romances, and in general they have had greater impact on relations between the two feuding union families than on management rights or management decision processes. Systems of equity were based on the historic past—traditional jurisdictions and established work relationships. Of these two categories, the former was favored by the outside unions and the latter by the inside. But when measured against a dynamic situation, both yielded poor results. The logic of the established work relationship provided no tools for coping with new matters of interest. Clinging to the past-practice criterion undoubtedly provided short-run benefits for those currently on the job, but in the long run this approach could involve costly sacrifices, to the extent that its use discouraged the channeling of energies into more realistic attempts to deal with change.

ARBITRATION

As we moved from interunion pacts to the arbitration of disputes under the labor-management contract, we also seemed to move one step closer to day-to-day operating problems regarding contracting-out. Jurisdictional claims to whole categories of work were abandoned in favor of consideration of the equities in the individual case. Moreover, the identity of the key figures changed. Industrial management, a shadowy figure in the interunion pacts, was directly involved. The inside union was a main actor in both proceedings, but while the outside union and the contractor may have been affected by the arbitration decisions, they were relegated to the sidelines.

As indicated in Chapter 5, the arbitration process regarding contracting-out inevitably was shaped by both the immediate organizational and the larger cultural matrix in which it was placed. Moreover, in the case of contracting-out, the existence of a complex multiple-interest group structure for the problem seemed to dictate flexibility as a prime requirement for the survival of arbitration as an effective contributing institution. Adherence to a legalistic model for behavior was found in Canada, and this course of action also represented a possibility for the United States arbitrator (see Chapter 5), but it would not have been in keeping with the character of institutions that lent only token support to legalism as a way of life in collective bargaining relations.

The identification of the role of arbitrator with that of a judge has tended to make flexibility and adaptability incongruous characteristics. Yet the environing parties at interest and the arbitrators themselves have supported changes in the nature of the arbitrator's role and in patterns of usage regarding key elements such as decision criteria. These changes in approach were in part reflected in a contrast between two separate sets of studies, the first two dealing with arbitration decisions on contracting-out from the middle of 1947 to the middle of 1959 and the third with decisions from the middle of 1959 to the middle of 1962 (Dash, 1960, Crawford, 1960, and Greenbaum, 1963).

The arbitrator has served as an auxiliary, rather than a primary, divider of the industrial work pie and definer of fair shares. However, from the late 1940s to the early 1960s his role in this area became increasingly important. His greater significance was reflected in Greenbaum's (1963) observation that in the twelve-year period 1947–1959, sixty-four contracting-out cases appeared in *Labor Arbitration Reports,* while in a relatively short time, namely, the subsequent three years, a total of fifty cases were reported.

In addition to the economic and technological factors that served to bring this issue increasingly to arbitration, the 1960 Warrior-Gulf decision of the United States Supreme Court [27] also underlined the role of the arbitrator as a crucial third party in contracting-out disputes. In the Warrior-Gulf decision, the high court declared contracting-out an arbitrable issue and thus in a sense designated these cases as the property of the arbitrator, who would then constitute the final "legal" authority for the two disputing parties. Some of our management

[27] *United Steelworkers of America v. Warrior and Gulf Navigation Co.,* 363 U.S. 574 (1960).

and union informants noted that, after Warrior-Gulf, arbitrators seemed to adopt a new outlook on their role in contracting-out cases. Whether or not this observation was generally true, this decision set the scene for downward displacement of the final determination of disputes and for increased prominence for the arbitrator's role.

Decision criteria: symbolism and utility

The arbitration system in the United States was not destined to produce definitive legal solutions or a body of firm rules regarding rights and equities as these relate to contracting-out. Some of the reasons for this situation are indicated above; others stem from the problems of measurement discussed in Chapter 10. Legalistic questions of rights have served as a symbolic mantle for contracting-out issues, and arbitrators dutifully have debated the conflict between the inherent rights of management and union rights implied by the very existence of a contract, sometimes styled the "benefits" or "fruits of the bargain."

If the arbitrator accepted only one set of rights as valid, then an automatic solution to the case was provided. (For an illustration of this position, see page 64.) However, the prevalent tendency to recognize a confrontation between two sets of rights blocked the attainment of a definitive answer, and the black-or-white scale of the rights issue offered no basis for resolving this dilemma. Indeed, the arbitrator was faced with the same measurement problem that plagued all the parties at interest in contracting-out. In brief, this was the problem of devising a scale of values along which one could move in order to achieve a reasonable decision or settlement. As no such scale existed, the task of devising one fell to the arbitrator.

Testimony of the authors of the three studies on arbitration decisions indicated that the inherent rights of the parties played a negligible role in the final pronouncement of the arbitrator. According to Dash (1963, p. 214), "The reserved rights theory is given lip service by a minority of arbitrators, but little, if any, real recognition." (In reserved rights theory, management retains all rights not expressly "given away" in the agreement.) Evidence of the changing position of the arbitrator was indicated in the Greenbaum (1963) and Dash (1960) findings regarding the implied limitations theory. (This theory maintains that management's recognition of the union reserves to the union's members the right to work of the bargaining unit.) Dash found that this theory was on the rise, but Greenbaum's later cases revealed that its use had declined and that arbitrators were substituting, for implied rights, applied standards of their own.

Crawford (1960, p. 72) presented an interesting list of nine rejected criteria that arbitrators typically discussed but generally did not use as determining criteria in their awards. Included among these items were all the standard legalistic arguments. This list provides a good picture of the kinds of measuring sticks that have been suggested in an effort to assess the extent of the employee's equity in the work of the firm. The following criteria were enumerated: management's reserved right, the union's right to the available work of the bargaining unit, the union's right to the benefits of the bargain, "authority to contract-out is authority to void the agreement," past practice in the company, past practice in the industry, the number of jobs involved, whether or not the work is integral to the regular business of the company, and whether or not an emergency exists.

In common with all questions of rights and precedents, the great majority of these criteria permit no more than "yes or no" judgments— the use of a simple dichotomous scale. If both sides in a dispute can establish rights and precedents in their favor—and inevitably they can —then the arbitrator can determine only that conflicting positions exist. He is faced with the problem of devising another scale for the purpose of resolving the conflict. Thus, he may introduce a time limit which will serve to diminish the claim of one of the groups, or he may devise a means for measuring which side has the more substantial claim.

On the other hand, the last three criteria, the number of jobs involved, the degree to which the work is integral to the regular business of the company, and the degree to which an emergency exists, conceivably could be measured along a continuous scale of values. But none of these criteria serves as an equally good measure of equities on both sides. The number of jobs involved is essentially a measure of the inside union's equity, and the degree to which work is regular business may have a similar function. The degree-of-emergency scale might act as a measure of management's equity. However, even in the case of measurable criteria there was a tendency to move, not in the direction of greater precision, but rather toward assessment in terms of general categories. Thus, number of jobs involved was summarized as either a "substantial" or a "not substantial" figure. The Greenbaum survey revealed that numbers of jobs ranging from one to thirteen were cited as not substantial and an overlapping range of from one to forty-three was considered substantial. From this observation, one could conclude that, in addition to having a simple structure, these measurements also were not referred to generalized scales but rather were specific to a given case.

In summary, the arbitrator's assessments of equities did not appear to be based on the traditional "rights" criteria or for that matter to hinge on any one key criterion. Instead, judgments apparently were based on a composite scale of values. Measurements were simple in structure, and the values assigned were meaningful largely in terms of the data for a given case. Crawford (1960) attempted to define what we have designated as the elements of a composite set of scales. Again, evidence of change in decision patterns was reflected in Greenbaum's (1963) modifications. The Crawford (1960, p. 72) scale included the following elements:

> To put it too boldly and too simply, the decisions measured against the underlying factual situations seem quite consistent and quite logical. Rightly or wrongly, up to now, the published awards convey that the issue of contracting-out is:
>
> First, is the contracting-out apparently based on economies available to the subcontractor of lower wage rates including fringe benefits rather than other economies of operation or special advantage? If so, the contracting-out will be found in violation of the implied limitation from the Recognition Clause.
>
> Second, if not, is permanent continuing work being contracted-out? If not, the work may be contracted-out. If so, is the contracting-out of the permanent work based on *compelling* logic or economies of operation that justify such action? The doctrine seems to be that the company cannot undermine the status of the collective bargaining agent by contracting-out work primarily to beat the union prices, nor can the company contract-out permanent work without compelling reasons other than a seeming desire to reduce the status of the exclusive agent.
>
> Otherwise and generally, therefore, contracting-out is a management decision since the status of the bargaining agent is not involved.

Crawford felt that a pattern of consistent decision-making emerged from the awards, however inconsistently they may have been articulated. Unfortunately, our satisfaction at discovering an agreed-upon formula for dividing the work of the industrial firm between the inside and outside forces was destined to be diminished by subsequent research findings.

Greenbaum found somewhat different patterns emerging from her data. She concluded that tests for savings in labor costs were no longer useful in determining a pattern. Use of this criterion appeared in only a minority of four cases, and in two of these the contracting-out was upheld. One decision even praised management for cutting labor costs by subcontracting! All three studies agreed that arbitrators were more likely to be critical of contracting-out when the work involved was permanent rather than temporary. However, there was no consensus that "permanent work was the property of the inside forces and temporary work of the outside forces," to paraphrase the jurisdictional allocations of the interunion pacts. In fact, arbitrators upheld contracting of permanent work in seventeen of twenty-six Greenbaum cases and in twenty out of thirty-five for Crawford. The later Greenbaum

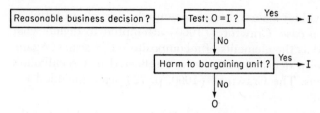

Fig. 11-2 *Division of work between the inside and outside forces: Arbitration.*

study also seemed to place more emphasis on layoffs as a factor influencing the arbitrator's decision.

In conclusion, the study of the 1959–1962 cases produced a more general statement of the arbitration decision process rather than a more detailed refinement of the earlier Crawford formula. In our terminology, two scales were delineated, one judging the positive and the other the negative aspects of the management action—the degree to which contracting-out was a reasonable business decision and the degree to which contracting-out was designed to undermine the inside union (see Figure 11-2). Thus, specific data, such as the existence of savings on labor costs and temporary versus permanent work, were assessed, not independently, but rather on the basis of their contribution to position on the above scales. In an even more general statement, both these scales could be combined into one measure of management's "good faith," with the reasonable business decision at one end of the scale and actions undermining the union at the other.

Our own study of arbitration cases focused primarily on their effect at the plant level (see Chapter 5), but an independent reading of the decisions used as the basis for the above studies led to some further general conclusions about the contribution of the arbitration process to the contracting-out problem. We have been critical of the wins-losses, scorekeeping approach to management decision-making, and yet, by the very nature of his task, the arbitrator was forced into the role of an ex post facto scorekeeper. His task was very different from that of the initial management decision-maker. In fact, we perceived a close similarity to some aspects of the role of the judge settling a personal injury suit. However, in this case there were two sets of damages to be considered—damages the union suffered due to work losses incurred by members of the bargaining unit and damages management potentially would suffer in losses of efficiency in the business.

The hard core of the arbitration decision seemed to involve a process of balancing off these two sets of losses. Clearly, this was no simple task, but from a study of the cases certain patterns emerged. If the work losses seemed to be extreme, the arbitrators generally decided for the union. If the work losses were not extreme and management losses could be established, the decision favored the company. But if management losses were not clear, the decision might sustain the union's position even though the bargaining-unit losses were not substantial. In other words, the burden fell on management to show some gain in business efficiency.

The limits of the arbitration process

Upon measuring the arbitrator's treatment of contracting-out against the total framework for the problem, it seemed apparent that the "consistency and logic" of his analysis were not of a generally applicable type but rather constituted primarily a system for reaching solutions via arbitration. Settlement clearly involved moving beyond the black-and-white aspects of rights formulations, but the arbitrator could not encompass the entire contracting-out problem. He had to be selective, and his selection of elements quite logically flowed from the need to solve the problems of two parties in dispute. Therefore, he tended to limit his considerations to their immediate complaints. The further selection of a framework wherein relative damages were measured served as a device that was acceptable to both parties. While other criteria could have been chosen, these served to limit the proceedings to the dispute at hand and to the kind of data that the parties seemed to be willing to furnish to the arbitrator. Each one essentially was trying to prove that he would be grievously hurt if the will of the other prevailed.

The arbitrator's ability to be original was curtailed by the felt need to work with the concepts of both parties within a limited framework. Thus, the *status quo* was pictured largely in terms of the inside union's construction of the problem. Integrity of the bargaining unit was viewed in terms of its historic constitution, and the concept of permanent work was based on the "hard core" category of the historical past. Outside interests and possible alternative restructuring to accommodate these matters went beyond the limits of this conceptualization. Judgment of the union's claims seemed to reflect largely concern about the possibility that the extent of the damages was overstated.

On the other hand, there was some question about the moral rightness of management's position. Management may have been attempting to undermine the integrity of the bargaining unit, and to exonerate management it was necessary to establish that it was not intent upon inflicting damages upon the union but rather was pursuing another course of action. If management was clearly on the side of economic and technological progress, this alliance served to obliterate the past and the basis for the damage claims of the inside union. Actions involving the replacement of (inside) labor with (outside) labor, two seemingly identical entities, raised more questions of a moral nature than actions involving the replacement of labor with capital or with capital plus labor. Practically speaking, the test of management's good faith could be summarized briefly in the following question: Is the contracted work (A) like an existing inside operation (B)? If $A = B$, the decision tended to favor the plaintiff (the inside union). On the other hand, if $A \neq B$, the defendant's (management's) case was strengthened. In general, the greater the similarity between the two operations, the greater the probability of "poor faith" on the part of management. Essentially, then, the handicap of the likeness had to be overcome. Questions of change and dynamism entered the arbitration model at this point and seemed to lend to it a measure of reality that was largely absent from the interunion pacts.

The parties and the arbitrator

The cases that found their way to arbitration unquestionably represented a selected group, but the basis for their selection was far from being either uniform or clear. Both management and labor liked to think that they permitted only the "good" cases to go to arbitration, but the astuteness of their judgments was impaired by the fact that each one focused on his own damages and did not study his position in the light of the full model employed by the arbitrators. Both parties were well acquainted with the fact that neither the presence nor the absence of a contract clause limiting contracting-out was a clue to eventual victory. But despite the thoroughness with which some managers and union officials studied arbitration decisions on contracting-out, most of them felt that, in the final analysis, the outcome of an individual case was unpredictable. (In part, of course, this feeling was a product of the failure to recognize the "dynamism" in the arbitration process.)

Some prediction of the risk involved in arbitration could be made on the basis of the results for the Dash (1960) and Greenbaum (1963) samples. In both studies, management had roughly a 3:1 edge over the union. Management won forty-four and lost eighteen cases in the Dash sample and was the victor in thirty-nine and loser in eleven in the later group. If these cases were representative of the entire population, it certainly seemed safe to conclude that management had at least a better than even chance of receiving a favorable decision.

Predicting a management loss on the basis of advance examination of the union case was at best an uncertain matter. Management losses generally were associated with the presence of several "adverse" factors such as the contracting-out of permanent work either when men were on layoff or to achieve a savings in labor costs, but these were more in the nature of necessary rather than sufficient conditions for sustaining a union grievance. Thus, they did not serve as reliable predictors of the arbitrator's decision. Another reason for inability to predict outcome stemmed from the nature of the arbitrator's criteria. These criteria were tooled to catch the obvious case of managerial "bad faith," but their meaning in intermediate situations was much less certain.

Those who anticipated that every arbitration case would have a clear implication for the rights of the parties involved were doomed to disappointment. In fact, even the arbitrators did not always agree about the implications of a given decision. Crawford (1960) found that, in classifying nineteen identical cases, two arbitrators disagreed in four instances—a 21 per cent difference—on whether or not the full right to contract-out had been retained. As for the immediate management and union parties, a given decision's significance for the rights question generally was left open to a variety of interpretations.

In Chapter 5, we described the effect of the ten arbitration cases found in our sample. For the six management "winners" and the four "losers," the results generally proved to be inconclusive. The parties adjusted to the decision and proceeded much as before. When the arbitrator's decision rejoined the reality from which the case was abstracted, the decision lost its character of finality and was shaped and molded in the course of everyday organizational life.

There was some evidence of changeover time in the criteria that the arbitrator employed, as well as in the manner in which he employed them. Some may condemn this behavior as an indication of lack of principle: actually it represented an adjustment to a dynamic situation in which the context and meaning of contracting-out were changing. For instance, in the late 1940s, contracting-out as an adaptation to technological change may have been the exception, but as this step became the rule in the early 1960s, the significance of the exceptional case criterion vanished and, along with it, established conceptions of the inside union's fair share of the work. Thus, a new assessment of standards for judgment was made in order to compensate for the change in conditions. Other types of adjustment took place as the parties adapted to the message contained in past arbitration cases. Thus, management may have learned to avoid those which tended to project an unfavorable image, e.g., contracting-out for the sole purpose of saving on labor costs.

As the parties accommodated to the specifics of the arbitration process and, conversely, as the arbitrator adjusted to the behavior of the parties in a changing industrial situation, special criteria might become obsolete, as, for instance, when behavior generally began to conform to the definition of a former exceptional case. An unintended bias crept in, and change was required in order to achieve a new and equitable definition of fair shares, which in a sense was measured in reverse in the assessment of damages suffered by each party.

Arbitration and contracting-out: an assessment

On the positive side, arbitration has not led to the development of a formidable legal structure for contracting-out. Nor has it fostered a situation in which every instance of contracting-out became a Supreme Court case. Wisely, the rights issue has been played down, and, by and large, arbitrators have acted in a manner that should have served to encourage the development of responsible relationships among the parties themselves. On the other hand, arbitration has not succeeded in developing much in the way of creative guidelines for future action. However, this contribution simply may have been outside the scope of its function. Those who hoped for more probably did not possess a realistic view of the uses of the arbitration process.

The same can be said of those who, in line with the scorekeeping, wins-losses approach, declared that a single decision deprived them eternally of their fair share of the work or of the ability to manage the business efficiently.

Moreover, arbitrators have shared a limitation commonly faced by many other decision-makers who deal with a select group or groups rather than with the total number of parties involved in a given problem area. They could only surmise many of the data that related to the absent groups. In this case, the very significant role of the inside forces in management and of the outside management and union could not be considered officially. Essentially, the arbitrator was in the position of dealing with a two-dimensional figure from a multidimensional universe.

As for the two "client" parties, industrial management and the inside union, arbitration has left the fair shares of both in a state of flux. The arbitrator has assigned no territory and has honored no jurisdictional claims, beyond a nodding recognition of the distinction between permanent and temporary work and some concern for the man on layoff. A general inside workers' claim to all the available work of a given type has not been recognized. In fact, no firm property claim of any kind has been established for the inside workers. It might be added that the same generalization applies to management.

COLLECTIVE BARGAINING

The bargaining structure

Through collective bargaining, the inside workers and their unions attempted to ensure a fair share of the maintenance and construction work of the industrial firm. This was an enterprise not easily accomplished. Not all inside workers felt equally committed to this problem, and "fair share" did not have the same meaning for all members of the work force or for all levels of the union hierarchy. Restrictions on contracting-out served as a solution to a variety of inside union problems, such as questions of workers' job rights, declining membership rolls, and competition from outside unions. Moreover, inside union enthusiasts for restrictions on contracting-out were counterbalanced by outside union opponents of these measures. Seniority clauses redistribute benefits within the work force by favoring older workers in preference to younger ones, just as anti-contracting-out agreements favor inside workers in preference to those employed by outside contractors.

In the case of the interunion pacts, inside management was the major unrepresented party at interest. Similarly, the outside forces—the contractors and craft unions—played this role in the case of collective bargaining over contracting-out, and the inside forces were an unrepresented party at interest in management agreements with contractors and in agreements between contractors and craft unions. The parties to the collective bargaining relationship were well aware of the fact that they were participating in a multigroup bargaining structure. When an unrepresented "other" party became an active participant in a relationship, he sometimes attempted to recoup the losses suffered in the role of the "other." Thus, some managements stated that the interunion pacts had caused them to make "adjustments" in their bargaining approach to the inside union. With some uneasiness, the participants in a given bargain recognized that they also were silent parties in other battles that might produce a different and conflicting solution to the issue in question.

The need to defend a given group's position in relationships in which it was not an immediate party undoubtedly caused collective bargaining activities regarding contracting-out to "spill over" readily into other theaters. Both the directly and secondarily involved parties sought support from sources such as Federal regulatory bodies and legislation, the courts, and a variety of private "third parties." For example, in the late 1950s while the industrial unions were attempting to negotiate stronger clauses on contracting-out, both union and management members of the outside forces were urging that these agreements be outlawed.

In its efforts to divide the industrial work pie, collective bargaining did not prove to be a source of innovation. In essence, negotiations formalized previously existing principles developed by industrial management. Many persons, especially members of the outside forces, felt that collective bargaining had a critical effect on contracting-out, in part, because the initial divider of the pie, industrial management, was directly involved. However, the solutions that collective bargaining did not achieve proved to be more significant than those which it did.

The failure of collective bargaining to realize definitive solutions could be attributed to a variety of factors. Thus emphasis on contracting-out as a rights issue dictated a "no yield" strategy. In addition, the measurement problems discussed in Chapter 10 led to ambiguous descriptions of equities—to solutions notable for vagueness rather than clarity. Even more significant may have been the fact that collective bargaining was environed by other, competing agreements which served to lessen the impetus to achieve a solution in this particular arena. The existence of diverse and conflicting views within both inside management and inside union groups similarly discouraged effective problem-solving approaches. The resulting postponement of solution invited the efforts of others and probably increased the notoriety achieved by those who finally produced definitive answers, both good and bad.

Divisions in the inside union: craft splinter movements

Members of industrial management held conflicting interest positions with regard to contracting-out (see Chapter 8). One might have assumed that the inside union would hold a more solidary position, and, to some extent, this was true. Within industrial management, there was both opposition to and support for management's right to contract-out. On the other hand, the inside union members generally were united in opposition to this right, but there was variation in the conviction behind the opposition. Most inside unionists shared a general symbolic hostility toward the outside craft unions, especially when the latter proposed to "invade" the industrial plant, but some inside workers threatened to bolt the plant union in favor of a craft affiliation. In addition, the various levels of the union hierarchy had differing preferences regarding solutions to the contracting-out problem.

Contrasting the early 1950s with the early 1960s, one could note a solidification of the inside union's position on contracting-out. In the early 1960s increasing production work job losses raised the removal of work from the bargaining unit from the level of a special interest demand to a general issue. Prior to this time, contracting-out tended to be a question of limited interest that frequently "washed out" in the last rounds of negotiations. This item often was traded off for other gains that would benefit a larger number of workers. Thus, within the plant, one sometimes found a small replica of the larger craft and industrial union schism. As indicated in Chapter 6, inside craft groups were able to push for agreements on contracting-out when these men constituted a substantial proportion of the total force, but when this situation did not prevail, a minority group of craft workers faced real limitations in their ability to gain support for their programs from the majority group, the production forces.

The contracting-out issue might have had a different fate if the craft splinter movements of the late 1950s had developed into real and widespread secession from the industrial unions. Much of this discontent sprang from what the craft groups regarded as inadequate wage differentials between skilled and semiskilled work. Craftsmen felt that some unions representing the mass of semiskilled production workers were not sufficiently interested in obtaining appropriate rewards for their more highly skilled members.

Threats of craft splintering were displeasing to both inside unions and management. Contracting-out was an auxiliary issue in this move, and some managements considered concessions on contracting-out as a possible means of stemming the tide of revolt. In fact, some managers in our fabrication industry cases expressed the hope that this gesture would enable the inside union to hold its members. Valuable though it was, management's right to contract-out also had its price. In this case, the price of protecting this right—dealing with a separate craft group—apparently was too high. Of course, the threat of potential revolt was not universal. Rather, it was concentrated in those industries, such as transportation equipment and rubber, where the skilled groups were fairly strong in numbers although not a dominant force (Weber, 1963).

Among industrial managements, there was a strong sentiment in favor of a unified structure for the inside union group. Managers were not enthusiastic about the prospect of dealing with additional unions, especially craft groups from whom they anticipated sizable wage demands. Fifty-one companies in our seventy-four plant sample had maintenance and construction forces organized in industrial unions. In this group, forty-eight managements were opposed to splintering, and only three said that they were indifferent about the matter. None of them favored the move. One-half the "opposed" managements said that the splintering of their maintenance and construction forces would encourage more contracting-out.

In general, inside craft groups probably were searching in the right market in considering a shift to outside craft representation to achieve increases in wages. But drawbacks were involved in turning to craft unionism, for the findings of our research indicated that this was the wrong market for those shopping for assistance with a contracting-out problem. Thirty per cent of the firms in our sample had separately organized craft groups, and the great majority of these had very weak representation on the contracting-out question (see Chapter 6).

Threats to "splinter off" generally were not carried out. Instead, the matter tended to be settled by arrangements that gave the craft groups at least nominally greater representation in the inside union. On the whole, our research did not produce much evidence that indicated that the contracting-out issue served to induce serious schisms in the industrial unionized work forces.

Diversity in union goals and concepts of equity

From the top leadership to the lowest rank and file levels of the industrial union, there was general agreement on the principle of "keeping the work inside." But this consensus on goals, if strictly followed, involved a sacrifice at the top levels of the organization, where a healthy interest in gaining more members prevailed. Insistence on "keeping the work inside" could hamper the development of new fields for organizing, for instance, the potential enrollment of the increasing numbers of workers employed in contract maintenance operations. Top union officials had to weigh the potential strength to be gained in growing areas against a strategy of expending energy in order to retain current possessions, the inside jobs in plants presently organized. Decisions did not always favor exclusive focus on the latter course of action. As indicated in Chapter 9, some inside unions were organizing outside contract forces that performed maintenance work in industrial plants. Future growth of the union may have been contingent upon organizing, not just inside workers, but rather all those associated with a given process. But to the men "boxed into" a relationship with an "old-style" inside establishment, these activities seemed to indicate that ultimately their fair share of the work was an expendable item.

However, top union officials also were concerned about the "erosion of the bargaining unit" and about the necessity of returning lost jobs to it. According to their standards, a successful operation involved the retention of a full complement of positions in a given plant. In the course of the research, we found cases in which there was an inconsistency between this goal and the individual worker's interest in higher earnings and other gains of that general nature. The men in the plant tended to take a dim view of contract clauses that defined fair shares only in terms of protecting jobs. They also were interested in expanding available overtime work and in attaching to contracting-out penalty provisions that would add to the total earnings of the existing inside work force.

This difference in the approach of the leadership and the rank and file was clearly illustrated in a case at a food-processing plant. By exerting considerable time and energy, the regional union officers had succeeded in convincing management that a proposed modernization project should not be contracted-out. When the head of the maintenance and construction department objected to the proposal on the grounds that his men could not complete the project within the required time limits, the union officers suggested that additional workers could be employed. However, when the new recruits appeared on the site, the inside craftsmen walked out. The men argued that the newly inducted workers lacked the necessary skills, but the real issue was the overtime they would be losing by dividing the work with the newcomers. Needless to say, the union officials were irked at the actions of the established workers, who wanted the modernization project to serve as an avenue toward higher rates of pay and increased income. The organizational roles of the union officers and members resulted in differing conceptions of an equitable answer to a contracting-out problem. Again, the differences in solutions were due to differences in the problems that each group was attempting to solve.

These discrepancies between rank and file and union officer views were not resolved by compromise. Rather, both themes appeared in collective bargaining agreements, although at a formal level the union officials' philosophy predominated over that of the inside workers.

Collective bargaining and the inside workers' fair share

The presence of a contract clause was not necessarily a good measure of the inside union's strength regarding contracting-out. Of the fourteen firms having the highest union influence ratings, one-half had no formal agreement on contracting-out. Moreover, three-fifths of those managements with clauses reported no real sense of restriction in their operations (see Chapter 6). At present we are interested, not in the degree of effectiveness of the clauses, but rather in their contribution to the concept of the inside worker's fair share of the maintenance and construction work of the industrial firm. It has already been indicated in Chapter 10 that the problems the unions faced in the development of this concept were fairly severe, but nevertheless a substantial proportion felt that the undertaking was worthwhile.

In our seventy-four plant sample, unions had successfully negotiated clauses governing contracting-out in twenty-four companies (32 per cent of the total) and sixteen unions (16 per cent) had failed in the attempt. In a Bureau of Labor Statistics study of contracts in manufacturing and nonmanufacturing plants employing over 1,000, the proportion with agreements was smaller but still substantial. This BLS review of 1,687 agreements, excluding only those in the airline and railroad industries, revealed that 378 (22 per cent) had limitations on subcontracting or contracting-out (Lunden, June, 1961).

Only four agreements in the comprehensive BLS survey expressly prohibited contracting-out. These included a single instance in the food, lumber, "miscellaneous," and service industries, respectively. Thus, formal definitions of the inside workers' share as all the work of the firm were exceedingly rare. As noted in Chapter 6, our study encountered one craft-organized case that reversed the above situation and required that all work be contracted. Equally rare were agreements affirming management's right to contract-out, thus implicitly denying that the inside employees had an equity in their work. Lunden (June, 1961, p. 3) found the following agreements in textile and paper mills: "Among the rights and responsibilities which shall continue to be vested in the company shall be: The right . . . to contract work in its discretion." "It is understood that the company may employ outside contractors to perform work in the mill."

Firm, unyielding agreements of this type clearly were the exception and not the rule. The BLS study uncovered some clauses that mimicked the formulas of the initial interunion pacts, designating the fair share of the inside employees in terms of certain categories of work. Thus in one case the agreement noted, "No job shall be let to outside contractors, other than major construction and major repair, and fabrication, and installation, and use of patented or highly specialized equipment . . ." (Lunden, June, 1961, p. 8). However, the usual agreement did not focus on rigid definitions of jurisdiction. Such prescriptions generally were no more acceptable to inside management than they were to the inside unions in peace-pact negotiations with their outside counterparts. Clauses of this type appeared largely when a definition of territory was mutually agreeable to at least some elements in both inside union and management groups.

The typical agreement set no firm boundaries delineating the inside employees' share of the work. In fact, there seemed to be an implicit recognition that almost any kind of maintenance and construction work could be contracted or, conversely, could be performed by the inside forces. Thus, questions of past practice and established work relationships appeared in agreements between inside and outside unions and were injected into arbitration hearings on contract disputes, but the contracts between management and union did not cite this criterion. We found no clauses stating that the inside workers were entitled to all the maintenance and construction work that they customarily performed. Instead, agreements tended to operate within the framework of the management decision process, specifying conditions under which contracting was either fair or unfair (see Figure 11-3).

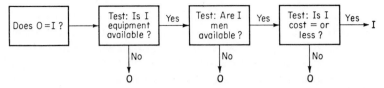

Fig. 11-3 *Division of work between the inside and outside forces: Collective bargaining.*

Collective bargaining assigned to the inside employee a conditional equity in his work. Depending on the circumstances of a particular case, the strength of his claim was either increased or decreased. And in recognition of the fact that "conditions" might reveal a strong claim on the part of the inside worker, his position sometimes was buttressed with an assurance that he would be informed of a pending or actual contract. The above description covered almost all the agreements in our sample. The greatest proportion, three-eighths, stressed layoffs as a significant conditional criterion, and one-fourth specified other criteria of this nature. One-third of the clauses provided for notification of the inside union. The contracts fell far short of establishing a firm equity in the work in question. For the inside workers, they were more in the nature of a foot in the door—a recognition of interest.

Men on layoff

The occurrence of layoffs constituted a measure of the inside workers' need for the available work of the firm—and of the potential or actual harm that an individual might suffer as a result of contracting. A man who was working full time at another task may have suffered some loss, for instance, in the inability to take advantage of an opportunity to gain new experience. But the case against contracting-out was much clearer when the individual either was out of work and not called back or was laid off as a consequence of the practice.

One of the stronger clauses in our sample held that "The Company agrees that it will not contract any work which is ordinarily and customarily done by its regular employees if, as a result thereof, it would become necessary to lay off any such employees." Some provisions simply stated that, when contracts were let, idle employees would be provided with work whenever possible. Other contracts limited grievances to cases in which the union could prove that the layoffs in question directly resulted from a given contract. While these agreements established a claim to not being rendered idle by contracting—or to not remaining idle during contracting—they often were hedged with qualifications and enforcement required proof of managerial "guilt" that was difficult to obtain.

Establishing a cause-and-effect relationship between layoffs and contracting-out was far from simple. Contracting that directly preceded or followed layoffs of men performing the same class of work provided the union with a strong case. But the timing of both these actions was a manipulable entity from the standpoint of management. When the two events were separated by a substantial stretch of time, layoffs could be attributed to other causes. Moreover, restrictions concerning men on layoff could encourage more drastic measures such as progressive cutting back of the size of the work force through attrition and failure to make replacements.

Other conditional criteria

In addition, there was a general question that related to the equity of both laid-off and working employees. Would members of these groups have been able to perform the contracted jobs? To determine this point, there were a variety of tests for likeness or identity between the relevant inside operation and its outside counterparts. The greater the similarity, the stronger the inside workers' claim. If the inside men were available for work and the company possessed the means to perform the task in question, with supervisors and equipment ready to go at no added cost, the inside workers would have appeared to have a cogent case. Conversely, as inside conditions began to deviate from this standard, the strength of the workers' claim diminished.

As noted above, one-fourth of the agreements in our sample specified various conditional criteria relevant to contracting-out. A typical example was a clause in a fabrication (electrical machinery) firm's collective bargaining contract that stated:

> It is the intention of the Company to provide full and regular employment for its employees at all times. In accordance with that intention, the Company shall make every effort to use its available working force and equipment in order to avoid having its work performed outside.

This company had a policy of contracting-out as much as possible; as a matter of fact, outsiders performed two-thirds of its maintenance and construction work. Insiders engaged in this field constituted a small proportion, 2 per cent, of the total work force of 1,200. Actual union voice in the management decision was rated as very weak, with a score of 5 (see Chapter 6). As a rule, the inside craft workers were employed six days a week, and thus they lacked some of the usual stimuli for complaints regarding contracting-out. Only two formal grievances had been filed under the agreement. In one case, the men wanted to tar a roof, but management felt that they were interested only in the overtime pay that the work would involve. A contractor was hired for the job. In the other case, the union successfully convinced management that two laid-off workers should be called back to paint an office because they could do it "just as cheaply" as an outsider. Apparently, the agreement had little effect on management "rights." A company official noted that the document merely expressed the company's intent, in any case, and therefore was not restrictive. He remarked, "We anticipate no problems. We already contract-out practically everything."

In light of the general or specific conditional phrases attached to some agreements governing contracting-out, these became little more than statements of everyday management policy and practice. Compliance often meant not contracting when it would have been unwise in any case. For instance, a company may have had its own resources in supervision, men, and equipment readily available. To contract work under these circumstances would be largely a matter of perversity. Moreover, at times management found to its delight and unions to their sorrow that the clauses served to clear the way for contracting-out. The contract legitimated the exceptions that were, in fact, the grounds for contracting-out which management ordinarily would use. Specific criteria, such as provisions in some of our cases that work might be contracted-out only if completion time was a factor, if peculiar skills were involved, if specialized equipment was not available, or if cost was less, belonged in this category, and in addition these proved to be operationally ambiguous and manipulable limits at best. A machinery plant manager with a clause of this type pointed to the four conditional criteria that were mentioned and noted, "You see that these are not really restrictions on management. The clause favors us much more than it does the union. In fact, these are all things we should consider in making this decision. In a sense, it helps us by making them explicit."

Notification

Notification clauses seemed to provide the inside forces with about the same level of benefit as those specifying conditional decision criteria. Some union leaders expressed doubt that these provisions had any value. In one of our cases, officials from union headquarters removed "notification in advance" from a local fabricated-metals plant agreement because they felt that this clause was "worse than nothing"—that it provided no means for effective control. However, if union officers were so inclined, they would gain satisfaction from their symbolic inclusion in the management decision process via the notification clauses. Notification also provided a formal recognition of union interest and an opportunity for efforts at bargaining, but, in general, management was not obliged to deviate from its original position.

Some arbitrators tended to rate notification as a fairly weak provision, presumably because there was little in the way of a concrete and enforceable end product. Notification was a "right" to be about something, rather than a right to "something" per se—to some clearly specified consideration. However, as later discussion in this chapter will reveal, in 1962 the National Labor Relations Board made some rulings that may have served to elevate the significance of notification in the eyes of the arbitrator.

Management's view of notification revealed a great deal of ambivalence. Inclusion of the union in face-to-face discussion about contracting-out symbolized a greater concession than the conditional decision criteria, for, in the case of the latter, management still appeared to be acting unilaterally, with the union consigned to its customary role of griever. Yet notification was a common practice. As indicated in Chapter 6, forty-seven per cent of the companies employed it, casually more often than consistently, as a management defense. A much smaller proportion, 11 per cent, had contractual provisions specifying notification. In our sample the majority of these agreements, six out of the eight, stated that notification should be made before the contracts were let. One agreement mentioned notification at the time when contracts were let, and another noted that "The company will advise the union when construction work contracts have been made."

It is significant that seven of the eight companies had policies of contracting-out as little work as possible. A manager in an industrial fabrics firm noted, "This is our policy anyhow. We try to use our own men whenever possible, even by giving them a certain phase of a contracted job they can handle." Most of these managements felt that their employees received a fair share of the work of the firm. All except one expressed some chagrin that the workers had chosen to reduce the matter of notification to contractual form. The transportation-equipment management in the exceptional case regarded a contract clause that provided for discussion with the union in the case of major jobs as "most favorable to us" because it concluded with the statement that "The final decision, however, shall rest exclusively with the Management." In practice, however, this union was the strongest in the group in exercising control over contracting-out.

The above also was the only case in our sample in which notification was limited to a special class of work, such as major jobs. A refinery manager reported that another plant in his firm had an agreement that the union would be notified before the contracting of any job in excess of $10,000. Of course, in the administration of notification clauses, cases were informally screened to cut down the work load and at the same time to include instances of contracting-out that were likely to become controversial. However, specification of a screening criterion in the contract was fairly rare.

In one sense, notification agreements represented an implicit recognition of the inside workers' "interest" in jobs that were slated for contracting. But the problem of converting this interest in a share of the work into a tangible good was left "up in the air." A union leader described the notification procedure of a heavy-equipment manufacturer as "complying with the letter of the contract but violating its spirit." Being given the "facts" fulfilled the requirement, and management held the line at this point. However, union leaders and members generally wanted an opportunity to react freely and fully and to urge certain changes.

The agreements described thus far specified conditions under which an inside worker's claim to a share of the work presumably either was strengthened or was provided with a foot-in-the-door mechanism for discussing the matter. These essentially were tests of management's good faith and good intentions. The more closely inside conditions approximated those obtainable outside, the stronger the evidence of poor faith. The more covert the action, the greater the suspicion of "dishonorable" intentions. A verdict of "guilty" or "not guilty" could be obtained, but none of these agreements specified a means for sharing or dividing work between the inside and outside forces. To find agreements of this type, one had to turn to contracts governing the contracting of production work in the garment industry.

Work-sharing and featherbedding

Work-sharing agreements found in union-management contracts in the garment industry accomplished what those governing industrial maintenance and construction had failed to achieve. These provisions simultaneously coped with the relationship of management to both the inside and the outside work forces. The arrangements cited above dealt with only one relationship—that between management and the inside workers—and left the other suspended on a thread of conditional avenues of escape.

In the garment industry agreements, there were two commonly used bases for sharing the production work. The one more frequently employed divided work during slack periods on the basis of the number of machine operators employed in the inside and outside shops. Less popular was a percentage plan wherein the inside and outside employees received their respective proportions of the total work performed during the busy season (Lunden, July, 1961). While obviously still subject to manipulation, these agreements provided a clear statement for determining the fair shares of the inside and outside forces.

The absence of these provisions in the industrial maintenance and construction field could be explained by several factors. In the first place, while production work easily could be divided into independent units, construction and maintenance lent itself to this treatment only in specific cases. In the second place, rival unionism of the type that plagued the industrial maintenance and construction field did not present problems in the garment industry. Conflict between the inside forces serving under the prime employer and the outside contractor's forces existed, but it was mitigated by the presence of a single union that functioned as a unifying and controlling force in a highly competitive and insecure industry.

Some ill-specified informal sharing of maintenance and construction work was found in plants organized by craft unions that represented both inside and outside workers. However, in union-management contracts the closest parallel to work-sharing was found in featherbedding-type clauses. While the actual work was not shared, the "conditions" of work were. For instance, if the outside workers received overtime pay, the inside employees were entitled to an equivalent amount. In one of our process plants, management resisted a union demand for a clause that would have required the company to work on Saturdays 50 per cent of the major craft of the central service crews that would have performed the work in question, had it not been contracted. Thus, if electrical work were contracted-out, one-half the company's electricians would have received a week-end assignment. This agreement was found elsewhere in the chemical industry and applied only if the requisite skills and equipment were available internally.

Formal arrangements of this type were not common. In the Lunden survey (June, 1961) only 2 per cent of the clauses took this form, and in our study of seventy-four plants we found only one such provision. A utility firm agreed that under emergency conditions only, if the company was using contract crews who were receiving double time for overtime, the inside crews would be paid double time rather than their customary time and one-half. The inside men became interested in this provision as a result of circumstances that prevailed during a lengthy emergency period when the two groups worked side by side around the clock.

As noted in Chapter 6, management actually employed measures of this type as defenses designed to preserve control in this area. Thus, featherbedding practices sometimes were management-initiated, and, in the case of contracting-out, these practices probably tended to arise because devices such as work-sharing plans did not appear to be feasible. While pay for no work may have seemed to be the ultimate in union gains and something to be abhorred by management, for some firms it was little more than an overhead charge—the cost of "freedom" and flexibility in decision-making.

Major negotiations

In the late 1950s and early 1960s, contracting-out became a key issue in almost every major union-management negotiation, notably in the automobile, steel, and railroad industries, in all of which there were substantial groups of inside maintenance and construction employees. In 1960, steel and automobiles each had some 200,000 persons performing this work,[28] while the railroad industry had approximately 300,000, less than half the number employed in 1947.[29] Managers and union leaders troubled by contracting-out problems watched these bargaining speculators both expectantly and apprehensively. A victory for their side might enhance their own local cause; on the other hand they felt that a loss might set a precedent that would be their undoing. However, the actual effect of these major negotiating sessions was far from clear; on the whole, they did not yield readily communicable solutions to the problem of dividing work between the inside and outside forces. The steel negotiations of 1959 and 1962 and the Pennsylvania Railroad strike of 1960 produced answers to the contracting-out question that stood at opposite poles. Of the two, the steel industry's actions probably had the greater significance.

The steel industry

In steel, the wage question was hammered out in the 1959 agreement that concluded the long strike, but contracting-out joined medical insurance, seniority, incentives, job classification, and a host of other work rules problems that were referred to a newly constituted labor-management group, called the Human Relations Committee. A special subcommittee of the larger body began to work on the contracting-out problem. This step signified the changing status of contracting-out as a collective bargaining issue. It had moved to the position of a problem worthy of solution in its own right. But it had also become such a knotty problem that ready resolution was impossible, and referral to a committee seemed to be the only feasible alternative for the disputants.

In effect, this collective bargaining decision moved contracting-out away from the formal negotiating arena and into a new forum where settlements took a back seat and the functions of study and discussion assumed major proportions. Assigning work on issues, such as contracting-out, to study committees gave promise of side-stepping at least some of the legalism and focusing on rights that characterized

[28] *Factory*, 1960, 118(3):106.
[29] *New York Times*, Oct. 20, 1962, p. 29.

formal negotiations. For contracting-out in a process industry such as steel, this was a move in the right direction.

In June, 1963, the emphasis on informal talks rather than formal bargaining produced a historical peaceful contract settlement in the steel industry. Observers hailed the accomplishments of the committee as the beginning of a "new era in labor."[30] A tightening of restrictions on contracting-out joined control of work by supervisory personnel, discussion of the use of overtime in the face of layoffs, and abbreviated industrial sabbaticals as major elements in an agreement that granted no wage increases and instead concentrated on job and income security.

The customary stress on inside union members' "right" to work performed in the past and on management's "right" to make a reasonable business decision was supplemented by an agreement that in each plant joint labor-management committees on contracting-out would be established to resolve problems in connection with the operation and application of the agreement, as well as any other problems relating to contracting-out. In addition, the committee was to be notified before any work could be contracted-out, and at the request of the union members the matter would be discussed in an effort to reach agreement before action could be taken. If no amicable arrangement could be devised, the usual grievance and arbitration machinery would be brought into play.[31]

Despite its designation as an experimental agreement,[32] the substance of the clause certainly did not shake the world of settlements on contracting-out. However, the 1963 steel contract served to underline the change in the status of this issue, not only with regard to the growing stress placed on it but also with regard to the means employed for its resolution.

Upon contrasting contracting-out with other problems treated in this manner, it seemed fairly clear that the study group could produce improved answers to problems whose current solutions though formerly adequate required adjustment to new situations, for example, cases in which existing units needed to be combined or reshuffled. Thus, the committee's problem-solving approach facilitated alterations in the size of seniority units and in the number of steps in the grievance procedure.[33] But in the case of contracting-out and other problems that could not boast a preexisting formula or scheme, there was no established scale of values that could serve as the basis for new calculations. In the garment manufacture industry, for instance, a committee could

[30] *New York Times,* June 22, 1963, p. 11.
[31] *Steel Labor,* 1963, 28(7):8–9.
[32] *Ibid.,* p. 3.
[33] *Wall Street Journal,* Feb. 15, 1963, p. 1.

produce an improved version of a work-sharing plan, but in the absence of this type of groundwork the difficulty of the task was greatly increased.

To turn postponement, which is the immediate effect of referring a problem to a committee, into an organizationally meaningful solution was far from easy. Taking the heat off the collective bargaining table was one function that the study group could fulfill, at least temporarily, but providing answers to questions that collective bargaining could not solve represented a move to a higher level of difficulty. The Human Relations Committee and groups of this type formed in other industries served as a support, and perhaps even a substitute, for collective bargaining. Assessment of their total effect on contracting-out and other management rights issues seemed destined to be clouded by the fact that competing groups, notably *ad hoc* bodies such as presidential committees, regulatory agencies, administrative agencies, and inter-union pact umpires, were appearing on the scene as active contributors. Some of these were newly formed elements, and some represented old groups assuming new functions and interests. The formation of some groups clearly was stimulated by the desire to escape the bonds of legalism. Inevitably, these new and differently constituted bodies moved, and seemed bound to continue to move, in different directions from one another, producing a variety of solutions, some compatible and some inconsistent, to problems concerning contracting-out.

The railroad industry

The Pennsylvania Railroad negotiations of 1960 moved in the opposite direction from the intent if not the realities of the study committee approach. These sessions were characterized throughout by a property-oriented approach to the contracting-out problem and finally concluded with an attempt to infuse greater specificity into one of the conditional criteria for the management decision. At one time this railroad was a highly integrated operation. It built its own locomotives and passenger and freight cars, although it purchased some as well. When the contract dispute occurred, the company was constructing only freight cars although some of these were also obtained through purchase and leasing arrangements. Moreover, the firm hired contractors to rebuild and upgrade this equipment.

Needless to say, the Transport Workers Union and the System Federation of the International Association of Machinists, representing altogether 20,000 maintenance workers, were not pleased with these increases in the share of the work assigned to outside forces. The unions were seeking to end a sharp decline in the number of shop employees through a program wherein the railroad would do all repair work and equipment maintenance with its own facilities. Company officers characterized these demands as an invasion of managerial rights.[34] The controversy simmered for three years despite the efforts of an impartial referee and a presidential fact-finding board. Finally, on Sept. 1, 1960, a strike took place, the first in 114 years. Apparently, the railroad was willing to agree to do all repair work and equipment maintenance, on the condition that the work could be done as cheaply as by outside contractors, but the unions rejected this offer. However, at the end of the two-week strike, the unions accepted an agreement that completely abandoned the notion of establishing a firm property claim to all the maintenance and repair work of the firm.

Instead, in the later rounds of negotiations, union officials focused on revamping the conditional criteria for the management decision whether to contract-out or use inside forces in the rebuilding and up-grading of locomotives. They wanted margins specified regarding inside-outside cost differentials in order to prevent work from being contracted on the basis of an insignificant difference in cost. In addition, the unions requested that the company reveal all the correspondence with contractors and bids relating to a particular job. Such data would have been useful in cases in which the inside forces determined to underbid the outsiders via concessions, such as accepting overtime at straight time rates.

The final settlement made no mention of revealing correspondence, but management did agree to back up its cost argument with bids from the competing inside and outside units. With regard to cost differentials, a schedule of significant differences was drawn up. For contracts ranging from 0 to $10,000, any greater cost was determining. However, for jobs costing more than $10,000, rate penalties were introduced. Starting at 10 per cent for contracts in the $10,000 to $50,000 range, the rate dropped to 2 per cent for jobs in the "$500,000 and up" class. However, the dollar difference between the two alternatives would have had to be greater than 2 per cent for the latter category, because the rates for the previous categories were cumulated to this point.[35]

As a matter of fact, some managers told us that they employed less elegant but nevertheless similar rules of thumb in making a decision regarding the contracting-out of work, and most noted that small differences in cost were inconsequential. Again, one found evidence that collective bargaining provisions in this area tended to constitute a formalization of managerial practices.

This agreement was particularly interesting because it provided in some sense a concrete dollar-and-cents measure of the equity of the inside forces in the work of the firm—a statement of the precise "loss

[34] *New York Times*, Sept. 2, 1960, p. 9.
[35] *New York Times*, Sept. 15, 1960, p. 36M.

of efficiency" that management should be willing to undergo in order
to provide work for its own men. However, realistically, this could be
simply a measure of the point at which bringing in a contractor was
considered to be worthwhile.

This contract aroused considerable interest in management circles,
and some alarm as well, because of the explicit statement of cost
criteria and the presentation of data regarding contractors' bids. To
some, these provisions represented a means for establishing new union
beachheads in management decision territory. Of course, the agreement would have been much more unusual if it had been made by
Big Steel rather than the railroads, where labor-management relations
traditionally have been subjected to a high degree of regulation and
specification.

In its public reactions, railroad management professed to see no
inconsistency between this agreement and the notion that its rights had
been fully retained. A company official commented, "We are particularly glad that despite the unions' sweeping demands we were
able to make an agreement that retained our rights to manage the
railroad and which will not impair the efficiency of our operations."[36]
Another company statement noted that "The final settlement recog-
nizes the right of the railroad to contract work to outsiders."[37]

The contribution of collective bargaining

Pressures due to declining job opportunities caused the inside employees' desired share of the work of the industrial firm to become an expanding quantity. Inside union members sought to ensure a fair share
of the available work through collective bargaining, but vagueness
continued to characterize the notion of a fair share established through
this means. The task of actual definition was left to others—to the
parties in the course of day-to-day interaction and, when their efforts
failed, to third parties, such as arbitrators, who were expected to apply
to a particular dispute the standards formulated in the agreement. In
many cases, the arbitrators had to make an attempt at supplying
standards as well.

Some third parties apparently would have preferred to "farm out"
to labor and management the work of supplying a precise formula
through contract negotiation. This route for salvation was recommended by Schedler (1955, p. 137) when he noted, "The moral is
fairly obvious that it is incumbent on both parties to consider, either
alone or in conference, this problem of letting out work, to decide
under what conditions, if any, it should be done, and then to spell out,
insofar as possible, the agreed-on policy and incorporate it into the

[36] *New York Times*, Sept. 13, 1960, p. 40.
[37] *New York Times*, Sept. 15, 1960, p. 36M.

labor contract." Others also have hinted that the silent contract may be less appealing to management since the Supreme Court's Warrior-Gulf decision and that both parties might prefer their own agreement to some of those handed down by arbitrators and the courts (Crawford, 1960). However, there was no indication that labor and management were proceeding generally in the direction of more precise language.

More precise language, in the spirit of the Pennsylvania Railroad agreement, probably had two major effects, neither of which involved Schedler's promise of more "digestible" arbitration decisions. The first was the creation of substantial quantities of red tape that might have served better than the specific contents of the provision in question to ensure a larger share of the work for the inside forces. Our research indicated that complex procedures and red tape, whatever their source, made contracting-out lose its attractiveness. The union that succeeded in shifting contractually the task of proving "the case" from its shoulders to those of management may have been well on its way to achieving this result. Of course, the effect of the red-tape factor would be greatest in old plants; in new plants the threat of this development might bias management against establishing a substantial inside force.

Second, while agreements that specify rules for evidence and detailed decision criteria have not provided workable solutions to the contracting-out problem, they certainly could furnish a fine outlet for managerial innovation. Thus, in the case of the railroad contract, jobs could be broken down—or built up—into units that would fall in the most favorable category. Such procedures were well known to local managers who wished to avoid seeking headquarters' approval of construction and maintenance projects. In addition, "legalistic" provisions would make excellent ammunition in bargaining with contractors who, for instance, might have to adjust their bids to meet a required differential in cost.

Some of the union leaders with whom we spoke had a remarkably good understanding of contracting-out problems, but most of them admitted that they still were searching for the ideal clause. Frequently, tentative consideration was given to provisions that would serve to increase controls over management's procedures in the decision process as well as over the criteria management applied. Naturally, it was anticipated that the "restrictions" would introduce a bias toward the inside performance of work. A union official in a heavy fabricating industry remarked that he was contemplating further regulation of the management argument regarding the availability of facilities. He felt that management should be required to establish that the necessary equipment was "absolutely unavailable" and that purchase was "absolutely impossible." The argument against purchasing equipment would be acceptable only if the company officers could show either that the equipment in question would be used only once or that its cost would create a gross financial hardship. However, despite these unyielding tones, he noted that he had "gone along" with a management move to contract-out a paint job because some needed scaffolding was unavailable internally.

This example well illustrated the difference between the ideal and the real world in contracting-out. In formal negotiations, the parties moved over to extreme rules, designed to cope with all contingencies in general but with none in particular. Implicit in these rules was a model of the manager as a sly fellow out to hoodwink the workers through a series of sharp practices. The managerial image that developed in day-to-day relations was modified by the realities of the situation. Thus, the union official had to face the fact that, even though management purchased the equipment, the inside workers might not be willing to erect and climb scaffolding in order to paint a tower.

Because legalistic formulations could provide no answer to problems of this type, some authorities decried the pursuit of solutions in the form of more specific collective bargaining agreements. Kahn (1960, p. 77) favored instead a "just cause" approach and "a more fruitful posing of contracting-out issues in functional and practical terms." However, there was a caveat connected with this and other prescriptions to seek through collective bargaining more realistic, practical, and functional answers to contracting-out problems. These goals could have been achieved more readily had the divided world of multiple forces and diverse interest group pressures been replaced by another in which the contracting-out decision was measured on only one commonly accepted scale.

The products of the traditional collective bargaining process shared with the arbitration decision the necessity of facing the realities of everyday life in the plant, the problems of rival unionism and relations with active members of the outside interest group. Certainly, the observer had little reason to be surprised that collective bargaining over contracting-out did not succeed in establishing any clear rules governing the division of maintenance and construction work between the inside and outside forces. As we have seen, only a few agreements repeated the unworkable arrangements of the inter-union pacts in which gross categories of work, such as maintenance or minor construction, were declared to be the property of the inside workers. By implication, then, tasks that did not fall in these claimed categories could be assigned freely to the outside forces.

Schemes for dividing work within particular categories had not been developed beyond the general inference that outsiders had an equity in surplus, unfeasible, or uneconomical items within each class. The divisions were formulated quite naturally to favor the inside forces, saying in effect to outsiders, "After we have dined fully, you may have the remaining food." The unity supplied by membership in a common labor movement was not sufficient to overcome jurisdictional differences between inside and outside unions. Therefore, one found no cases of rules that applied equally to both sides and no parallels to the work-sharing regulations of the garment industry, where only one union was involved. Moreover, developments of this type were extremely unlikely.

Given the complex structural problems surrounding collective bargaining over contracting-out, equalization provisions offered, not necessarily a satisfactory solution for dividing work, but perhaps the only feasible one. Equalization avoided the difficulties of developing functional fair shares rules with respect to the work itself and simply assigned a value, such as "equal overtime," to the equity of the inside employees.

In summing up, it was clear that most of the collective bargaining agreements on contracting-out did, in fact, take cognizance of the interests of both industrial management and the outside forces. Despite union aims of a more sweeping nature, on the whole the provisions constituted no more and no less than a foot in the door for the inside workers.

EQUITY THROUGH LEGISLATION

The means for determining fair shares that have been described thus far—interunion pacts, arbitration, and collective bargaining—omitted from their direct course of action one or more of the immediate parties at interest. However, in the case of legislation, all the parties had an opportunity to lobby and to be heard at functions such as congressional hearings. In these proceedings, issues generally were viewed in black-and-white terms as both inside and outside organizations attempted to buttress their property claims with the force of law. Through legislation, some interests sought to increase their share of work, while opponents attempted to block this effort and substitute for it moves to better their own position.

Resort to legislative controls was contemplated by those parties at interest who believed they were adversely affected by the agreements of others, e.g., the interunion pacts or collective bargaining provisions regarding contracting-out. However, much more insistent were the pressures of competing inside and outside interests for legislative assistance in gaining footholds in new and growing areas. The missile field was a good example. In this case the main action involved jurisdictional conflicts between inside and outside industries rather than unions. In missiles, one witnessed a seeming countertrend to the general pattern, with manufacturers claiming rather than disowning construction work. Prime contractors, who often were air-frame manufacturers, held that testing and secrecy were their chief concerns in retaining work connected with the installation of missiles. On the other hand, the construction industry maintained that this work properly belonged in its jurisdiction and that the manufacturers were interested in installation primarily because it was their least standardized and therefore most profitable undertaking.

The Davis-Bacon Act

Members of the outside forces bitterly termed the missile sites "the empire of airframe and large industrial manufacturers."[38] The construction industry's foothold in this empire seemed to hinge in part on legislation that was conceived in a different era and for an entirely different purpose. This legislation was the Construction Industry Wage Statute (the Davis-Bacon Act) of 1931, and it was designed to control wage competition among construction contractors bidding for government work by requiring that the wage rates paid be those prevailing in a given area. In applying this law, the Wage Determination Section of the Department of Labor decided, first, whether or not given work was, in fact, construction and, second, the amount of the applicable prevailing rates for the area in question.

For the outside forces, this law provided an entering wedge into the domain of the missile manufacturer. But inside interests recognized this fact and supported moves to have the provisions and administrative procedures of the legislation altered. The inside industrial unions claimed that their members were being deprived of employment because, whenever the Department of Labor determined that work was governed by Davis-Bacon regulations, "industrial contractors too routinely subcontract work to a construction contractor with building trades labor, for the building trades threat to strike is ever present."[39]

The Holland Report

The immediate bone of contention was a report of the Missile Site Public Contracts Advisory Committee (the Holland Report), issued August 25, 1961. This report suggested guidelines that would have narrowed the area covered by Davis-Bacon and strengthened the industrial manufacturers' and unions' claim to certain activities, particu-

[38] *Qualified Contractor*, 1962, 27(8):66.
[39] *New York Times*, Sept. 1, 1962, p. 8.

larly launching control systems work that was being performed by the building trades unions.

Needless to say, the outside forces bitterly opposed the activation of this report. They argued against making changes in the traditional areas of outside and inside dominance, stating that this action would serve to harm even the inside unions by destroying an "age-old" division of work.[40] But, more than this, some members of the outside forces felt that one of the basic dimensions of fair sharing would be violated. In a reference to the program favored by the insiders, it was noted, "They suggest that the Act should be remedied so that the construction worker is restricted to that work which no one else might want to perform."[41] This last statement pointed to an important element in the notion of fair shares. A party at interest may have regarded work in a given category as his sole property, but he typically did not want to be limited to this category. If he was, then these tasks became the "dirty end of the stick," for he was being deprived of some of the good, profitable work in the categories that were closed to him.

Fair shares at the missile sites

Competition for work at the new missile sites did not result in a new conception of fair shares for the inside (manufacturers) and outside (construction industry) forces. From the beginning, members of both inside and outside organizations engaged in an active contest for position in this growing field. While the outsiders were determinedly trying to advance their foothold, the insiders were equally determined in their attempt to exclude them from certain territory. However, there were points of agreement. The manufacturers were willing to permit the construction industry to function in its traditional bricks-and-mortar role of builder of buildings. But the outsiders wanted a share of the work that included more than traditional construction. In the terms of the interunion pacts, this work fell in the gray area, but there were no past practices or established work relationships to serve as a base line for determining ownership.

Thus, the matter reverted to the familiar question of jurisdiction, with the Federal government playing a key role, both as the initial giver of a contract for work and as the source of a law that specified conditions for government contract work defined as construction. The outcome of the struggle hinged on the definition of the word "construction," for work that fell in this category had to be compensated at prevailing construction rates. The probability then was high that

[40] *Ibid.*
[41] *Qualified Contractor,* 1962, 27(8):68.

this work would be assigned to an outside contractor. Quite naturally, insiders moved for a redefinition of work included in the construction category, and, quite reasonably, outsiders opposed any such action. The Holland Report, while clearly acceptable to the insiders, was just as clearly unacceptable to the contractor-craft groups. But, neither government officials nor legislators relished the task of formulating overall rules that would be satisfactory to both sides. More appealing was the alternative of leaving things essentially as they were. A statute that was "neutral" in the sense that it was conceived for another purpose could continue to serve as a means for the assertion of construction contractors' claims to a share of the work. Competitive efforts seemed to turn to smaller adjustments within the given framework. For example, the inside unions bargained for and received Davis-Bacon rates for construction work at missile sites,[42] and the contractor-craft complex moved for the inclusion of fringes in the rate formula.[43]

As new fields develop, one can anticipate the growth of variously structured inside-outside struggles over a fair share of the work involved. In general, the outside forces have had better opportunities in new and developing fields, where they have not had to face the competition of the established inside operation. However, in some new areas one found essentially two contract groups competing for fair shares. At the missile sites a variation developed on the familiar theme of prime contractor-subcontractor differences. The construction crafts were faced with the age-old problem of controlling the advantage held by the prime contractor, who in this case was a manufacturer, a member of a group that was serving increasingly as both the outsiders' client and the outsiders' competitor.

FAIR SHARES AND THE ADMINISTRATION OF FEDERAL LABOR LEGISLATION

The role of the Federal government

The situation at the missile sites was indicative of the extent to which the Federal government had become involved in the competition between inside and outside interests, as well as in the business of defining the appropriate share of work to be accorded to each one. In the post-World War II period, the Federal government began to engage in fairly extensive subcontracting, in part to escape the bind of low civil service salaries, which made it impossible to incorporate needed talents

[42] *The Machinist,* Oct. 18, 1962, 17(33):2.
[43] *Qualified Contractor,* 1963, 28(4):13.

into the inside government organization. In addition, governmental subcontracting represented an effort to support private industry. For example, the maintenance of some Federal buildings was contracted-out. Moreover, contracting provided a means of expanding Federal employment without giving the appearance of expansion.

However, the position of the Federal government, when considered as a whole, assumed an ambivalent stance with regard to contracting. When the government conducted business, for instance as an agency that engaged defense contractors, it pressured for efficiency and the elimination of unnecessary overhead expense, which, of course, included the use of contracting when this was the most economical and effective business method. On the other hand, the government had to cope with the problems of workers plagued by a loss of job security, and thus those who conducted the Federal labor relations function viewed contracting-out in quite a different light—as a threat to inside employment opportunities. Thus, work could be contracted-out to meet the requirements of the Defense Department and then returned to the inside crew as a result of an "unfavorable" National Labor Relations Board decision.

NLRB decisions

In the years 1961 and 1962, the National Labor Relations Board, which administers and enforces the National Labor Relations Act, created considerable interest by issuing conflicting decisions on contracting-out. A 1961 decision seemed to say that the outside forces' share of the work of the firm was a matter of managerial discretion. But the following year the Board reversed itself in a manner that appeared to strengthen the position of the inside union (see Figure 11-4). In the process, the management rights issue came to the fore, the Board fell under attack for making "politically motivated" decisions, and the experts as usual extrapolated these decisions to the point where no act of contracting was left unaffected.

Fibreboard and Town and Country

The first of the cases involved the Fibreboard Paper Products Company and the Steelworkers and Machinists Unions. In 1959, this company assigned maintenance work to a contractor who employed members of the building trades unions. The inside workers were notified of the move and of their impending dismissal. Management maintained that it could save $225,000 a year by contracting this work—work formerly performed by seventy-three of its own maintenance and power-house employees.

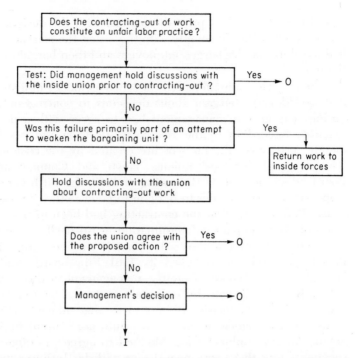

Fig. 11-4 *Division of work between the inside and outside forces: National Labor Relations Board* (1962).

The initial Board decision of March, 1961, upheld the right of Fibreboard management to contract-out for economic reasons without first consulting the workers' bargaining agent.[44] However, new factors entered the picture, such as changes in the membership of the Board that accompanied the change in 1961 from a Republican to a Democratic national administration. In addition, a new philosophical approach was generated by what one Board member described as "changing circumstances in the labor-management field."[45]

These changes were reflected in the case involving the Town and Country Manufacturing Company and the Teamsters Union.[46] Town and Country, a manufacturer of home trailers, contracted-out its trailer hauling after its workers voted to join the Teamsters. Early in 1962, the Board ruled that this contracting-out apparently had taken place in order to prevent unionization. But it added that, even if the move were undertaken solely for economic reasons, management

[44] 138 N.L.R.B. No. 1558.
[45] *IUD Bulletin*, 1963, 8(3):13.
[46] 136 N.L.R.B. No. 111.

would have to conduct prior discussions with the designated bargaining representative. To comply with the order, the company would have
had to rehire the discharged employees and then bargain with them on
the issue.

The majority opinion stated that management's obligation was limited to a duty to bargain about decisions to contract-out. There was
no implication that management had to agree with a negative union
reaction. According to the Board, its decision did not innovate. It
merely recognized the facts of life created by the customs and practices of employers and unions. Town and Country appealed the
Board's decision, but, in the spring of 1963, the Fifth Circuit Court of
Appeals upheld the order to bargain in good faith with the union. The
court cited the fact that the contracting had been in part, at least, the
result of "the company's determination to rid itself of the union."[47]

In the light of the above decision, it was not surprising that the
Board reviewed and reversed its 1961 Fibreboard Products ruling.
In contrast to Town and Country, management in this case seemed to
be motivated primarily by economic factors. The Board again gave
assurances that its decision did not mean that subcontracting was fore-
closed to management if the union would not consent to the action. It
noted that no employer was obligated to agree to union demands on
subcontracting that were inconsistent with his business judgment. Yet
management was ordered to reinstate the dismissed employees, with
back pay. After restoring the former *status quo*, it then could bargain
with the union on the question of contracting. The Board indicated
that this would be a useful procedure. It observed, ". . . candid discussion of mutual problems by labor and management frequently results in their resolution with attendant benefits to both sides. Business
operations may profitably continue and jobs may be preserved."[48]

When the U.S. Court of Appeals, District of Columbia Circuit,
heard the Fibreboard case, it upheld the NLRB position that the
Labor-Management Relations Act requires that the inside union be
given an opportunity to meet the employer's complaints concerning
the high cost of maintenance work before such work is contracted-
out.[49] The strict managerial "no discussion" defense again generated a
strong judicial counterreaction.

Additional troublesome questions were raised by instances in
which management contracted-out the work of employees who were on
strike. Their replacement has been justified by the need to protect the
business, but again the Board ruled that management would have to

[47] *IUD Bulletin*, 1963, 8(5):12.
[48] 138 N.L.R.B. No. 67.
[49] 53 L.R.R.M. 2667.

bargain with the union about this matter. In one case the Hawaii Meat Company permanently contracted-out its delivery service during an economic strike.[50] In another, the Abbott Publishing Company contracted-out the work of its mechanical department while the union, the Chicago Newspaper Guild, was conducting an unfair labor practice strike.[51] The latter case was similar to Town and Country in that the Board felt that the contracting was simply one of a large number of attempts to harass and weaken the union.

The implications of the new approach

Reactions to the Board's new decisions seemed to negate its disclaimer that nothing unusual was involved. While the National Association of Manufacturers and the Chamber of Commerce raised the prerogatives issue and charged that the rulings had eroded fundamental rights long established, industrial unions praised the rational nature of an approach that would serve to add to the stability of union bargaining relationships and help protect maintenance workers in their jobs.[52]

Even the Board members did not agree on the final effect of the decisions. A conservative member dissented in part because he felt that the requirement to bargain would initiate endless turmoil rather than peaceful settlement. He contended that the Board's new approach placed contracting-out in "the arena of economic struggle and industrial turmoil where strikes, picket lines, charges, counter-charges, protracted litigation and many other aspects of economic power possessed by unions are protected by this Board and are, therefore, legally available to a union to compel a complete abandonment by management of its proposal on the pain of suffering irreparable damage to every aspect of its business."[53]

This Board member also was alarmed at the prospect of burgeoning red tape: "The time involved in extensive negotiations and in protracted litigation before the Board, together with numerous technical vagaries, practical uncertainties, and changing concepts which abound in the area of so-called 'good faith bargaining,' makes it impossible for management to know when, if, or ever, any action on its part would be clearly permissible."[54]

The line of reasoning initiated in the Supreme Court's Warrior-Gulf decision that designated contracting-out a bargainable issue was extended through these new Labor Board interpretations that declared contracting-out a mandatory subject for collective bargaining. If man-

[50] 139 N.L.R.B. No. 75.
[51] 139 N.L.R.B. No. 118.
[52] *IUD Bulletin*, 1962, 7(10):15.
[53] *Factory*, 1963, 121(5):262.
[54] *Ibid.*, p. 265.

agement refused to bargain in good faith, it was guilty of a violation of section 8(a)(5) of the National Labor Relations Act.

On previous occasions, decisions such as Town and Country and Fibreboard have conjured up visions of the sheer destruction of management's freedom to conduct the operations of the firm. Our research indicated that decisions of this type tended to have largely short-run effects and that the validity of long-run projections was a much more precarious matter. In a similar vein, much of what the dissenting NLRB member projected into the future has had a plentiful existence in the past, e.g., contracting-out marked by strikes, picket lines, charges, and countercharges.

Moreover, the Board was concerned, not with contracting-out in all its facets, but rather with one particular problem, namely, a legalistic one. Did the act constitute an unfair labor practice? This criterion may have tended to move the Board closer to the inside forces, because "unfairness" was viewed from the standpoint of the person whose work was being contracted-out and not from the standpoint of the competing outside forces. Almost all the problem-solvers in this area were, as we have noted, working out unique problems. For those who cherished their "freedom," the limited focus that arbiters typically employed meant that many aspects of the total problem remained uncontrolled. On the darker side, the solutions arrived at through a limited approach could have unintended consequences of an undesirable nature.

Certainly, our research indicated that the orders of the Board did not constitute a literal bombshell in the field of labor-management relations. Only one-fifth of our cases pursued a no-discussion defense of the contracting-out decision. On the other hand, three-fourths employed a barter defense of some type, indicating that they were willing to trade some commodity or commodities in recognition of the equity of the inside employees. Almost one-half employed a notification defense, but the Board was ahead of industrial management if this body meant, by bargaining, a full and free discussion. Only a small minority of four firms felt that the union should be included fully in the decision process (see Chapter 6).

As far as effect on formal procedures was concerned, the new approach of the Board potentially would have a drastic effect on only a minority of firms. The others had proceeded some distance along the designated route, and again a minority was far beyond the point of involvement prescribed by the Board. Moreover, without the aid of the Board's ruling, a small number of local unions (four), in conjunction with an effective group of allies, had penetrated the decision process to the point of real control over it.

The effect of the Board's decisions on the fair shares of the inside and outside forces was not clear. The insider was entitled to a hearing, but the outsider could still get the work. But implicit in the orders was the notion that the inside workers were entitled to some consideration. The disputes that came before the Board represented fairly extreme cases, e.g., contracting-out designed apparently to break unions and punish strikers or contracting that was followed by mass dismissals of whole departments.

Therefore, it was not surprising that legalism as an approach to fair shares reached its zenith in the case of the NLRB, for the procedures the Board developed essentially were aimed at the strict managerial legalists, whose actions undoubtedly tended to produce the greater portion of the unfair labor practice cases. As noted earlier, strict legalism on the part of management was highly amenable to reverse controls of this type. Thus, the procedural tests of fairness, e.g., prior discussion or bargaining with the union, were aimed at the legalist, who insisted on his right to no discussion of any sort.

The rules for equitable division of work initiated by a particular source clearly were a function of the nature of its clientele. Both the NLRB and arbitrators typically dealt with problem relationships, and the program of the Board especially seemed to be geared for extreme management rights cases. For these cases, the message was clear. Some concessions should be made. If management contracted the work in question, the displaced workers should be paid an indemnity of some sort, such as equal assignments in some other part of the operation. However, the prescriptions of the Board understandably indicated a lack of appreciation of the facts of the "average" case, in which the shadings of gray predominated over black and white.

In the new approach of the Board there also was implicit a positive affirmation of the primacy of the inside relationship and the inside employment bond, in part born of a sympathy for the plight of the man who had based his expectations on its continuance. Presumably, the contractor's employee, noted for his flexible adaptation to the vagaries of the labor market, would be expected to weather employment crises without becoming an object of social concern.

In sum, the luster of management's rights may have been symbolically tarnished by the Board's decisions, but their effect on actual flexibility in the management decision process was less clear. It was erroneous to assume that these pronouncements were being visited upon a management freely conducting a completely rational decision-making process. As a matter of fact, even in the absence of the union, management generated substantial sources of restraint within its own organization (see Chapter 8).

Perhaps the main threat of the Board's new approach was, not the principle introduced, but rather the red tape, the potential created for stalling, delaying, and dragging matters out. Again red tape was not an innovation in this area, and that supplied by the Board simply could be added to the collection accumulated from a variety of other sources.

chapter 12

Inside and Outside Views
of Equity

Thus far, we have analyzed concepts of fair shares developed largely in formal proceedings by labor relations specialists and by those with middle- or top-level positions in companies and unions. The views of those who actually managed and performed the work in question were only indirectly represented. Nevertheless, the inside managers and their workers and the contractor and his employees embodied the institutional problems that others were attempting to solve and the interests that others were trying to protect. How did criteria for allocating work such as "black," "white," and "gray," established work relationships, good faith bargaining, and reasonable business decisions "shape up" in terms of the behavior and views of the direct participants?

Cases presented in previous chapters have illustrated the dilemma of the official bargain-maker who encountered work crews with contrary views of fair shares (see page 216). Our interview and observation data indicated that differences of this type were common and that, when one left the world of the dispute-solver and entered that of the personnel who actively managed and performed industrial maintenance and construction work, one encountered a different set of views regarding a fair share of this commodity.

THE INTERNAL SERVICE DEPARTMENT'S FAIR SHARE

In Chapter 8, we noted that the internal service department manager jealously guarded his jurisdiction against both inside and outside encroachment. But the concept "jurisdiction" implies a nonselective claim to all the work in a designated category. In general, we found that jurisdiction was only one side of the fair share coin; on the other side, one found selectivity and a notion of a balancing out over time in the quality of benefits received.

The inside manager's fair share

Quality of work

Within the firm, operating departments generally recognized that the service groups had definite, though often informal, rules regarding the type, quality, and quantity of work that they would accept. While favored parties could trade other goods for dispensations from the rules, these requirements applied generally and their waiving was not a free commodity. From the operating manager's point of view, the service department's code contained provisions of this type: "They do not want 'dirty end of the stick' jobs—unpleasant or dangerous work —jobs that yield a low return on their bookkeeping costs, or jobs that tend to cause bad relations within the work group." For example, internal problems arose when high-status workers attempted to force those of lower status to do more than their "share" of certain undesirable assignments.

With regard to work covered by all or part of the above description, the inside managers were not opposed to contracting. In fact, these were the jobs that they regarded as the contractor's fair share. We did not locate any service department heads who actually wanted to take over all the work in their domain. Even those in highly integrated operations saw a definite place for the contractor. One service manager remarked, "When we have something like sitting in a bosun's chair and painting a tower, I can't get my men to take that kind of work. They tell me to hire a contractor. They'd rather stay home on layoff."

While the inside manager did not want all the work in his field, he also resisted firm specification of the nature of his share. Absolute dominion developed a highly negative value when it was restricted to one or two categories of work, especially if these included less highly valued, routine maintenance activities. Confinement to certain categories of work inevitably assumed the proportions of the dirty end of the stick. The service officer wanted a richer diet—one that included some of the big jobs, some of the interesting work. The head of an inside maintenance department complained, "When a job we could get our teeth into comes along, they give it to a contractor. We never get a chance to show what we can do. Then, to add insult to injury, my people threaten to quit on me and go to work for the contractors."

In sociological terms, a pattern of reciprocity was involved. In return for handling small, routine, day-to-day tasks, the manager expected some larger, nonroutine jobs. Inevitably the latter involved construction craft work, to which the contractor asserted a prime property claim. The intensity of the inside department's counterclaim depended a great deal on the recent history of the group's activities. If the men had just completed some "good" work, the pressure was less. But when the head of the inside department pointed to a situation in which the plant manager had contracted five desirable jobs in a row, the pressure gauge might have read near the top of the scale. One inside maintenance manager reported that his predecessor had resigned because "contractors were being favored" and that he was considering the same step "if the situation didn't improve."

Scope of function

Another aspect of the fair shares question involved the scope of the task to be performed. Ideally, the inside service manager wanted to be treated as a professional, with the operating departments serving as his clients. For some, this goal could be satisfied through small changes. They wanted the operating departments to "show greater respect" and to consult in advance about certain matters. Others wished to integrate backward into the early stages of planning and design, in the fashion of the package contractor. In fact, some of these proposals seemed to be stimulated by the rise of the integrated contractor and a desire to emulate his pattern of operations. And in some cases the inside man moved to incorporate a contract function in his own operation. Instead of fighting contracting, he joined the movement. As a contractor he was able to compete for a share of some other firm's work as well as to increase the size and status of his function within his own organization. The expansionist theme was constant, but it assumed many forms, with modest plans the rule and large-scale efforts the exception.

Greater voice in the initial decisions concerning maintenance and construction work constituted an important avenue of approach toward ensuring a fair share for the inside service department. In contrast to the inside union, the service manager could employ a variety of organizational strategies for achieving this goal. As indicated in Chapter 8, these included a wide range of trading relations with operating departments. The exclusive use of formal routes to achieve expansionist goals was not common. We found only a few cases in which maintenance and construction heads attempted to work primarily through formal channels to increase the scope of their function. In one instance, the inside manager obtained from the plant manager a written directive instructing client departments to clear projects with maintenance prior to issuing a work order. But to be effective, a formal order apparently had to be the last step in an organizational process, rather than the first. For a strong inside department, the directive might serve merely as a confirmation of power. But in the above case it did little more than raise the hackles of the operating departments, who proceeded to side-step the maintenance man by contracting greater amounts of work than before.

In Chapter 8, we noted that inside service managers defended their jurisdiction in a manner that compared favorably with the efforts of the dyed-in-the-wool unionist. In common with the bargaining representatives of the workers, the manager attempted to resist the territorial encroachments of others. Moreover, there appeared to be specialization in the matter of defending the inside function's fair share of the work of the firm. The uttering of insistent outcries fell to the union. The subtler matter of organizational strategy fell to the internal department. The union took the public route, often through attempts to obtain formal agreements; the internal department followed private intra-organizational paths to achieve the same goal.

But as we have seen, the inside manager was not interested in merely retaining his present holdings. A knowledge of his past activities would yield a very incomplete picture of his present desires. His notion of equity, or fair share, was far from being purely defensive.

The inside workers' fair share

It is safe to say that the inside workers were the least sophisticated of the contending parties, but they also were the most sensitive to the immediate environment in relation to contracting-out. While the inter-union pact formulators focused on categories of work and established relationships, the arbitrator and the National Labor Relations Board on good faith bargaining, the collective bargainer on decision criteria, and the inside manager on a good and varied diet of work, the inside crews concerned themselves with the day-to-day process in the plant. They were sensitive to trends in the number of layoffs and in spending for maintenance and construction work. The workers' feeling that they were receiving a fair share of the work seemed to hinge on the rate of change of these variables. Data related to this process will be presented in Chapter 14. They are mentioned briefly at this point to indicate that the maintenance and construction crews in the plant had a system of equity with regard to the work of the industrial firm that was uniquely their own, although, in common with others engaged in this work, their notion of fair shares was cued to the current and immediately preceding flow of benefits.

Reactions of inside workers who felt that they were not getting their fair share were divested of the abstract, categorical considerations that characterized the deliberations of those called in to settle a question. In the workers' eyes, debates on the prerogatives aspects of the contracting-out issue were proper activities for those at higher levels. The workers were at the point of maximum impact in this process, and they reacted to the forces they experienced directly. Their fair share was a function of what they needed and of what was available to them. As we shall note in Chapter 14, special agreements and claims to specific categories of work played a secondary role in relation to these major considerations.

THE CONTRACTOR'S FAIR SHARE

The contractor's definition of a fair share of the industrial market was surprisingly similar to that of his inside counterpart. From the narrow specialty contractor to the broad-ranging integrated operator, there was a common desire for a good and varied diet of work. Confinement to a particular class or category of work was considered undesirable, and there was a general expectation that dirty, unpleasant, and low-paying jobs should be balanced with those of better quality. Contractors whose share of industrial work was protected by licensing requirements resented companies that called them in only for work that had to be contracted (see Chapter 7). Similarly, they were displeased at jobs that appeared to constitute the inside manager's "cast-offs." However, the contractors' flow of work typically had more than one source. Thus, a contractor might have accepted "bad work" from one firm that was balanced out by "good work" from another. On the other hand, the inside managers and workers generally did not have available this convenient source of compensatory adjustments. On the whole, they were limited to the resources within the firm, and balancing in the quality of assignments had to be achieved from among the requirements of the various operating units.

Sources of support

Still, as an outsider, the contractor was jealous of the inside manager, who, he erroneously felt, could pressure for and obtain almost any desired work. The lack of firm and binding commitments from the industrial firm was a source of both freedom and insecurity. To ensure a guaranteed core of work, contractors sought support from members of other groups such as craft unions, legislators, architects, and engineers. It was felt that, if members of the last two groups wrote specifications "properly," they could assist in directing work to particular outside organizations. And despite the shift from the labor-problem to the marketing approach noted in Chapter 7, for some the jurisdiction of the craft union continued to be regarded as a strong factor in defining the contractors' share of work. A specialty contractor noted in an interview, "The bigger the jurisdiction of the union, the bigger our market. We cannot ignore their problems. Our people have been losing work to other unions, and we are feeling the effects."

But some contractors' attempts to ensure a fair share of the work were thwarted by the reluctance of craftsmen in the local labor market to depart from their traditional concept of jurisdiction. Some contractors who obtained industrial maintenance contracts in order to stabilize their work load were dismayed to find that local craftsmen did not care to undertake this type of activity. The men frequently had a "new construction" bias, and any task with a maintenance tag had considerably less appeal. Contractors reported instances in which the men refused industrial service calls. They characterized this work as "shooting butterflies" and simply left the contractor in the lurch. Thus, defining a fair share inevitably involved efforts to adjust differences in the concepts of outside management and workers, specifically, to overcome traditional notions of suitable work held by both sides.

Inside management and the contractor's fair share

Despite the contractor's efforts to enlist the aid of others, his best source of support in gaining a fair share of industrial work came from within management itself. Industrial managers who were interested in availing themselves of contract services recognized the need to give the contractor an adequate portion of work. A plant manager remarked, "If you want the contractor when you need him, you have to give him enough work to keep him in business." Another plant manager expressed similar sentiments about the nature of the job assigned to a contractor, when he noted, "Several months ago we were installing a new machine. We had to rewire a panel board and finish the job in three days. We said we were short six hours, but our man said it was only two. If you bring in a contractor, you can't ask him to do the last six hours of work that your people can't possibly finish. The job has to be fair to him. We hired a contractor for the entire job and the two crews worked together."

On the other hand, industrial management expected the contractor to relinquish a share of his work if inside "politics" necessitated this move. In one plant the mechanical workers were cut from forty-eight to less than forty hours per week. There were strong protests and demands that contracted work be pulled back in order to restore the inside forces to their old position. At the time, a number of contractors were remodeling the firm's offices. Management talked to them and explained the situation. Each contractor agreed to give up a part of his work. For instance, the electrical contractor let the company take back the installation of fluorescent fixtures but retained the major wiring. The plant engineer in this company noted that it was important to hire contractors who would be reasonable if the union "acted up." He commented, "They could hold you to the original bargain, but I think they see that they would lose by this action in the long run." Thus, in order to preserve his long-run share of the work, the contractor sometimes had to make short-run concessions.

While the contractor appreciated the industrial manager's efforts to give him an adequate share of the work, he concurred with the inside service manager's lack of enthusiasm for sharing arrangements. For both, a part of a job was definitely an inferior good. A whole job was much preferred. But the contractor seemed philosophically resigned to the notion that his fair share of industrial work was a tentative matter, dependent on the whims of others. As a contractor observed, "We're on the receiving end of everybody else's deals. After the unions and the companies agree among themselves, we try to find out what's left for us. Sometimes we can't even get that information."

While the industrial manager was worrying about threats to his "rights" to contract-out, the contractor seldom mentioned his rights or prerogatives. Instead, he was concerned about threats to his share of the market. Arbitrators, inside unions, and manufacturer-contractors were among the forces that might have served to diminish his holdings and his ability to expand. In common with his inside counterpart, the contractor was selective and "expansionist" in his approach to fair shares. Not even the highly specialized were interested in clinging to a rigidly defined jurisdiction. Movement in the direction of "better" work, and of industry-stabilizing work, constituted significant goals.

CONCEPTS OF EQUITY: A SUMMARY AND ANALYSIS

In labor-management relations, one is tempted to focus primarily on areas of disagreement, but in the groups studied, despite the sound and fury, there was substantial agreement on the basic foundations of contracting-out. There was no denial that it was a useful and desirable practice, at least under some circumstances. But given a considerable amount of agreement, one still was faced with a great diversity of plans for dividing the maintenance and construction work of the industrial firm. These diverse solutions were a function of the differing systems of values possessed by the various groups. Thus, in examining the various systems for the equitable distribution of work, one must not make the assumption that all were seeking answers to a common problem, for quite the reverse was true. The interunion pacts, collective bargaining, arbitration, and Federal legislation and its administration were aimed at solving problems unique to the relations among the parties directly concerned.

However, despite their parochial origins, the solutions were phrased in general form, and thus one was tempted to judge them on a common scale, as better or worse answers to the same problem. In our research, we were especially interested in determining how these solutions measured up against everyday organizational realities. The interunion peace pacts probably revealed the least appreciation of the facts of life in the industrial plant. Conversely, these were the programs most fully given over to other considerations. It was difficult to rank any scheme as "best," but collective bargaining probably came the closest to producing a body of realistic approaches to the problem. Of the "third parties" involved, arbitrators provided a better means for resolution than the efforts of governmental bodies such as the National Labor Relations Board.

In judging these systems of equity, the areas omitted from control spoke as eloquently as those which were included. The attention of the various parties centered largely in attempts to embed the present in the past and the future in the present. Potential or actual plans for future invasion of another party's territory were kept apart from the agreements. Should these plans prove successful, the new holdings would quickly develop a past history and a claim to respectability as the basis for a new concept of fair shares. Thus, there were problems that moved beyond the simple division of known territory. Devising means for controlling future developments challenged the ingenuity of both the immediate parties and those called in to settle disputes.

Past claims and present damages

Traditional formulas for dividing territory encountered problems with industrial maintenance and construction work. The outside forces had great difficulty as well as little success in pressing their customary territory-dividing solution of jurisdictional boundaries. The gross divisions finally established in the first verson of the interunion pact, e.g., construction, maintenance, and the "gray area," failed to gain acceptance. At first glance, some form of jurisdictional lines might have seemed to provide a simple and easy formula for dividing work. But while such an approach is possible in the new construction field, it had little meaning in the industrial organization, where in terms of function insiders and outsiders were spread "all over the lot," as one manager phrased it. At the missile sites and wherever government work was involved, the Bacon-Davis Act of 1931 furnished a jurisdictional wedge for the outside forces by establishing required wage rates for work designated as construction. But even the outside forces came to realize the weakness of the concept of rigid jurisdiction in the industrial field. In fact the notion of jurisdiction could be turned against its supporters, who, as in the case of the outside forces, might have found others attempting to confine them within the boundaries of a solidly claimed territory, such as new construction.

The general rejection of jurisdictional lines might have been interpreted as the result of an understanding of organizational reality, but unfortunately the substitutes used in their stead did little to further this cause. Rather, they focused largely on property rights based on customary practices. The use of past history in this manner is no stranger in labor-management relations, where it often has served as the operational expression of claims based on abstract principles. A prime example was the established work relationship of the second version of the interunion pacts. However, as in the case of other criteria applied to contracting-out, past practice has tended to be both ambiguous and manipulable. On the whole, the notion of jurisdiction based on the past practice criterion tended to militate against the outside forces, for it was difficult for them to establish ownership of inside work.

There seemed to be good reason for the tendency for property claims based on the past to be supplemented and supplanted by questions of damages and fair shares that related primarily to the present condition of the parties in a given case. Or it might be more accurate to say that data concerning the past were used to establish the initial property claim but that actual settlements stemmed from questions concerning the present. The segment of the past that had a crucial effect on cases in dispute often was a rather small one, primarily the immediate past, which provided a measure of how a given interest group currently was faring.

Assessing the contributions

The third parties

Reviewing the contributions of the various dividers of the industrial work pie, one found the National Labor Relations Board attempting to cope with the extreme managerial legalist with equally legalistic procedures. The new approach of the Board began by rejecting contracting-out that constituted an "unfair labor practice," in the sense that this move was undertaken to weaken or destroy a union, but, in addition the Board introduced some procedural tests of fairness, e.g., prior discussion or bargaining with the union.

On the other hand, the arbitrator, the other potential source of legalism, primarily focused on individual cases. While the governmental agency assumed the task of beating down the extreme management rights enthusiast, the arbitrator could afford the luxury of substantially ignoring the rights question and of producing a less virulent brand of legalism. But the arbitrator, too, was faced with only a limited slice of a total problem, with selected groups rather than the total number of parties involved, and with restricted means for developing solutions. Moreover, he generally was presented with *fait accompli,* and thus he examined fair shares after the fact, asking in essence: What damages did the parties suffer? As a measure, he employed a scale assessing management's "good faith," with the reasonable business decision on one end and actions undermining the union on the other. In general, the arbitrator assigned no territory, honored no jurisdictional claims, and, indeed, established no firm property claims for anyone, beyond a nodding recognition of the distinction between permanent and temporary work and some concern for the man on layoff. As in the case of the NLRB, the arbitrator's criteria were tooled to catch the obvious instance of managerial "bad faith," but their meaning in intermediate situations was much less certain.

The parties in major disputes

Through the interunion pacts and collective bargaining, the parties directly involved in contracting-out problems attempted to formulate their own definitions of fair shares. The pacts were distinctive because they focused most specifically on the division of work between the two contending groups. In part, this phenomenon could be attributed to the absence of a crucial party in the actual decision process, namely, industrial management. Thus, managerial factors, such as questions of cost and efficiency, did not cloud the picture. On the other hand, when measured against a dynamic situation, the pacts provided little in the way of useful guidelines for decisions regarding the equitable sharing of work.

Turning to collective bargaining between inside managements and unions, the contract clauses definitely reflected the complexities of the management decision process but said little or nothing about dividing work between the inside and outside forces. Rival unionism, among other factors, rendered this a subject for silence. The agreements tended to operate within the framework of the management decision process, specifying conditions under which contracting was either fair or unfair. Far from innovating, collective bargaining sometimes simply produced written specifications of former management practices. In general, the specifications were vague and ambiguous, and the actual definition of the inside worker's fair share was left open—to be supplied by the parties in the course of day-to-day interaction or by others called in to settle disputes.

The immediate parties: the managers and workers

The various parties actually performing industrial maintenance and construction work, contractors and inside managers and their respective work crews, proved to be both selective and expansionist in their approach to fair shares. While each recognized some appropriate share for the others, none was interested in limiting aspirations to particular categories and classes of work. In fact, at the operating level, the notion of fair shares was cued to the current and immediately preceding flow of benefits. Moreover, this concept involved a measure of reciprocity, receiving "good" work in return for doing "bad" work in order to provide a varied diet, for the contractor it also meant receiving work that would serve to maintain a steady flow, in return for performing needed jobs. Formal dispute-settlers, applying the logic of good faith bargaining, established work relationships, and the reasonable business decision, could take no cognizance of factors that involved give-and-take in relationships extending over time. The problem-solvers were limited either to single cases or to making pronouncements that applied to an entire class of cases. Unquestionably, their decisions could have unintended consequences for operating-level relationships.

A final assessment

The competing and coexisting systems for determining equity in the work of the industrial firm by and large tackled short-run rather than long-run problems. Major questions, such as the optimal structure of the employment relationship for a given activity, were not considered. Consistently lacking, too, were efforts to deal with more than one "share" at a time. On the whole, the greater amount of attention was accorded to the inside employees' share of the work. In many of those deliberations, the outside forces were little more than shadowy figures.

None of these systems provided final answers to a question. None caused the others to disappear or become obsolete. One found not only competing inside and outside parties but also competing agreements regarding fair shares of the work. The effect of the existence of competing solutions could only be surmised. Inexorably, the efforts of the various dividers of the industrial work pie seemed to move toward an increasing number of formal pronouncements on the subject and toward at least the appearance of greater control by the proliferating group of "third parties" brought in to solve specific problems. The legalism of the management rights proponent seemed to generate its own undoing as the "unbiased" answers to the question of determining fair shares piled up an impressive mound of red tape, if nothing else.

Despite isolated instances in which agreements moved toward greater specificity, there appeared to be an overall trend toward more general notions of equity. A persisting theme was the testing of managerial good faith. Bad faith was revealed in a close similarity between the contracted work and an existing inside operation, and the more covert the action, the greater the suspicion of "dishonorable" intentions. Failure to observe the dictates of these requirements could serve to strengthen the inside employees' claim to a share of the work in question. But criteria for determining fair shares were themselves an uncertain factor. Criteria designed to detect the isolated or extreme case no longer served this function as the exceptional instance became the rule. Criteria themselves can become obsolete and require replacement. Contracting-out gradually has moved from the status of an absolute management right to a mandatory subject for collective bargaining, but the criteria for judging this action still tended to reflect its former status and the need to punish those who abused its "privileges."

part vi

Management Rights
and the Decision Process

chapter 13

The Management Decision

In this chapter, we shall examine the decision process management has sought so ardently to defend—and the union to invade. We have discussed management rights. Now we are asking: The right to do what? To defend what? This author and others (Slichter et al., 1960) have found that collective bargaining solutions to contracting-out problems were both vague and ambiguous, but what about the management decision process collective bargaining attempted to control? Did this process stand in sharp and rational contrast, or did the agreements merely reflect the confusion inside management?

THE REAL AND THE IDEAL DECISION

The literature provided little basis for optimism concerning the relative proportions of rationality and unreason in contracting-out and related decisions, such as make or buy. However, a pessimistic view has arisen, in part because the implicit models of both the ideal and the real situation have tended to assume an extreme form. While appropriately complex, the "ideal" has tended to constitute an overly neat representation of a unilateral management action. On the other hand, the contrasting version of "reality" generally has been nothing more than a simplified one-factor model of the true process.

One finds the ideal decision model in the writings of Culliton (1941) and Oxenfeldt (1956). These models typically have involved only one point of view, that of the manager or management group moving through a series of logically arranged and thoroughly explored steps. In brief, the manager draws up a clear set of specifications for the job in question and exhaustively searches the market alternatives to the inside operation. Then he takes a hard look at relative cost data, obtaining a very careful estimate of inside costs and actual bids from the outside. But, in addition, he projects the present relative cost picture into the future and weighs the price of the inside alternative to the business as a whole, in terms of factors such as the absorption of funds that could be used for other purposes.

However, turning to the real world, Culliton (1941, p. 98), who developed a precise normative model for the make or buy decision, presented the following bleak version: "The basis for most current actions of making or buying is not a current decision but either a decision consciously made sometime in the past or a decision flowing unconsciously out of previously established practices or habits."

Oxenfeldt (1956) recommended a rigorous course for the decision-maker, but he, too, viewed the actual process as one submerged in bias, controlled by a single factor assigned a weight completely out of proportion to its true significance. To round out this picture of managerial bungling, one can quote Higgins's (1955, p. 113) defense of the instinctual approach to the make or buy decision: "The truth is that some decisions made instinctively without elaborate study may be more correct than those checked by reams of reports."

These examples of unreason and bias undoubtedly represented small slices of reality, but they also drastically oversimplified the whole truth. At the same time, the ideal models erred on the side of unreality and impracticality, for they failed to recognize the organizational aspects of the decision process, including the very important challenges to management's "right" to a unilateral role.

Observations such as the above provide an impressive basis for despair regarding the feasibility of definitive research on this management decision process. Apparently, this was one of those areas of business activity which favored models of an indeterminate nature, in which recent events dominated thinking, as did satisfactory procedures already used, evidence at hand, and subjective probability calculations.

AN ORGANIZATIONAL DECISION MODEL

In developing a model for the contracting-out decision, one might very well have accomplished little more than the precise pinning down of imprecise data. However, our approach was not normative, and we did not have the goal of reforming managerial thought processes. Rather, we wanted to treat the decision as an organizational process—to study the flow of events and changes in the process over time.

Obviously, specifying the elements and relationships for a model fulfilling these requirements was a large order. Moreover, it could not be accomplished solely by means of study and observation in the field. In the language of the computer, this was not a question of programming a known system of behavior, such as the procedure for calculating the payroll of a given firm. The contracting-out decision was not a routinized matter, and, despite the extensive research on which our study was based, we were forced to make certain assumptions about the behavior of this system.

Our model was based on the conviction that there was, after all, some rigor in the process and that, to a certain extent, it was dominated by a limited number of objective and measurable factors. Thus, some of the very interesting realities of this decision process were not relevant for our purposes, for we were concerned only with those aspects of the total behavior pattern which played a determining role in the decision. In the later stages of this research, the model was used as the basis for computer simulation of the decision process.

Analyzing the decision process

The initial stages of our effort involved the simple determination of the main units of analysis and of the relationships among them. Figure 13-1 presents the results of this work. The units included, importantly, members of the "partisan" inside and outside forces. For the inside forces, these were: the maintenance and construction department, informal work groups, and the inside union. The outside forces were

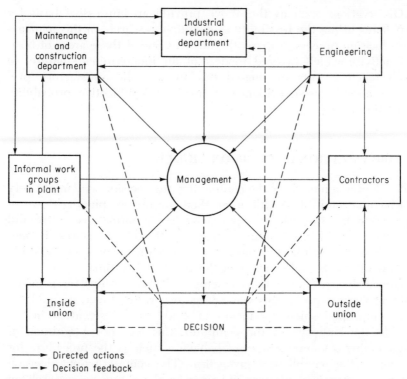

Fig. 13-1   *The contracting-out decision: main units of analysis.*

represented by the contractors and craft unions. In Chapters 7 and 8, we discussed at length the institutional roles and relationships of these groups.

Other units were the industrial relations and plant engineering departments in the industrial firm. Members of these groups served both as decision-makers and as representatives of special interests. As one might have anticipated, engineering had a larger initial decision function than industrial relations. Apart from handling worker complaints about contracting-out, industrial relations rarely had active decision-making powers in this area. There were only two exceptions to this rule among the seventy-four plants in the sample (see Chapter 15). On the other hand, in roughly one-half of the firms, engineering was a key decision-maker in minor projects and played the same role in major projects in over one-fourth. However, in our analysis, the decision function was subsumed in the unit "management," and these two departments were considered as separate entities because of their institutional roles as pressure groups. Their functioning as distinct interests was underlined by the fact that three-fourths of the plant engineers and four-fifths of the industrial relations officers disagreed at some point with operating management on basic questions of contracting-out practices, policies, costs, and union influences.

All the above units constituted the main sources of pressure on the decision. The unit designated as management represented the decision-making function. In the case of contracting-out, the decision-maker clearly had a double task. Naturally, he served the usual active management function of observing the "interests of the business" as dictated by factors such as market conditions and the rate of technological change. But, in addition, management served as a focal point for all the pressures generated by the various units and acted both to evaluate and to resolve these forces. If management failed to fulfill this role of conciliator, it might be laying the groundwork for third-party intervention and for a third-party decision in which management, too, would be treated simply as a special interest.

As indicated in Figure 13-1, a given decision did not represent the final step in the process, for each new decision was "fed back" to the various units and might become the basis for further action as one or more units issued a protest or simply took the decision into account in planning new pressure actions.

The total process: a flow chart analysis

Thus far, we have established the basic units in the decision process, limiting these to the immediate parties. Third parties, such as arbitrators, the National Labor Relations Board, and the courts have not been included, nor has the manner in which the total process is organized been made explicit. Figure 13-2 presents the total process, from its initiation to its possible culmination in legal proceedings. A given decision process may end at any of the indicated points along the way, or it may extend the entire route through arbitration and court action. An exceptional case, such as the Warrior-Gulf decision, finally was resolved by no less than the Supreme Court of the United States.[1]

The managerial function

The flow chart summarizes the crucial steps in the decision process as they were revealed in our individual case studies. The first twelve boxes comprise the heart of the managerial function, as it is traditionally conceived. Objective data regarding factors such as the availability of contractors and inside facilities and crews and the prices of labor and materials are used as the basis for making an estimate of

[1] *United Steelworkers of America v. Warrior and Gulf Navigation Co.,* 363 U.S. 574 (1960).

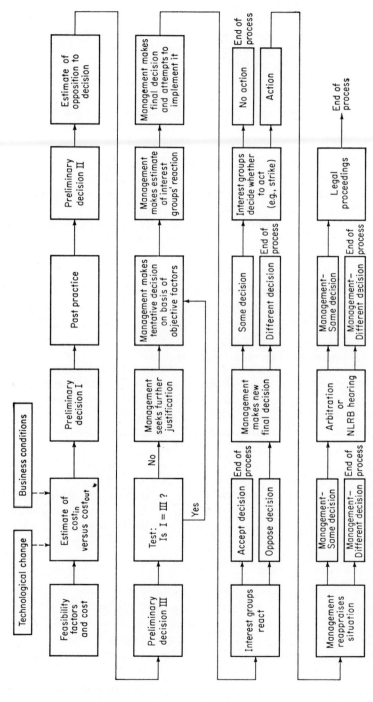

Fig. 13-2 *Flow chart: the contracting-out decision.*

the relative costs of the two alternatives. These estimates are made in the light of environmental factors such as current business conditions and the rate of technological change. This part of the total process, if carefully conducted, approximates the prescription for the ideal management decision. However, the inclusion of these factors was not intended as an indication that they necessarily were explored thoroughly. The model was designed to accommodate all situations, including those in which these factors received little more than a nodding recognition. As one manager observed, "At times we just 'eyeball' the job and let it go at that." At any rate, Preliminary Decision I is reached, and it is possible for the process to end at this point.

On the other hand, the direction of this decision may be shifted as a result of the impingement of other factors. An evaluation of Decision I in the light of past practice may lead to Preliminary Decision II. (For our operational definition of past practice, see page 271.) Then, an estimate of the potential opposition to the proposed action may result in Preliminary Decision III. In some cases, the latter estimate apparently was made routinely. A manager in a metal-fabricating plant commented, "Whenever we make a decision on contracting, we consider what the union's feelings might be, and we are swayed by what we think would be their possible reactions."

At this point, we are interested in learning whether or not consideration of past practice and the estimate of the opposition to the decision have caused a change in the direction of the decision. Thus, we perform a test to determine whether or not Decision I equals Decision III. If the two decisions are different, then management faces a dilemma and must attempt to resolve it by seeking further justification for its action. Having completed this step, management makes another tentative decision on the basis of the objective factors. Management also makes a new estimate of the interest groups' reaction to the decision. This step may include discussion of the matter with them. Now management makes a final decision and attempts to implement it.

The generation of group pressures

The interest groups are faced with a definite decision, and they react to it. If the reaction is negative, members of either the inside or the outside forces may pressure for a change. According to our model, the strength of the reaction is a function of the pressure factors in operation at that time. Figure 13-1 presents a scheme for evaluating the amount of pressure that potentially can be generated by the inside workers.

In the first step, the group appraises its current status to determine whether or not it is receiving its fair share of the work. It reacts in

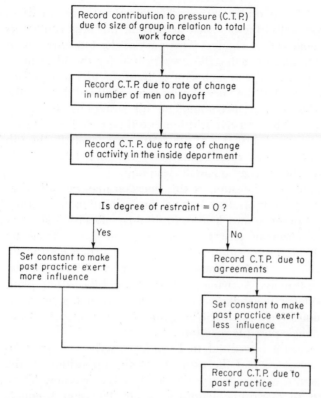

Fig. 13-3   *Pressure against the decision to contract-out: the inside workers.*

terms of the current rate of change in the number of men on layoff
and in terms of the current rate of change in the activity of the inside
maintenance and construction department. If these factors yield a
a degree of restraint greater than zero, then pressure to enforce any
existing union-management agreements on contracting-out will be
accentuated.

If the group's appraisal of its current status produces no basis for
pressure activity, then the inside workers' notion of whether or not
they have been receiving a fair share may be contingent upon the
status of past practice. In brief, according to our definition of past
practice, the workers assess the contribution of the last ten decisions.
If all these favored the outside forces, the insiders may generate considerable heat for a reversal of this pattern. Or, conversely, if all the
last ten decisions favored the insiders, they may exert strong pressures
against a change in this pattern (see page 287).

If agreements existed, the effect of past practice was weighed
in order to take account of this reinforcing source of pressure. Our

field research indicated that past practice exerted less influence in cases in which restraints were generated by the group's appraisal of its current status. As a final step, the pressure generated by the combination of the group's self-appraisal of status, agreements, and past practice should be weighted by a measure of ability to exert pressure in the organization, the group's numerical strength in relation to the total numbers in the work force.

Of course, the inside workers constituted only one of a number of interest groups acting in this area. But the general nature of the sources of pressure activity was similar for all of them. Pressures from any of the groups at interest had a complex rather than a simple basis. Certain pressure-stimulating factors were basic and took precedence over others, while some served primarily as reinforcing agents.

When all the interest groups have reacted to the decision, the process will come to an end if all of them accept it. The term "accept" may provide an overstrong description of cases in which groups low on pressure-inducing factors simply fail to concern themselves with the matter. However, groups high on pressure-inducing factors may oppose the decision and take steps to register their displeasure. Management, in turn, will react to their presentation and make a new final decision. Company officers may respond to the pressures by issuing a different decision—one that will disappoint the current recipients of the work by reassigning it to the "opposition." In some cases, the "different" decision may involve postponement of the work until a more propitious time. Of course, this tactic is possible only in cases in which postponement is a feasible alternative.

The new final decision also may be a repetition of the original one. Having received a counterchallenge, the interest groups will then consider a future course of action. They may simply drop the matter or decide to trade their grievance for other concessions. In either instance, the process has reached its end point, and management may proceed with its original decision. On the other hand, if the pressure-generating factors are strong, the interest groups may take further action.

The inside workers through their unions have fullest access to means for persisting challenge, and therefore these are the groups most likely to follow this course. Other groups at interest, such as the inside maintenance and construction manager and the contractor, generally have receded from the picture as active opponents. Continuing protest actions are the forte of the inside workers and unions, although others may support these efforts.

In the face of pressures such as strike actions, management again will appraise the situation. If company officials do not yield at this point or produce an acceptable compromise solution, the door is opened for the entry of a third party, who will attempt to resolve the matter. Occasionally, an outside union will persevere to this point. It may have thrown a picket line around work management has been performing with inside forces and also may have threatened to refuse to fulfill future assignments, but if management does not yield, the outsiders can file a claim under the internal disputes plan of the craft and industrial unions or appeal to the National Labor Relations Board on the same basis. However, as indicated in Chapter 11, these actions might constitute little more than futile gestures.

The inside union is much better able to extend the process beyond the point of management's final refusal. It may take the matter to arbitration, to the National Labor Relations Board, and finally it may resort to legal proceedings. A series of court and NLRB decisions that followed in the wake of the 1960 Warrior-Gulf decision[2] have served to legitimate extension of the decision process in this matter. When the final third party decision is received, the process has reached its fullest extent, excluding, of course, this decision's inevitable contribution to the future actions of the various parties at interest.

This model was limited to the flow of events surrounding a particular decision. As we have seen, the process might end simply, or it might become complex and involved. In reality, of course, the various groups were constantly pressuring for a fair share of the work, and the events associated with any one decision merely recorded this continuing process at a given point in time. All the groups faced the common problem of having to estimate one another's reactions. When a group reacted on its own behalf, it looked at the total organizational process and its progress to date in relation to it, but in considering another group's position, it was inclined to focus on the individual case and to make its predictions on that basis. This phenomenon was not solely a function of lack of perspicacity. Information about another group's position in relation to the total process usually was not available to the outsider. Thus, he could not understand the basis upon which another group was calculating its fair share or estimate correctly the amount of pressure that it was willing to exert on its behalf.

The nature of the decision model that we developed should be interpreted, not as a denial of the significance of the industrial manager as a decision-maker, but rather as a recognition of the fact that, in the case of the contracting-out decision, the core of the process often lay in the interactions of pressure or interest groups inside and outside the industrial firm. Moreover, the final direction of the decision often was a product of the pressures the various groups could mobilize behind their particular position.

2 *Ibid.*

THE RESEARCH DESIGN

Needless to say, contracting-out did not always involve pressure group activity, but we were interested in developing this model in order to pursue further the study of pressure activities in this particular decision process. As we have noted previously, contracting-out was an ideal subject for this type of investigation.

As a first step, we specified a simple pressure group model for the contracting-out decision. The model assumed that the decision was the result of the pressure of the following groups: management M; the inside interests I, for example, the inside union and maintenance and construction department; the outside interests O, for example, the outside craft unions and the contractors.

In explaining the pressure activities of these basic groups, we were interested in variables that served as independent stimuli of the pressures exerted—variables whose changes over time would serve to predict various aspects of the decision process. The pressure that each group might exert was assumed to depend on a number of these variables: $X_{M_1}, X_{M_2}, \ldots, X_{M_k}$ for management; $X_{I_1}, X_{I_2}, \ldots, X_{I_k}$ for inside interests; $X_{O_1}, X_{O_2}, \ldots, X_{O_k}$ for outside interests. The actual amount of pressure was assumed to be the sum of some functions of the variables. (The functions referred to here were discrete functions expressed as weights.) The pressure of management was expressed as

$$\sum_{i=1}^{k} f\left[M_i(X_{M_i}) \right]$$

and the resultant pressure of the three groups as

$$\sum_{i=1}^{k} f\left[M_i(X_{M_i}) \right] + \sum_{i=1}^{l} f\left[I_i(X_{I_i}) \right] + \sum_{i=1}^{m} f\left[O_i(X_{O_i}) \right]$$

The above model stopped the decision process at a given point in time, but our research indicated that each decision was not an independent unit. Past decisions very obviously influenced the present one. Our observations in the field prior to conducting the formal study of the decision process had confirmed this fact. The actions and reactions of the parties were shaped by events in the immediate and recent past.

Thus, a significant aspect of the research design involved the specification that the decision process be studied over time. Data relating to our variables were collected for series of at least thirty consecutive decisions in any one division or other unit in the firm. In this manner, our variables were located not only at a given point in time but also in relation to their antecedents and successors in previous and subsequent decisions. We also were able to measure the rate of change of each variable and relate the rate of change of one variable to that of the others.

The variables selected for study were fairly simple aspects of the contracting-out problem—"hard," or objective, rather than subjective data and, in general, elements that our prior research had indicated would be significant and truly independent aspects of the total situation and not simply other manifestations of the dependent variable. For each decision in a consecutive series, we obtained the following data:

1. Estimate of $cost_{in}$ versus $cost_{out}$. The estimated difference between the cost of doing work inside and contracting-out, if the firm made this calculation.
2. The final decision. Was the job assigned to inplant forces or to a contractor?
3. Date of the decision.
4. Amount of money involved. The size of the job as reflected in its total cost to the firm.
5. Inside union challenges, if any.
6. Outside union challenges, if any.

The following background data were gathered at the time of each decision:

1. Employment size of plant
    a. Number of hourly employees
    b. Proportion of total hourly employees engaged in maintenance and construction work
2. Number of workers on layoff
    a. Data for maintenance and construction forces
    b. Data for other hourly employees
3. Agreements with the inside union that applied to the decision in question

This research model was based on our observation that the interest group examined more than just the single event and did more than just compare present events with past instances of the same nature to determine whether the former were equal to or different from the latter. This description would aptly fit the legalistic approach and procedures used to determine ex post facto questions of rights and equities. But the individual and group in the organization proved to be sensitive to other kinds of information—information about the rate of change of factors that constituted the relevant environment of a given problem, such as contracting-out. Thus, a factor such as number of men on layoff was not simply a specific quantity. It was a dynamic function that may have been increasing, decreasing, or proceeding at a constant rate.

Some of the benefits of devising a model of this type stemmed from its forcing the researcher to be extremely specific about the nature of the phenomenon he was studying. General references to "forces" that stimulated "pressures" had to be abandoned in favor of a specific listing of these factors, and those which were incidental had to be distinguished from those which were of major significance. Moreover, operational measures of these factors had to be devised. At this point, the experience of extensive field work and the supporting data from the survey became highly valuable. These sources indicated clearly that, while some pressures might arise from wounded psyche, the great majority also had firm roots in the hard data of the contracting-out problem. Our observations had confirmed the fact that, while contracting-out was justly described as a complex problem, this description applied most aptly to its group structure. On the other hand, the factors that stimulated pressure actions seemed to be limited in number and fairly consistent in their impact.

In order to construct a "working" model, we had to determine the various routes by which interests inside and outside the firm were attuned to the total process. While establishing these routes, we also were obliged to operationalize pleasantly vague concepts such as past practice and fair share. The model that resulted was used to predict the direction of the final decision, although in this book we are focusing on its role in predicting challenges to management's "right" to contract-out.

Data collection for this aspect of the research on contracting-out was an arduous and time-consuming process and required extensive cooperation on the part of informants. Therefore, the sample was necessarily small, numbering five process and five fabrication plants. Needless to say, selection was made in a nonrandom fashion, for willingness to participate was essential, although seven companies actually were members of the original random sample of seventy-four. All the cooperating plants were fairly large, employing over one thousand. The maintenance and construction forces ranged in size from sixty to nineteen hundred workers.

QUESTIONS AND ANSWERS REGARDING THE MANAGEMENT DECISION PROCESS

In Chapter 14 we shall present the major findings of this research in relation to the problem of predicting union challenge to management decisions. At this point we are going to review some of our general

observations regarding aspects of the decision process that seemed to
have significance for industrial relations questions. Some of these elements have been noted briefly in prior sections of this book.

The effect of the past on the present

The past history of the contracting-out decision certainly seemed destined to have an effect on questions such as the inside workers' notion
of fair shares and on the future expectations of all the parties concerned. Initially, it was assumed that the past history would reveal
more variability—more shifting back and forth between the two
alternatives—than actually was the case. If one considered the plant
or firm as a whole, variation did exist, but in a given division or other
decision unit the more characteristic pattern for decisions for which
consideration of the two alternatives was relevant tended to be fairly
long runs for a given alternative, either to contract-out or to do work
with inside forces.

When informants explained their decision process in interviews in
our initial survey, they cited criteria that seemed to indicate that a
fair amount of variability would be present. For instance, managers
described systems in which the number of inside workers available in
each trade and the number of hours required for scheduled work
were monitored daily, and on this basis the current backlog of work
was calculated. If the backlog exceeded an arbitrary limit, for some
twenty to thirty days and for others six weeks, work then would be
contracted. However, our field studies revealed that these systems were
amenable to a fair amount of control, and generally a backlog of
sufficient size was present either chronically or not at all. In a transportation-equipment plant in which management used this criterion,
there was a high level of contracting, whereas, in a machinery company employing a similar standard, almost all the work was done with
inside forces.

On the whole, then, our research upheld the finding of Cyert,
Feigenbaum, and March (1959, p. 93) that in the managerial decision
process, a high premium is placed on alternatives similar to those
chosen in the recent past. Our data seemed to indicate that there were
organizational commitments to one route or the other over the short
run, say, one year. Of course, there were occasional deviations from the
ongoing pattern, but these did not continue. We noted, that, for fairly
long stretches of time, members of the inside and outside forces became accustomed to persisting decision patterns, either favoring or
disfavoring them. This situation also promised to be a rich source of
crises in cases in which management finally failed to conform to the
anticipated pattern.

For our decision model, we operationally defined past practice as the contribution of the last ten decisions to the present one. Obviously a given past history did not have the same significance for all parties. Thus, if the last ten decisions favored contracting-out, this factor had a variable weighting in the eyes of the diverse inside and outside pressure groups. Of course, the parties' actual perception of past practice could have deviated significantly from the true history, and, in this case, using the actual data to predict behavior would have introduced a source of error. Although one would assume that management had the best information on past practice, a maintenance manager in an automobile factory cited a case in which this was not true. During the course of a dispute over past practices with regard to contracting-out, he pulled out a list he had compiled for the purpose, and when the inside union officers countered with one of their own, he discovered three jobs that had escaped his attention. Moreover, they favored his side of the argument!

Our field contacts indicated that inside workers and unions were not able to detect unfailingly all instances of contracting-out. However, big jobs, a prime source of trouble, retained their customary visibility, as did actions that deviated from an ongoing pattern. Naturally, the outside forces, the contractor and his craft union employees, had a far from perfect view of past practice in the firm. Data reported in Chapter 14 upheld the latter point and also indicated that imperfect knowledge on the part of the inside workers was a matter of little consequence.

Other aspects of decision patterns

The term "past practice" generally was used to refer to the gross direction of a decision, i.e., was work assigned to the inside or outside forces? But our research indicated that other aspects of the decision process could and did affect its potential for creating industrial relations issues.

In Chapter 14, we shall note the effect of factors such as the rate of change in the amount of money spent on maintenance and construction. Thus, we found that fair shares was not a constant notion, an entity established in tradition. Rather, the notion of what was fair changed in response to changes in the rate of departmental activity.

Spacing and timing

Other factors of this same general nature deserved further investigation, e.g., the effect of the spacing and timing of decisions. Was there a pressure-generating differential between situations in which decisions were made at an even pace throughout the year and those in which long periods of quiescence were followed by feverish activity?

Differential cost calculations

We have been looking at the implications of the decision process for industrial relations questions. But in our research we found that industrial relations matters or other anticipated sources of challenge also had implications for the manner in which the decision process was conducted. We expected, for instance, that the cost differential between the inside and outside alternatives would be a significant dimension of the decision process. However, as in the case of past practice, the actual facts did not conform to our original expectations. The competing inside and outside forces were not subjected continuously to the scrutiny of full cost estimates that included labor, materials, overhead, etc. This statement applied even in cases in which both alternatives were being considered very actively. In fact, a decision to "go outside" frequently was not accompanied by an estimate of inside costs.

An examination of our decision series data revealed that the rate at which full cost estimates were made was rather low, ranging from a high of one in six decisions to a low of one in thirty. Such estimates generally were made when pressures or questions clearly were anticipated (see Cases 2 and 3, Chapter 14).

Order in the decision process

A final question is that of the order of appearance of the various factors in the decision process. Our research was not specifically directed toward the systematic study of this problem. Yet, industrial relations issues inevitably turned on the question of order in the decision process. The measures recommended usually did not tamper with the activities of a given decision-maker. Questions of order typically involved bringing in new groups or moving old groups into positions closer to the initial steps in the process. These basic changes in the group structure of the decision process had tremendous symbolic significance. The various interest groups attempted to have the factors that best expressed their point of view evaluated prior to the reaching of a first decision.

Inclusion of the factors in question usually took the form of including the group itself in the deliberations, an action which confirmed the now vital nature of these considerations. In essence, when a dispute-settling agency required management discussion with the union prior to contracting, it was underlining the importance of variables relating to the inside interests. But another question was involved. Did a change in order of occurrence of the factors have a real as well as a

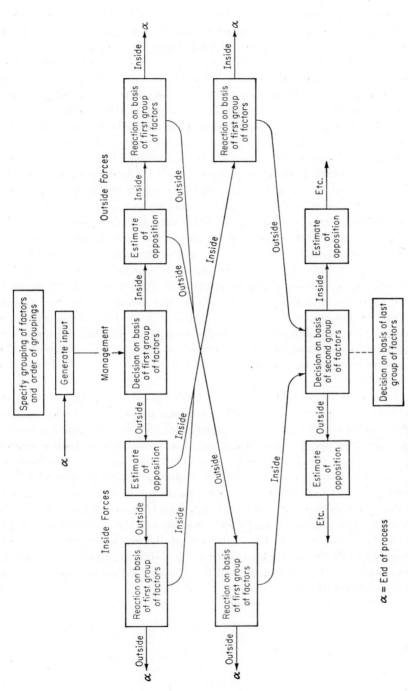

Fig. 13-4 *The contracting-out decision: the ordering of factors.*

α = End of process

273

symbolic significance? Early entry into a process was not necessarily equivalent to having the influence that prior consultation symbolized. In several of our cases management found that it was simpler to dispose of a factor early in the process, with the status-giving value of early inclusion counterbalancing the absence of actual effect on the final decision.

The question of the ordering of factors in the management decision process probably arose even more importantly at the informal level in the case of the complex or involved decision regarding contracting-out. Such decisions, while not rare, were in the minority in both our process and fabrication industry samples of consecutive decision series. For both the fabrication and the process samples, about one-third of the decisions were concluded rather easily. One-half of the process decisions were somewhat more involved but were still resolvable. One-third of the fabrication group fell in this category. But one-sixth of the process decisions and one-third of the fabrication became a source of difficulties, in the sense that some group or groups pressured fairly actively for a change in the direction of the decision. In these cases, the ordering of factors became important. Who came in, when, and how assumed significance. Potentially the decision process might extend for the entire route prescribed in Figure 13-2. Management's changing the initial decision depended in part on whether the inside or the outside pressure groups succeeded in taking the next play and initiating a supporting chain of relationships that would enable them to hold it.

Figure 13-4 presents a flow chart version of the resolution of the "problematical" decision regarding contracting-out. Practically speaking, some events in a decision process cannot occur simultaneously, and therefore one finds ordering solely a convenience. In the initial phases of the decision process it seemed to make little difference whether the manager considered scheduling first and then availability of equipment or whether this order was reversed. But in other phases of the decision process, the ordering of factors might make a difference. A strategically placed factor might initiate a whole series of "favorable" events. In the research reported here we were concerned primarily with the prediction of protest. However, the more complex and equally significant question of the effect of the ordering of various factors deserves further study.

chapter 14

Prediction of Protest

This chapter will focus on the prediction of inside workers' challenges to management decisions to contract-out. Throughout this book, we have been concerned with various aspects of the management rights question. Persons concerned about rights generally have regarded challenge as a serious matter, for they have perceived it as the first step on the road to full-scale invasion. However, the cause of challenge often has been left as a moot question or has been attributed to the quixotic impulses of the work force. Prescriptions for prevention of protest often have stressed the "good management" formula. Our research was based on the thesis that challenges could be accounted for and that a significant part of this accounting involved a recognition of the intimate relationship between challenge and various aspects of the managerial decision process. Moreover, we were searching for factors that served as independent stimuli of challenge. We wanted to veer away from variables that simply tended to be other manifestations of the same phenomenon—variables that led to almost self-fulfilling conclusions such as the following: "Challenge was a product of worker dissatisfaction."

Inside workers' interest groups proved to be cued to selective aspects of the total organizational process—those which served to measure the rate of change in the groups' welfare function, regarding job property rights and the equitable distribution of available work opportunities. It will be shown that the rate of protest increased in response to increases in the rate of change for these particular factors.

BACKGROUND FACTORS:
THE CHARACTER OF THE WORK GROUP

It should be noted that our study was limited to a particular work group, whose characteristic functioning in the organization could have had a definite effect on its grievance activity. Thus, conclusions regarding the maintenance and construction workers' protest behavior might not be applicable to other groups. At any rate, it was important to place these groups in relation to other members of the industrial work force.

The research of Sayles (1958) indicated that structural characteristics and the technological organization of the work were the prime components of work-group protest behavior. Technological factors acted to limit severely the range of possible behavior, and thus common patterns emerged among those at similar points in the organization or flow of work. These factors proved to be such powerful determinants of behavior that it was not necessary to have information about the specific composition of the group, the qualities of the supervisor, or the state of union-management relations. Moreover, Sayles found that it was possible to predict not only which groups will protest and which will tend to accept their conditions of work but also the methods used by a given group.

Four types of protest groups were distinguished by Sayles: the "apathetics," low-paid, low-skilled members of mixed crews or long assembly lines who rarely challenged decisions; the "erratics," members of homogeneous, interdependent crews and short assembly lines who protested in a spontaneous, demonstrative, and unpredictable fashion; the "strategics," who were indispensable, highly skilled operators manifesting a persistent and calculated self-interest activity; and, finally, the "conservatives," skilled individual functionaries whose overall level of grievance was moderate and characterized by restraint.

The conservatives were of special interest to us because maintenance and construction workers were included in this group. Conservatives were self-sufficient, often doing their own bargaining apart from the union. They were concerned about specific self-interest issues, and when a matter of this type arose, a key question was: Are we going to get our share (Sayles, 1958, p. 34)? In addition, the conservatives engaged in a cyclical type of grievance activity. A period of passivity, in which there was a gradual rise in the feeling of being left out, was followed by an active phase, wherein the group improved its position and then fell back into a satisfied state of inaction.

Field work conducted in connection with our research confirmed the above picture of the inside maintenance and construction worker. He was not a persistent challenger of management decisions, but he was a predictable one. In our study, a "cyclical" form of protest behavior also was found—behavior that had its immediate surface roots in the management decision process. But this behavior also most certainly had its deep roots in the technological organization of the work of the maintenance and construction trademan.

Of course, maintenance and construction work varied greatly in skill level, and we observed differences in the bargaining behavior of the high- and low-skilled. On the whole, we found that members of more highly skilled groups, such as electricians, were more likely to have agreements with management concerning the extent of their job territory, but they also conformed to the requirements of the conservative model in the sense that they did not insist on enforcing these agreements at all times. The lower levels, millwrights and laborers, for example, were more likely to react spontaneously and to assume some of the behavioral trappings of the erratic model. However, the lower levels in maintenance often regarded the upper levels as pattern-setters, and thus their deviance from the conservative model was limited in extent. The higher levels also were more likely to be active in the union, and in a few cases in which maintenance forces were a strong and numerically large element in the plant we found their members serving as leaders in the local.

This picture of the total maintenance and construction grievance syndrome—independence of action and careful rather than chronic "griping"—needed one more element to round it out. In our studies of these groups, we found that, within the limited sphere of their function, there was little disposition to distinguish between management problems and bargaining issues. They may have agreed that management had the "right" to determine the production workers' schedule, but the concept of a "prerogative" had no meaning within their own area of concern. The men were likely to be interested in any and all aspects of the department's operation.

RATE AND TIMING OF PROTEST

How often did the inside crews contest a management decision? At one extreme, the workers might object to every instance of outside contracting. But following this course would suggest a prohibitively high rate of activity, as well as one that would have been inconsistent with the behavior of the conservative type. However, one of the interesting sidelights revealed by our research was the pervasiveness of the assumption that challenge to outside contracting was a consistent occurrence. Of course, those directly involved at the plant level rarely made this mistake, but those on the periphery of the process, such as persons called in to solve a particular dispute, frequently had this impression. The basis for this erroneous assumption was the notion that each contract represented a perceived property loss for the inside men and therefore, of necessity, stimulated an objection. However, objection did not prove to be a simple stimulus-response phenomenon. Contracting-out was a necessary but not a sufficient condition for protest.

Protest and decision patterns

Yet some situations did seem almost to dictate protest. One might have assumed that, if a given series of decisions predominantly favored the inside workers, they would not object to a single "deviant" instance of contracting, but the reverse was true. With only ten series of decisions as our total sample, we can indicate only what appear to be points of high agreement within the limits of these data. In four of the series, the majority of the decisions favored the use of the inside forces, and, in each case, the plant union challenged the occasional decision to contract-out. These breaks with current tradition evidently were regarded as a serious matter, and those directly concerned seemed to be urged by others to "nip this thing in the bud."

The remaining decision series, six in number, predominantly favored contracting-out. Reasons for protest will be discussed later, but the findings confirmed one of the specifications of the conservative model. The workers did not prove to be in a state of continual upset over contracting-out. In all cases, less than half the actual contracts became the object of protest. Proportions in the individual plants ranged from slightly under one-third to slightly over two-fifths. The decisions comprised a series in the sense that all were made by management in a given section of the plant, usually the mechanical division or its equivalent, but, of necessity, these decisions involved different jobs and work groups.

Protest in relation to type of work and work goups

However, protests were scattered among the various categories of work. Thus, there was no indication that some areas were trouble-free, while others continually produced challenge. Data from the decision series revealed that grievances were distributed as follows: 25 per cent involved maintenance work; 43 per cent, modernization; 32 per cent, major construction. While the problematical "in-between" area did have an edge on the others, there was a notable degree of interest in all categories of work. Protest clearly was not limited to certain types or kinds of contracting, and the rate of protest was not simply a function of the proportion of, say, routine maintenance jobs in the total series.

The work groups involved in the decisions were divided into two categories: high-skilled, e.g., electricians and plumbers, and low-skilled, e.g., millwrights and laborers. Combining the data for all the plants revealed that the highly skilled had a somewhat lower rate of protest than the less-skilled group. The latter objected two-fifths of the time when their work was involved in contracting, while the highly skilled responded in this manner slightly under one-third of the time. Again, these data substantiate the impression that the true conservatives were the more highly skilled members of the maintenance and construction crews.

In Chapter 13, it was noted that the inside workers generally did not have perfect knowledge of outside contracting. Inevitably, some jobs were overlooked, and of course we were concerned about this point because failure to object could have been due to lack of information. However, investigation revealed that this was not a serious problem. In six of the companies the insiders apparently did have the complete facts, and in the other four they missed only a small fraction —one or two instances. Interestingly, these occurred at times when group pressures on the decision process were low.

Protests by outsiders

This chapter deals primarily with the protest behavior of the inside workers. However, in gathering the decision series, all instances of objections from the outside forces also were recorded. Looking in from the street, the outside contractors and craft unions obviously were limited in their ability to monitor the day-to-day situation in the plant.

Thus, pressures and protests from the outsiders were less frequent, but their occurrence could be predicted rather readily. Their activities focused on the big jobs, for these had the combined qualities of visibility and desirability. A case of this type is noted in Figure 14-3.

Timing of protest

Still unanswered is the very significant question of the rate and timing of protests. Our research was designed primarily to shed light on this problem. Certain aspects of the occurrence of objections could be inferred from the work-group typology presented above. An affinity for spontaneous reactions to stimuli suggested patterns of protest different from those based on careful calculations. Any and all predictive schemes have assumed the existence of some underlying logic to the process of objection, but for our purposes the "character of the group" did not provide an adequate explanation, for we wanted to determine where protest would be generated within this context. In so doing, we were moving away from merely characterizing a response pattern and turning our attention to an analysis of response in terms of reactions to specific stimuli.

Changes in the rate of protest were related to the following: changes in the rate of spending for maintenance and construction and changes in the rate of layoffs. We hypothesized that increases in the rate of expenditure for this work would generate increased pressure activity on the part of the inside crew and that increases in the rate of layoffs would have the same effect.

While the above data comprised the heart of the analysis, additional factors were investigated. We were interested in determining the effect of special labor-management agreements that particular jobs were the "property" of the inside workers. It was hypothesized that workers would be more likely to protest contracting-out when it involved tasks governed by special agreements than they would in cases in which agreements did not exist. In addition, increases in the rate at which agreements were broken by contracting-out should have served to stimulate increases in pressure activity on the part of inside crews.

FACTORS PREDICTIVE OF PROTEST: GENERAL FINDINGS

Our analysis proceeded by plotting cumulated data for the elements in each decision series and then observing the degree of correlation in the rate of change of the various factors. Examples of this type of analysis are found in Figures 14-1 to 14-3. Before we turn to these data, we shall present some general findings with regard to the independent variables affecting protest: special agreements, amount of money involved, and number of men on layoff.

Special agreements

Those with a property-oriented view of the protest process should assume that objections automatically would follow the contracting of work governed by special labor-management agreements. Data for our decision series permitted the testing of this proposition, for in four of the cases, one-fifth to two-fifths of the contracted jobs fell in this category. Surprisingly, the existence of agreements that certain work belonged to the inside men did not serve to predict their behavior. One could not conclude that agreements were always weak predictors; on the other hand, there was no particular reason to believe that these cases were different from the average.

In Case 1 (see page 284), the inside union contested twelve in a series of thirty consecutive decisions favoring contracting-out. Examination of the data for the total group of decisions indicated that twelve involved work that was covered by prior agreements. It would have seemed logical to assume that these were the twelve that the inside union contested. However, this did not prove to be the case. Of the twelve decisions governed by special agreements, only four were the object of complaint. No protest was issued in the case of the other eight. The other plants revealed similar patterns of variable response. The union complained in one-fourth to two-fifths of these cases.

Why did these unions fail to complain despite the existence of a "legitimate" grievance? The agreements certainly applied to the work in question. All in all, this finding constituted something of a revelation, for such agreements usually have been regarded as definitive settlements of issues.

There were two possible explanations for this phenomenon. The first that came to mind was managerial design. That is, foresighted managers took the agreement into account and proceeded to contract such jobs when, in the vernacular, the "heat was off." Thus we noted that decisions governed by special agreements tended to take place at times when pressures from layoff and spending activities were minimized. Thus, special agreements were out of phase with the other factors. The additional impetus for action was absent. But whether one attributed this occurrence to managerial astuteness or simply good fortune, the fact remained that it was not an adequate explanation of the failure to protest. One still had to determine why the agreements, in and of themselves, did not serve as a sufficient stimulus to challenge. One possible clue centered in the nature of this type of agreement. The assumption that such agreements were long-run phenomena may not have been warranted. Apparently, these were essentially short-run settlements, largely applicable in full force to the case or cases that originally prompted them. Subsequently, then, both union and management chose to ignore the agreement. Basically, the situation could have been viewed in terms of the inside workers' current assessments of fair shares, and the fate of these so-called "fixed" agreements then was shaped in this mold. It should be noted that special agreements were not ignored when the "heat was on."

While special agreements failed to qualify as a predictor of protest, the other factors provided a much better vehicle for this purpose. For the indivdual decision, these data could be used as rule-of-thumb predictors of the possibility of internal protests.

Amount of money involved

Pure dollars and cents constituted the basis for the best predictor. The size of the job, as measured by the amount of money involved, was related firmly to union protest. For each company an appropriate dividing line between large and small jobs was selected. The location of the line varied from one plant to another. The smallest figure was $2,500, and the largest was $10,000. On the whole, proportions of jobs on either side of the line were roughly equal. In Case 1, the dividing line fell at $5,000. The inside union contested only four out of seventeen jobs under $5,000. On the other hand, it objected to the contracting of eight out of thirteen jobs that involved an expenditure of over $5,000. In another plant with an identical number of union protests, the figures were surprisingly similar. The union challenged the contracting of only three out of seventeen jobs under $10,000 but protested nine out of thirteen over $10,000.

To summarize the findings for the entire group, 15 to 27 per cent of the "small" contracted jobs were the object of protest, while 60 to 75 per cent of the "large" jobs merited this attention. It was apparent that overall figures for the proportion of jobs challenged tended to obscure the concentration of this activity in the large-job category.

Number of men on layoff

Number of men on layoff also proved to be a good predictor of union challenge. In two plants a similar measure was substituted—the number of men working out of their craft at lower-rated, less desirable jobs. A line of division between high and low rates of layoff was established for each plant. Again, the proportions falling on either side of the line were roughly equivalent. Whether workers were on layoff or out of craft, in all cases there was pressure from candidates hoping to regain either their former jobs or an equivalent position.

In Case 1, the dividing line between a high and low level of lay-offs was 5 per cent of the work force. The union objected to contracting in seven out of twelve cases when the level of layoffs was high, but it challenged contracting in only five out of thirteen cases when the level was low. In this decision series, "low" signified a figure either close to or actually zero.

To summarize the findings for the entire group, 18 to 31 per cent of the low layoff contracting was the object of protest, while challenge took place in 53 to 66 per cent of the high layoff cases.

CUMULATIVE SERIES ANALYSIS

Data for the series of consecutive management decisions were plotted cumulatively in order to indicate the rate of change for the various factors. On the horizontal scale, we plotted the number of the decision, with spacing to indicate the time interval between decisions, and, on the vertical scale, we plotted the cumulative dollars spent on maintenance and construction, the cumulative number of layoffs, and the cumulative number of union objections.

Analysis of the data for the various consecutive decision series revealed that the dependent variable "inside union objections" and the independent variables "dollars spent on maintenance and construction" and "number of men on layoff" had a highly correlated rate of change. In the case of the individual decision, when both the dollars involved and layoffs were high, according to the definitions presented above, the probability of objection also was high. In this sample, objections to contracting occurred in four-fifths of such cases. On the other hand, when both money involved and layoffs were low, the probability of challenges to contracting was significantly lower. In four out of five of such cases, there were no objections.

The reasons for simultaneous increases in layoffs and in amount spent for maintenance and construction varied, but many reflected the shifting nature of the talents required on the industrial scene and/or the effect of economy drives such as "profitability performance" programs. Thus, during cost-cutting drives in a period of technological change, unprofitable activities were reduced in scope, and therefore the rate of layoffs was increasing. At the same time, the need to meet competition stimulated expansion into new fields and the employment of new technologies. However, this expansion did not necessarily lead to investment in new plant and equipment. In the interest of conserving funds, the firm may have taken advantage of leasing arrangements and contracting-out. Under these circumstances, inside employee pressure on the management decision process inevitably tended to increase.

The individual cases

In this section, graphs of specific cases will be presented, primarily to indicate in detail how these variables were related to one another and to demonstrate how the acceleration and deceleration of the independent variables was related to the acceleration and deceleration of the protest process. The three cases were selected because they seemed to illustrate well the full range of types found within our limited sample of data. Case 1 is a process industry firm in which the consecutive decisions in the series largely favored contracting-out. Case 2 presents a fabrication company with the same decision pattern. Finally, Case 3 is a process industry firm in which the series of decisions largely favored use of the inside forces.

Case 1

The series of decisions presented in Figure 14-1 covered a period of nine months. Arrangement of the decisions along the abscissa is based on their consecutive ordering, but, in addition, their specific placement indicates the approximate interval of time that had elapsed between each pair. Decisions tended to be bunched in groups, and definite periods of high and low activity can be noted. Spending activity was concentrated in the periods when management made decisions 7 through 11 and 22 through 29. Between these two periods, there was an interval of four relatively inactive months. Protest did not assume great proportions during the first high-activity period. At this time, the level of layoffs was both low and unchanging. Decisions 1 to 11 involved the "breaking" of six special agreements and three protests. The inside workers did not protest four of the "special agreement" cases, but they did challenge the other two.

As far as the major variables were concerned, the following "inactive" period presented a different picture. The level of layoffs changed rapidly after decision 11, but the number did not continue to mount. Spending activity was increasing at a low rate from decisions 12 through 19. Most of the jobs were small, in the $5,000 or under category. Special agreements covered five of the cases in which work was assigned to outsiders, but only one instance of contracting-out was the object of protests. In periods of this type, management "rights" went largely unchallenged, and the incidence of "broken" agreements was at a maximum. Specialists in the labor-management field frequently attribute union challenge to the failure of management to

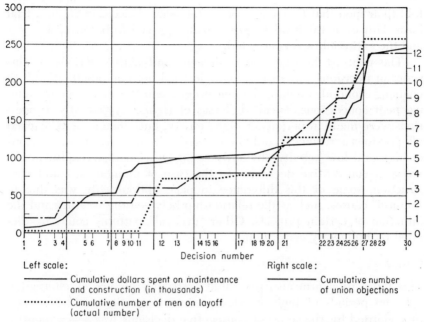

Left scale:
———— Cumulative dollars spent on maintenance
        and construction (in thousands)

············ Cumulative number of men on layoff
        (actual number)

Right scale:
——·—— Cumulative number
        of union objections

Note: Vertical lines separating groups of decisions indicate that one month has elapsed.

Fig. 14-1 *Cumulative number of dollars spent on maintenance and construction, cumulative number of men on layoff, and cumulative number of union objections, for a series of thirty consecutive management decisions: Case 1.*

comply with agreements, but, evidently, failure to comply did not always have the same significance.

Decisions 20 and 21 marked a transition between the previous period of quiescence and one of high activity. Decision 20 represented a sudden shift to a "big" job, and between decisions 20 and 21 pressures due to layoffs increased. Both decisions to contract-out were challenged. The most extended period of high activity began with decision 22 and stretched through 28. Pressures from increasing spending and layoffs combined to produce an extremely high rate of protest. Six of these seven contracts were contested. As if anticipating the coming difficulties, management had yielded on decision 20, giving half this job to the inside forces. One might have expected concessions of this type—concessions made in an attempt to reduce the level of agitation during a high-pressure period. The letting of $125,000 worth of contracts in a period of three weeks certainly had provided ample stimulus. Actually, management made another concession just prior to the awarding of the biggest contract in the series. Company officials told their men that they could have the work of decision 26 on a trial basis. However, the insiders' performance proved to be unsatisfactory, and the entire job was contracted.

The contrast between the quiescent and active periods in this series of decisions was striking. One learned not only about stimuli to challenge; one also obtained some insight into the incidence of management concessions, so-called "losses of rights." Apparently, concessions were made in periods of high activity, but when activity slacked off, previous agreements could be ignored. Alternation between periods of high and low activity obviously could be a characteristic of many series of consecutive decisions. In the case of maintenance and construction, some of this difference in pace undoubtedly was due to "natural" causes, such as the relationship between the weather and the initiation of certain projects. Other "cyclical" patterns could be dictated by budgetary constraints.

Case 2

This fabrication firm also presented a striking picture of alternation between periods of high and low activity (see Figure 14-2). Total time elapsed for the series of consecutive decisions was seven months. High activity began in the second month and extended into the first half of the third. Another active phase took place during the sixth month. Challenges to management decisions numbered twelve in all and were markedly concentrated in the periods of great activity.

Technological improvements had caused an intermittent stream of layoffs in the plant, and thus the union was particularly sensitive when large contracts were let. In each case, the company officials argued either that the men lacked the necessary skills or that the firm lacked the needed equipment. Special agreements applied to decisions 8, 17, and 18, but only decision 8 became the subject of protest. Decisions 5, 13, and 26 assigned work to the inside forces. The last two assignments apparently constituted indirect responses to grievances regarding the decision that had preceded each one.

An examination of Figure 14-2 reveals a rapid change in the rate of expenditure after decision 8. In fact, in the period between decisions 8 and 12, $190,000 worth of contracts was awarded, and each contract was the subject of complaint. The union was especially vociferous about decision 10 because it promised to involve a long-term relationship with the contractor. At this point, management made the only differential cost calculation in the series, and this rather detailed computation indicated that using inside forces would cost 55 per cent more than contracting. In the case of decisions 8 through 12, the stimulus to object was reinforced by pressures from layoffs. The same

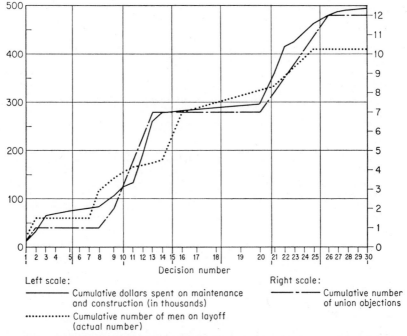

Left scale:
——— Cumulative dollars spent on maintenance and construction (in thousands)

Right scale:
— - — Cumulative number of union objections

············· Cumulative number of men on layoff (actual number)

Note: Vertical lines separating groups of decisions indicate that one month has elapsed.

Fig. 14-2 *Cumulative number of dollars spent on maintenance and construction, cumulative number of men on layoff, and cumulative number of union objections for a series of thirty consecutive management decisions: Case 2.*

pattern of response was found in the case of decisions 21 through 25, when management contracted jobs totaling $120,000.

Case 3

Case 3 was a process plant in which the great majority of the decisions favored the inside forces (see Figure 14-3). Expenditures for maintenance and construction were the highest for any one case, and only one moderate-sized job, by decision 11, was assigned to the outside forces. As indicated earlier, the inside workers were very apt to object to a "deviant" action of this type. In this instance, they did issue a complaint. Management proceeded to perform one of the two differential cost calculations for the series and produced a finding that outside contracting was 20 per cent cheaper than the inside operation. Despite the objection, the work was contracted.

The next decision, decision 12, represented an interesting reversal of the normal situation with regard to challenges to management deci-

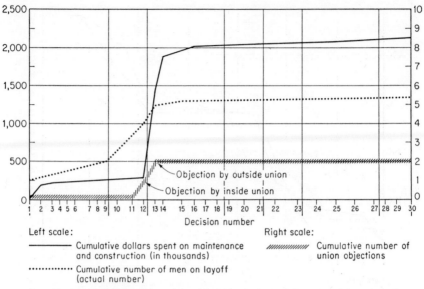

Left scale:

———— Cumulative dollars spent on maintenance and construction (in thousands)

·············· Cumulative number of men on layoff (actual number)

Right scale:

////////// Cumulative number of union objections

Note: Vertical lines separating groups of decisions indicate that one month has elapsed.

Fig. 14-3 *Cumulative number of dollars spent on maintenance and construction, cumulative number of men on layoff, and cumulative number of union objections, for a series of thirty consecutive management decisions: Case 3.*

sions. This assignment involved a large construction project that company officers wanted to give to the inside forces. Although layoffs were being made at an increasing rate, it still was difficult to find enough work for the remaining men. Technological changes were eliminating some of the workers' customary functions, and therefore a major project seemed to be a device for holding the group together. Managerial computations indicated that contracting would be approximately 3 per cent more costly than using inside crews. When the outside forces learned of the plans for this highly visible project, they brought pressure to bear through community officials. This effort was unsuccessful. It is evident that pressures from the outside had a characteristic in common with those originating on the inside. Both often were related to the size of the job, as measured by the amount of money involved.

MANAGEMENT CONTROL OF CHALLENGE

This research suggests ways in which the nature of the managerial decision process may stimulate protest. For instance, our study showed that inside union challenges to decisions to contract-out constituted dramatic responses to changes in the rate of spending for maintenance and construction. In addition, the inside group was sensitive to the rate of change in the number of men on layoff. Were managers conscious of these facts? In any case, what efforts did they make to control protests to contracting-out?

The majority of the managers interviewed noted some measures that they employed to control inside union challenges. In reality, examination of our data revealed that the probability of the inside crews' halting a particular contracted job or obtaining a change in a decision to contract-out was low. Less than half the contracted jobs were challenged, and, of these challenges, only a few resulted in a different "new final decision" in terms of the flow chart presented in Figure 13-3. But the possibility of demands for restrictive contract clauses, arbitration, NLRB hearings, and court suits loomed in the background and served as an ever-present stimulus of management interest in programs for control.

One of the basic managerial motivations had a legalistic slant—the use of controls to prevent the inside union from developing a "good case." Controls on the decision process involved measures such as clearing with higher levels in the organization. According to the rationale for these programs, they were aimed at cutting down protests and "trouble" in general. However, in reality management seemed to direct its efforts to building up a "good case" of its own, with a view to winning disputes should they arise.

Systems of control of this type obviously suffered from the blind spots of a case-by-case treatment and usually were ineffective in controlling the incidence of challenge. This task required great skill in controlling organizational process. A few managers were able to conduct fairly effective programs of this sort; others simply used a strategy of retreat. Thus, in several extreme cases of rank-and-file agitation over contracting-out, management postponed all projected work that was amenable to this action. Through this step, the manager moved, either by design or by accident, into the low-activity-rate low-protest-rate phase of our decision series. The problems of coping with challenge obviously were relieved, but a backlog of work was created that subsequently might have served to generate even worse troubles when it finally was restored to active status. An ensuing period of high activity almost certainly would instigate a new round of protests.

Declaring a moratorium on postponable work obviously was not an acceptable long-run solution for the control of protest. A few firms had initiated programs which more fully constituted attempts to "play the organizational process" observed in our research.

A metal-products firm initiated a program of this type after undergoing a year of hard-fought disputes over contracting-out. Most of the difficulties centered in a large project that was farmed out as a package. The various craft groups in the plant continuously pressured for the return of some of the work. An arbitration case resulted, and although the company emerged "victorious," the manager of the mechanical department determined that these incidents would not be repeated.

The year in which the program was undertaken actually was not comparable with the previous one, for no jobs of large dimensions were undertaken, and the work force had diminished in size through a process of attrition and early retirement. Under the new program, the inside men were permitted to develop a good backlog of their own work, including overtime. In addition, when contracting was initiated, the choice jobs were spaced out so that contractors would not seem to be getting all the "plums" at once. With this system, the manager reported that the number of grievances was reduced to four or five "weak gripes" for the whole year. The only formal grievance seemed to be the result of a visit by an official from union headquarters, who was upset by the reduction in the size of the work force and also was still attuned to the conflict situation of the previous year. The case indicated that, in "low-heat" years, the temperature could be reduced even further by proper spacing and control of the work load. However, in a high-activity year, the value of these practices may have been considerably diminished.

PRESCRIPTIONS FOR AVOIDING CHALLENGE

We have indicated the weakness of systems of controls that were directed at the preparation of a good case for arbitration or NLRB hearings. Such systems of control basically were not designed to alleviate the incidence of challenge. However, to what extent could management afford to alter its decision pattern in order to avoid challenges to its "rights"?

If no other goals were considered important, then the findings of our research could be used as the blueprint for a new, challenge-free mode of operation. The program would involve the spacing of activities to obtain an even flow, a constant rate of change. Moreover, as protests were highly likely when several heat-inducing factors became active simultaneously, the objection-minimizing manager should avoid this situation. At the most, only one friction-prone factor should be permitted to operate at a time.

For a given series of decisions, characteristically long runs for one outcome should be shunned. Long runs, especially with regard to the assignment of work to the inside forces, undoubtedly did serve to reinforce worker expectations that this course would continue. Consequently, the severity of their reaction to a change to contracting-out tended to be heightened. More frequent alternation between decisions to use inside and outside forces might tend to reduce the status of these expectations from a major to a minor factor.

However, there are real limitations to the feasibility of many of these measures. For one thing, long-run commitments may prohibit alternation between the two courses of action as well as the employment of strategically designed spacing of events. Perhaps the manager will have to accept the role of his decision process as an inevitable generator of challenge, and the major use of findings such as ours may thus be confined to the prediction of the rate and timing of protest.

chapter 15

The Management Decision Process: Unity and Diversity in Patt

In our research it was not unreasonable to assume that technological factors would affect the contracting-out decision process, all the way from the number of levels involved to the criteria used for evaluating the final results. The continuous flow requirement in process industries and the emphasis on quantities of discrete items of consistent quality in fabrication dictated decision-making procedures that would serve these disparate needs adequately. Nor was it unreasonable to assume that diversity of approach to this decision would exist within the industrial organization—among persons fulfilling differing institutional roles. However, the exact nature of these technologically and institutionally imposed differences was much less apparent.

Our approach to the relationship between technology and managerial decision processes was limited to a particular problem area. For a more general picture, the reader is referred to an excellent British study of the relationships between systems of production and their associated organizational patterns of behavior (Woodward, 1958). This research found that, in contrast to fabrication industries, those of the process type had both a more flexible and a tighter organization. In process industries, duties and responsibilities were less clearly defined, and there were fewer management specialists. The distinction between line and staff was not so sharp, for technical proficiency was essential in line supervision. Structurally, the process firm had more levels of authority—a median of six as compared with four for mass-production fabrication firms—but the greater number of levels was combined with a shorter span of managerial control and consequently smaller work groups. Woodward concluded that process technology permitted less pressured, more relaxed human relations in the organization. Process technology was rated as more complex than fabrication, and this greater complexity was viewed as being conducive to the development of a more rational environment. Features of this environment were: centralized control, consistent bases for judgments and decisions, ease of measuring management performance objectively, and ease of replacing managers without disrupting the organization.

THE DECISION STRUCTURE

Centralization

Some of our findings were consistent with the Woodward portrayal of the relationship between technology and organizational structure. In the light of our discussion in Chapter 3, it seemed logical to expect that process technology would require a greater degree of centralized control of the maintenance function. Our survey data confirmed this fact. It was found that, in fabrication as in process industries, decisions involving major expenditures were made at the highest levels in the organization, although seven exceptions to this rule were found in fabrication and none in process. But in process industry firms, minor decisions also tended to move to the higher levels more frequently—in 40 per cent of the process plants and in only 16 per cent of the fabrication. The definition of major and minor decisions varied from plant to plant. In our research the relevant criterion for distinguishing between them was the one employed by management in a given company, rather than an arbitrary distinction that we might have established independently. The dividing line often was expressed in terms of dollar amounts.

The role of staff specialists

Another striking difference between the decision process in the two industry groups involved the extent to which various staff specialists participated. Industrial relations was a good example. In process firms, the decision tended to be confined more fully to those in the line. Thus, an operating division head would assume the industrial relations function and conduct relations with the union on matters concerning the decision to contract-out. Beyond this level, there may have remained only appeals to the plant manager and to arbitration.

The head of the mechanical division in a process plant regarded the time he devoted to industrial relations as a good investment. He noted:

> You win the cases right here in this office. You can tell it to them [the workers] in a way that makes sense. We impress on them that they have to compete with the contractors. I say to them, "If your wife hired a plumber for $5.00 an hour, and he didn't do a good job, you wouldn't have him come back again, would you?" They see that. The work goes to the man who does a good job at a reasonable price.

In most cases, industrial relations entered the scene during contract negotiations and whenever trouble erupted, but thus far we have not established the place of these specialists in the initial decision process. Quite the contrary, we have indicated that others were "infringing" on their jurisdiction. As a matter of fact, actual entry of industrial relations specialists into the decision process prior to union protests was rather rare, occurring in only 18 per cent of the companies. In most of these cases, the industrial relations manager gave advice in the initial stages of the decision, but in two firms industrial relations took an active role in the entire process.

Interestingly, all but one of the firms in which industrial relations entered in the initial stages fell in the same general category—large fabrication plants that had at one time done a considerable amount of their own maintenance and construction work. As a result of the heavy negative pressures, contracting-out became a labor relations issue, and the role of the industrial relations manager, which originally was limited to handling grievances over contracting-out, was "integrated backward" into the initial decision process.

The two cases in which industrial relations played a leading role in the decision were large fabricating plants, one in transportation equipment and the other in metal products. Both had separate internal construction divisions and had been accustomed to building plants in addition to performing craft maintenance work. Thus, the pressures to keep work inside were strong and were reinforced by a vigorous inside union stand. These factors plus the red tape of the industrial relations machinery discouraged wholesale contracting-out, to say the least. Nevertheless, the larger of the two companies farmed out about one hundred jobs a year. Top management was extremely anxious that nothing should go amiss. As trouble was most likely to arise in the industrial relations field, these specialists shepherded the entire process from the initial decision regarding the feasibility of the action to laying the groundwork in the plant and in the community and monitoring the process after work was underway in order to detect signs of potential trouble.

These specialists' influence on the decision process was not easy to measure. Initially their counsel tended to be conservative, for if trouble should develop, the responsibility was theirs. However, after a contract was let, they were eager to see that it was completed successfully. Inevitably, some cases wound up in the hands of an umpire or arbitrator, and in these instances the industrial relations manager forcibly defended management's right to contract-out. One of the two men noted that he "hated to lose a case on contracting-out." The company that contracted about one hundred jobs a year generally had to retract two or three of these. On the whole, the industrial relations managers ran safe, conservative programs, probably better suited to stable than to dynamic periods in the firm's history.

INFORMATION NEEDS

Information needs cited by managers in process and fabrication firms reflected differences in their orientation toward the contracting-out problem. Fifty-six per cent of the process managers gave first place to better information on costs as a means of improving their decision process. A refinery manager remarked, "We need better cost yardsticks for our decisions. We want to know the minimum number of people required to maintain this refinery. What is the best balance between contracting and doing work with our men? Where would we realize the greatest savings?"

Needless to say, fabrication company officers were not indifferent to the question of improving cost data. A smaller proportion, 32 per cent, cited this as their greatest information requirement. However,

their primary concern with other areas was notably greater. Labor relations and organizational problems assumed higher significance. Thus, forty per cent gave priority to better information about the implications that contracting-out policies and practices had for the union-management relationship, and 24 per cent accorded the same importance to contracting-out's effect on the internal organization of the company. In addition, a small group, 4 per cent, was concerned primarily about the impact of outside factors such as jurisdictional battles between unions and union-contractor relations. A manager in an electrical machinery plant noted, "We need information that will expose corrupt situations. At present, we have unions telling us which contractors to use, and we find our union people hitting the contractors for 'contributions.' We want to know how to bring an end to the politics in this decision."

In the process firms, smaller proportions expressed concern about developing information in the above areas. Twenty-five per cent primarily desired more knowledge about the effect of contracting-out policies and practices on the union-management relationship, and 19 per cent assigned first place to data regarding the effect on the internal organization of the company.

These differences in priorities assigned to various types of information again reflected the fact that management in fabrication firms recognized that contracting-out had undergone a substantial degree of institutionalization as a problem involving diverse interests. Management in process firms, on the other hand, was slower about coming around to this point of view and more inclined to regard this decision area as a part of management's "property."

MANAGEMENT CONSENSUS

In dealing with the union or other outside groups, the firm may appear to present a united decision front, especially when defending a completed action. However, our research indicated that management actually was far from being united on the contracting-out question. Special and conflicting interests existed. But one often assumes that these divergent interests exist only "unofficially"—that everyone has the same understanding about the nature of company policy and practice, even though they may disagree privately. Nevertheless, we found that differences in point of view were accompanied by differences in conceptions of the actual nature of matters such as company policy.

No one would anticipate complete agreement among members of management who were responding to a total of 160 coded items. Yet the amount of disagreement was surprising, especially in view of the fact that the questions involved perceptions of the ongoing situation rather than attitudes. As noted in Chapter 13, three-fourths of the plant engineers and four-fifths of the industrial relations officers disagreed at some point with operating management. Far from being random in nature, the direction and character of the disagreements were consistent with the institutional roles of the various parties. In the following pages we shall explore briefly some of the salient differences between various levels of operating management, engineering, and industrial relations with regard to decision structure, practice, policy, costs, and union influence.

Decision structure

Disagreement about the formal structure for the contracting-out decision was evidenced by managers in slightly over one-half the firms. Industrial relations specialists tended to describe the decision structure as more highly centralized than it actually was. Operating management generally "disagreed" in the direction of making a more accurate assessment of the true situation. This finding probably reflected the fact that industrial relations generally became involved in the kinds of decisions that demanded the attention of the higher echelons.

Practice

With reference to actual practices in the firm, some disagreement regarding the extent of contracting-out was found almost universally —in 90 per cent of the companies. Of all management groups, industrial relations erred most consistently in the direction of overestimating the actual amount of work being farmed out. Again the institutional role of the industrial relations manager typically meant that he became involved in disputes over actual or potential contracting-out, while jobs assigned to the inside forces were not called to his attention.

Had detailed records of contracting-out practice been maintained and disseminated throughout the firm, the widespread disagreement about the facts undoubtedly could have been reduced. However, such records often were assembled only after trouble stimulated their accumulation, and these often were only as accurate as ex post facto data collection permitted.

Policy

The general absence of systematic data collection and dissemination was associated with divergent views of company practice. However, it would seem that information with regard to basic company policy could be communicated with a fair degree of success, and, as a matter of fact, common understandings about the nature of company policy were fairly widespread. Yet, in one-third of the firms, disagreements existed, and, interestingly, all but one of these firms belonged in the fabrication category. The single exception in the process field was a rubber company. Top management expounded a policy of contracting-out as much work as possible, but middle management, industrial relations, and engineering cited a reverse policy of keeping work inside. In this case, the disagreement seemed to be caused by a lag in communicating a drastic shift in policy.

In general, the disagreements on the nature of company policy tended to follow patterns consistent with the institutional roles of the various managers and thus could be construed as selective perceptions of a problem area whose ambiguous and changing character fostered variability of this type. One-third of the firms reported recent policy changes with regard to contracting-out, with a 2:1 ratio in favor of moves toward increased contracting. Again, there was disagreement over the direction of the changes. Lower levels of management tended to exhibit an "inside" bias in giving their version, whereas engineering had a slight "outside" bias. Of all those who disagreed, the position of industrial relations was the most complex from the standpoint of analysis. There was no clear line of bias pro or con the two alternatives. A pattern of deviation not found among the other groups appeared. One might describe this pattern as the "no policy, no change" syndrome. In contrast to the specific positions taken by the other interests in the firm, industrial relations tended to view contracting-out as a less clear-cut area. Where others reported definite policies or changes, the industrial relations manager saw none. One-half of the industrial relations deviations took this form.

Industrial relations' view of management policy easily could have been conditioned by its organizationally ambiguous situation. It was placed squarely in the middle, between the inside and outside interests within the organization, and its assignments in effect involved the zealous defense of both. From the standpoint of the firm, the industrial relations function was expected to keep management's right to contract-out intact. While industrial relations was held responsible for losses in this area, these specialists often felt frustrated about their ability to fulfill the role of protector of rights. Industrial relations managers noted that they lacked control over potential sources of loss. In describing his situation, one of them commented about the lack of cooperation from line management:

> What do those fellows care? They want to look good right now. Losing rights doesn't bother them. They'll make a deal with the union or take chances on a risky contract that opens up the whole issue. By the time the thing catches up with us, they're promoted to headquarters or they're

a big boss at some other company. They leave us holding the bag, and we get the blame when there's trouble over contracting-out. That's what happens if we don't stand over them day and night, and how are we going to do that?

At the same time, these managers were assigned the task of holding down inside work force agitation for restrictions on contracting-out. Therefore, industrial relations also had to pursue a program of defending the interests of the inside worker. A department manager benefited directly if contracting-out improved his cost position, but industrial relations received no accolades for accomplishments of this type. For the industrial relations manager, rewards were forthcoming when contracting-out involved "no trouble" for the firm.

The total result was a favoring of a flexible, "take-it-easy" strategy and an avoidance of definite commitments that might serve to stir up trouble. Thus, the industrial relations manager's view of policy conformed to a need for a shifting base for operations. In addition to those who claimed "no policy" when one actually existed, there were others who tended to compensate for the prevailing position by taking a contrary view of current policy. In an automobile plant universally noted for its extensive contracting, the head of industrial relations stated, "We try to give our men as much work as we possibly can. We believe that they must come first."

Costs

Lack of consensus on cost matters was found in one-third of the companies. Interestingly, only 10 per cent of these represented firms in which there also was disagreement about policy. Thus, by and large, these were not overlapping groups. Again, all except one case of disagreement on costs were found in fabrication firms. The incidence of disagreement in the single process (chemical) plant was the lowest of the entire group. While both the plant engineer and the industrial relations manager agreed that contracting-out was cheaper, the latter presented a more conservative estimate of the extent of actual savings. The two also disagreed on the size of the overhead charge used in calculating internal costs. Industrial relations reported that 100 per cent of direct labor cost was added; the plant engineer stated that the figure ranged between 40 and 55 per cent.

Almost to a man, lower-level operating management tended to rate contracting-out as more costly. However, in about 70 per cent of the cases in which top management and engineering presented deviant views, their disagreements were biased in the opposite direction. Industrial relations was split in direction of disagreement, with half these managers tending toward higher and half toward lower estimates of costs for the internal operation.

For the sample as a whole, slightly over 20 per cent of the companies lacked the information needed to make judgments regarding the relative cost differential for specific activities. However, among the nearly 80 per cent of the firms in which at least some data had been assembled, it was found that 30 per cent of the industrial relations managers did not have these data. (Twenty-two per cent of this group were in fabrication firms and 8 per cent in process establishments.) A small group, 5 per cent, stated that they had great difficulty in obtaining cost data and attributed this to the fact that they dealt with an outside group, namely, the union. One of these industrial relations men remarked, "Cost information is treated like a military secret in this company. Even when this office is called in we have trouble getting the information. They don't trust us with cost figures because we deal with the union. We are supposed to argue about timing and skills and keep costs out of the picture."

However, the others who were not given cost information seemed to be in this position simply because their need for it was not recognized. Their function apparently was defined as defender of an absolute entity, rights, and, for this role, cost data were regarded as irrelevant.

Union influence

Our research revealed that there was no united front of management agreement about the extent of union influence on the contracting-out decision. In fact, there was disagreement on this matter in two-fifths of the firms, and again the patterns of disagreement were consistent with the institutional roles of the various managerial interest groups. The nonspecialists in this area—top and middle management and plant engineering—tended to overrate the extent of the union's influence. Among the firms with disagreements, half the top and middle managers made this error, as well as one-fourth of the engineers. In cases in which the union, as indicated by our ratings (see Chapter 6), did exert at least some influence on the decision, 30 per cent of the engineers still were unable to make a judgment.

In general, those who were remote from the union tended to overestimate its influence on the contracting-out decision, while those who engaged in day-to-day dealings with the union were able to make a more accurate assessment of its impact. In one-half the cases of disagreement, the industrial relations manager tended to rate the union's influence lower than the other managers. In the remainder of the sample, industrial relations' rating was equal to that of the other management groups, with the exception of one instance of a higher rating. Interestingly, in this single case, a process plant engineer handled union relations with regard to contracting-out, while the industrial relations manager stood on the side lines.

Management disagreements in process and fabrication industries

Our discussion of management disagreements regarding various facets of the contracting-out decision process has emphasized the differences between process and fabrication industries. In our research we noted that, in contrast to process industries, fabrication had many more disagreements on matters of policy and costs. This situation was reflected in the differences between the average disagreement scores for plants in the two industry groups. The average number of disagreements in process industry firms was significantly smaller than the number in fabrication. In fabrication, the average was 9.64 per plant; in process, it was only 5.83.

Our findings regarding industry-based differences in respect to the extent of management agreement were especially interesting in light of Woodward's work (1958). This study reported differences in the extent of management agreement that favored process over mass and unit production. However, the data were expressed in general terms and made no reference to specific decisions or managerial problems such as contracting-out. Woodward attributed the higher agreement in process management to the greater rationality that was possible under this system. In other words, disagreement apparently could not be attributed largely to poor management or poor communication. Rather, disagreement was found to be a product of technologies that produced poor or uncertain information.

The British study also pointed to an era when many of our findings about the management decision process presumably will fade away. In the place of the pressure group and separable managerial interests, one can look forward to an era of rationality when managers generally will become interchangeable units from the standpoint of the operation of the decision process. Decisions will no longer be reversed as they move up the plant hierarchy, and a manager's replacement will make decisions in much the same way as his predecessor.

Certainly, in our sample the influence of pressure groups in management was enhanced by uncertainties in information, for these uncertainties provided the leeway for maneuvering and gaining position. In the course of future technological development, it is possible that the pressure-group model for the contracting-out decision may become obsolete.

MANAGEMENT RIGHTS AND THE DECISION PROCESS: SUMMARY AND ANALYSIS

In Part VI, we have turned the tables: instead of scrutinizing the union, we have examined seldom recognized ways in which management has generated challenges to its rights. Usually, management has been given credit for accomplishing this negatively valued mission on the basis of actions in a single case. Thus, an industrial relations expert may point the finger of scorn at a manager who contracted-out a big job at the very moment when qualified inside men were being placed on layoff status.

But why should such an incident take place? One might attribute it to managerial obtuseness or bullheaded insistence on "rights," but at this point our research findings will prove to be useful. The manager who undertook such an action might do so, in part, because prior experience indicated that no serious consequences would ensue. He might not realize that past successes could provide no security because of the instability of the underlying situation. In our study we found that the worker's concept of a fair share was not a constant quantity derived from a body of tradition. Rather, the calculation of a fair share changed in response to what was both needed and available—more specifically, in terms of our findings, in response to changes in departmental activities and in the number of men on layoff. Thus, although the mere existence of layoffs might serve as a tentative warning, a manager should be doubly alert if the rate of layoffs has been increasing or, even more seriously, if this increasing rate of layoffs also has been accompanied by an increasing rate of departmental activity.

In estimating their own reaction to a situation, we found that the various inside and outside interests intuitively assessed their position in terms of the ongoing process in the firm. But in assessing the position of other parties, these interest groups focused on the case at hand and, in so doing, missed critical data necessary for the calculation of the strength of potential counterpressures.

Lacking information about the nature of the total process, an outside observer also might have encountered seemingly inexplicable phenomena. For instance, he might have wondered why workers failed to object to management's "breaking" prior labor-management agreements with regard to contracting out—failed to the extent that prior agreements did not serve as a satisfactory predictor of challenge. Yet these events became comprehensible when we examined the individual case from the standpoint of its relation to various key aspects of the decision process.

In this research, we attempted to pinpoint the dynamic aspects of the management decision process that served to generate protest. We found that the best predictors of challenge were the status of the maintenance and construction function as measured by the current rate of spending for this activity and the status of layoffs as reflected in the rate of change in their number. Thus, layoffs did not represent simply a specific quantity, registered at a particular point in time. Rather, layoffs were a dynamic function proceeding variously at an increasing, decreasing, or constant rate. An increasing rate of change in layoffs served as a stimulus to a higher rate of challenge, and when both predictors recorded increasing rates of change, the protest function generally moved into high gear. We found a situation in which agreements and management concessions were made during active periods when the pressure was high and were ignored subsequently in "latent" periods when pressures diminished. The concept of job property proved to be a variable phenomenon despite the fact that collective bargainers and other dispute-settlers have treated it as a fixed entity. A realistic contract clause probably should provide for "contingent" enforcement!

Operationalizing our pressure-group decision model involved the specification and testing of independent stimuli of challenge. We have moved some distance from the initial stages of vague conceptualization, but much work remains to be done. The findings reported here could very well be subject to qualifications that have yet to be established. As far as our methodological approach is concerned, the measurement of the rate of change of the key factors operating in a given situation gives promise of having considerable value in the development of predictors of behavior in the field of labor-management relations—a field in which "hard" data and responsive group reactions are intimately intermixed.

Our research indicated that members of management in a given firm had diverse perceptions of their company's actual situation with regard to contracting-out. The proportion of firms exhibiting this diversity ranged from 90 per cent for data regarding actual practice to one-third for information on policies and differential costs. These findings served to underline the existence of diverse interests in management as well as the extent to which institutional roles and systems of reward dictated managerial position on contracting-out.

These data also provided a clue to factors that served to enhance the significance of the pressure-group model for the contracting-out decision. Insofar as the successful exertion of pressures was facilitated by the uncertainty and disparity of information in the system, the various interests possessed a fairly fertile field for pressure activities.

The relationship of technological factors to the disparity in managerial perceptions proved to be an interesting area. Our data indicated that, in contrast to managers in process industries, those in fabrication showed a much greater diversity of perception regarding the nature of policies and differential costs; in process industries, the contracting-out problem was more closely tied to the central core of the operation and was handled in a more highly centralized decision structure. The research of others has indicated a strong relationship between modern process technology and a rational approach to decision-making. But a more exact answer to the question asked at the beginning of Part VI—Management's right to defend what?—seemed to be: the right to defend a complex process that has fathered group-pressure activities and has played a part in the generation of protest to its output.

Conclusion

In this book we have explored the organizational meaning of the management rights issue and tested some of the major tenets of the rights approach to industrial relations. We have examined the management rights issue in general, and we have also looked at it in greater detail through the "eyes" of a problem involving changes in the organization of the work of the industrial firm—the contracting-out of maintenance and construction activities. In so doing, we were burdened to some extent with whatever was unique about this particular problem, but, at the same time, we could trace its origins in depth and move beyond the commonly found inventory-taking approach to the management rights field.

Contracting-out, we found, was not necessarily a "typical" management rights question, if such a question exists. But it was a crucial one, and the kind of issue that was coming increasingly to the fore—the work rules dispute that opens up in the face of technological change and diminishing job opportunities. In the light of rivalry between inside and outside unions, competition among contractors' organizations, manufacturers serving both as the independent contractors' client and competitor, inside service departments opposed to contracting by others in the same firm, etc., questions of rights constituted a superstructure resting on a base of strong and conflicting interests within management and within labor. In the process, a classical economic problem—the vertical integration or disintegration of the firm—was converted into a highly "political" affair.

In some ways this issue may provide a blueprint for a growing group of management rights questions that possess a complex structure of interests, that are neither clear-cut nor readily communicable to neutral observers, and that have variables that defy attempts at measurement. To complicate our study further, serious flaws appeared when we attempted to apply traditional management rights "dogma" to a problem of this type. Neat pronouncements that management did or did not have the right to contract-out proved to be only temporary matters, applicable largely to the immediate case.

In general, management seemed to gain by default its "right" to contract-out. Flexibility, sufficient to adapt to current needs, was provided, not by grace of foresighted planning or insightful dispute settlement, but rather by virtue of the difficulty of any one group's mapping out and effectuating a strong program of control. The diverse and competing groups were limited to competition within the range of the few, and not always significant, variables they were able to control.

Our data gave no indication that within industry the management rights theme was either extinct or in the process of being submerged by more "modern" approaches. However, strict no discussion legalists were rare—as were those who conducted cooperative union-management relations with respect to our substantive issue. But the practicing legalist may have had an influence far beyond his numbers, for, ironically, his activities encouraged the counterlegalism of other groups, such as governmental boards. Less avid advocates of rights dogma stood in danger of being swept up in the mass of red tape that potentially could emerge.

The strong rights position of certain firms has been attributed to managerial philosophy, but we found that with respect to our substantive issue a firm stand on management rights was neither idiosyncratic nor automatic. Rather, it was a function of the structure of the organization and of the requirements of the technological organization of work, especially in relation to the distinction between process and fabrication industries. The ability of the inside union to "invade" management territory also was related to factors of structure and technology.

Did the management rights focus on industrial relations have an effect on organizational process? In day-to-day organizational life this approach found expression in programs designed to defend rights. While defenses of rights presumably were conducted in the interest of more efficient operation, did these programs actually serve this objective? Or did efforts to retain and regain rights introduce practices that hampered organizational effectiveness? Too frequently, little consideration was given to the latter possibility. Our data seemed to indicate that these programs had blind spots. They concentrated either on the immediate defense of management property or, if this strategy had failed, on a wholesale recovery of the same. Middle-range solutions, based on a sensitivity to the build-up of pressures and directed at the smoothing and regulating of organizational process, were largely missing. Moreover, some short-run defenses were readily taken over by the union, and, in this sense, managerial legalists actually engineered invasion routes for others.

But the recurring theme in our data on this particular rights issue was relativism, not absolutism—attention with half an ear, not a whole ear. Thus, the ultimate effect of both union "offenses" and management "defenses" was cushioned by their inconsistent usage. In terms of day-to-day relations among those inside and outside the firm, the really basic property concept for management and workers alike involved not absolute notions such as rights, but rather the notion of equity— was one receiving a fair share of current activities, a fair share of the work available? As we have seen, the rate at which workers' protests (challenges to management "rights") took place was a function of this type of calculation regarding fair shares. Thus, in practice, the concept of workers' job property rights—and of managerial rights—proved to be a variable rather than a constantly active phenomenon. In effect, rights often became a grander cause with which to associate one's concept of a fair share.

It was a big leap from the variable world of organizational life to that of the collective bargainers and dispute-settlers, who in effect had the task, not of bringing order out of chaos as some have hinted, but rather of making fixed pronouncements on a variable process. While the inside and outside managers and crews concerned themselves with getting a fair share and a good and varied diet of work, the collective bargainer focused on abstractions such as decision criteria, the arbitrator and the National Labor Relations Board on managerial good faith, and the interunion peace-pact formulators on black, white, and gray areas and established work relationships. The collective bargainers and dispute-settlers typically dealt with only a small slice of the total organizational problem and a select few of the relationships involved, most frequently that between inside workers and management. In addition, they added problems that they themselves uniquely defined and attempted to solve.

Much in the fashion of the immediate parties, dispute-settlers sidestepped the absolute question of rights and instead turned their attention to other property-based questions, such as the damages suffered by those involved in a controversy. Middle-range organizational reasons for contracting-out were not considered, as the managerial action now might become simply a reasonable business decision or an attempt to undermine the bargaining unit—an action with either good or evil intent. When these decisions were returned to the organization, diverse —not united—interests within it "processed" the output of the arbiters and at times quickly turned awards and agreements that might have appeared to initiate long-run programs into short-run propositions.

Clearly, strict legalism lost out in its bid for status as a vital force, for bargaining over rights issues such as contracting-out was a diffuse process, spreading far beyond the confines of formal structures. Inevitably, study committees and other more diffuse means were devised to solve disputes relating to contracting-out and other issues of equal complexity.

But devising better battlegrounds will not, in the end, win the battle in an organizational and managerial sense. In the final analysis, the basic determinants of the use of inside or outside forces were technological and economic factors. Moreover, the key to advancement was flexible adaptation to new situations, not protecting ephemeral rights or clinging to obsolete property. As so often is the case, "victory" belongs to the group that is seeking new opportunities: to the inside union that accommodated to a changing concept of the employment relationship by organizing all workers associated with a given process, regardless of their source of employment; to the inside service manager who added a contract operation to his roster of activities; to the contractor and craft union who adapted their organizations to the requirements of continuing inside work. All these were taking steps away from a base in the past. Moreover, lack of ability to adapt in this fashion often stemmed from organizationally imposed rigidities that had little or nothing to do with having "lost one's rights."

The management rights problems that we observed arose partly because of the absence of smoothly functioning, organizational bases for the conduct of continuing relations between insiders and outsiders. In order to end this organizational blocking, there was a need to restructure organizations, rather than work within their limitations. In the course of technological developments, it is possible that, in some cases, the distinction between the inside and outside forces will diminish to the point where the differential view of the rights and equities of those inside and outside the firm gradually will be erased. In turn, some of the impetus for the power struggle that we observed may disappear as moves to reorganize the work of the industrial firm are reflected in a restructuring of the organization of inside and outside management and of their respective work forces.

In this sense, management rights issues of this type are not grand causes but rather just another aspect of organizational life—symptomatic of problems that can be ameliorated, not through legalistic affirmations or denial, but rather through means such as structural adjustments that will eliminate their underlying cause.

Bibliography

Abbott, Charles G. Buy, Lease, Share a Computer—or Utilize a Service Bureau. *Computers and Automation*, 1960, 9(2):2–26.

Abegglen, James G. *The Japanese Factory*. The Free Press of Glencoe, New York, 1957.

Adelman, M. A. Concept and Statistical Measurement of Vertical Integration. In *Business Concentration and Price Policy*. (A Report of the National Bureau of Economic Research.) Princeton University Press, Princeton, N.J., 1955.

Alger, Chadwick F. The External Bureaucracy in U.S. Foreign Affairs. *Administrative Science Quarterly*, 1962, 7(1): 50–78.

Bain, J. S. *Industrial Organization*. John Wiley & Sons, Inc., New York, 1959.

Bendix, Reinhard. *Work and Authority in Industry*. John Wiley & Sons, Inc., New York, 1956.

Bergen, Harold B. Management Prerogatives. *Harvard Business Review*, 1940, 18(2):275–284.

Berliner, Joseph S. *Factory and Manager in the U.S.S.R.* Harvard University Press, Cambridge, Mass., 1957, pp. 175–177.

Blough, Roger M. My Side of the Steel Price Story. *Look,* 1963, 27(2):19–23.

Born, Roscoe. Labor Split. *Wall Street Journal,* Jan. 15, 1959, pp. 1 and 12.
————. Rift in Labor. *Wall Street Journal,* May 23, 1961, pp. 1 and 16.
Boyce, Carroll W., and Carl G. Wyder. Maintenance Management Practices Today. *Factory,* 1958, 116(10): 90–107.
Brandt, Floyd S. *Independent and National Unionism in the Oil Refining Industry.* Ph.D thesis. Harvard University Graduate School of Business Administration, 1960.
British Productivity Council. *Industrial Engineering.* British Productivity Council, London, England, 1954.
Brown, Emily C. Interests and Rights of Soviet Workers. *Industrial and Labor Relations Review,* 1963, 16(2):254–278.
Brown, Leo C. The Shifting Distribution of the Right to Manage. *Proceedings of the First Annual Meeting, Industrial Relations Research Association.* Champaign, Ill., 1949, pp. 132–144.
Burns, A. R. *Decline of Competition.* McGraw-Hill Book Company, Inc., New York, 1936.
Bussard, B., and F. Schlessel. Trouble-shooter Tells the Ups and Downs of Subcontracting from Japan. *Factory,* 1961, 119(2):84–89.
Caples, W. G. Keeping Management Functions Out of Collective Bargaining. *American Economic Security,* 1955, 12:19–20.
Chamberlain, Neil W. *Union Challenge to Management Control.* Harper & Row, Publishers, Incorporated, New York, 1948.
————. Union Impact on the Management Function. In *Labor.* McGraw-Hill Book Company, Inc., New York, 1958, chap. 12.
Chandler, Margaret K. Garment Manufacture. In *Labor-Management Relations in Illini City, Vol. I.* University of Illinois Institute of Labor and Industrial Relations, Champaign, Ill., 1953, pp. 379–538.
————. Extent of Union Influence. In *Labor-Management Relations in Illini City, Vol. II.* University of Illinois Institute of Labor and Industrial Relations, Champaign, Ill., 1954, pp. 131–211.
————. Competition between the Inside and Outside Labor Force for the Work of the Industrial Firm. *Proceedings of the Fourteenth Annual Meeting, Industrial Relations Research Association.* Madison, Wis., 1962, pp. 334–345.
———— and Leonard R. Sayles. *Contracting-out: A Study of Management Decision-making.* Columbia University Graduate School of Business, New York, 1959.
Coase, R. H. The Nature of the Firm. *Economica,* 1937, 4(16):389.
Commons, John R. American Shoemakers, 1648–1895: A Sketch of Industrial Evolution. *Quarterly Journal of Economics,* 1909, 24:39–83.
————. Jurisdictional Disputes. In *Wertheim Lectures on Industrial Relations.* Harvard University Press, Cambridge, Mass., 1928, pp. 93–123.
Cook, Paul W. Decentralization and the Transfer Price Problem. *Journal of Business,* 1955, 28(2):87–94.
Crawford, Donald A. The Arbitration of Disputes over Subcontracting. In Jean T. McKelvey (ed.), *Challenges to Arbitration.* Proceedings of the Thirteenth Annual Meeting of the National Academy of Arbitrators. Bureau of National Affairs, Washington, 1960, pp. 51–72.

————. Contracting Out. In G. W. Taylor and E. D. Shils (eds.), *Industrial Relations in the 1960's*. University of Pennsylvania Labor Relations Council, Philadelphia, Pa., 1961.

Culliton, James W. *Make or Buy*. Business Research Study No. 27. Harvard Business School Division of Research, Boston, Mass., 1942.

Cyert, R.M., E. A. Feigenbaum, and J. G. March. Models in a Behavioral Theory of the Firm. *Behavioral Science*, 1959, 4(2):81–95.

Dalton, Melville, *Men Who Manage*. John Wiley & Sons, Inc., New York, 1959.

Dash, G. Allan, Jr. The Arbitration of Subcontracting Disputes. In *The Arbitration of Two Management Rights Issues: Work Assignment and Contracting Out*. New York State School of Industrial and Labor Relations, Ithaca, N.Y., 1960, pp. 70–84. Republished in *Industrial and Labor Relations Review*, 1963, 16(2):208–215.

Davis, H. S., G. W. Taylor, C. C. Balderston, and A. Bezanson. *Vertical Integration in the Textile Industries*. Wharton School, University of Pennsylvania, Philadelphia, Pa., 1938.

Davis, Louis E. The Effects of Automation on Job Design. *Industrial Relations*, 1962, 2(1):53–71.

Day, John S. *Subcontracting Policy in the Airframe Industry*. Harvard Business School Division of Research, Boston, Mass., 1956.

Dean, Joel. Decentralization and Intra-company Pricing. *Harvard Business Review*, 1955, 33 (4):65–74.

DeChazeau, M. G., and A. E. Kahn. *Integration and Competition in the Petroleum Industry*. Yale University Press, New Haven, Conn., 1959.

Derber, Milton. Management and Union Rights in Industrial Establishments. *Current Economic Comment*, 1960, 22(2):3–11.

————, W. E. Chalmers, and Milton Edelman. Union Participation in Plant Decision Making. *Industrial and Labor Relations Review*, 1961, 15(1):83–101.

Dobe, H. Donald. Fundamentals of Contract Maintenance. *Fourteenth Annual Plant Engineering and Maintenance Show*, a production of Clap and Poliak, Inc., Chicago, Ill., January, 1963.

Drucker, Peter F. Management Must Manage. *Harvard Business Review*, 1950, 28(2):80–87.

Dunlop, John T. *Industrial Relations Systems*. Holt, Rinehart and Winston, Inc., New York, 1958.

Edelman, Murray. Symbols and Political Quiescence. *American Political Science Review*, 1960, 54(3):695–704.

Elonka, Steve. Can CM Bring Down Your Zooming Costs? *Power*, 1961, 48(5):185–189.

Field, A. W. Shall We Subcontract? *The Manager*, 1955, 23(10):769–773.

Frank, L. K. Significance of Industrial Integration. *Journal of Political Economy*, 1925, 33(2):179–195.

Franklin, Roger. P.E.R.T. for the Electrical Contractor. *Qualified Contractor*, 1962, 27(10):85–90.

Gort, Michael. *Diversification and Integration in American Industry*. Princeton University Press, Princeton, N.J., 1962.

Greenbaum, Marcia L. The Arbitration of Subcontracting Disputes: An Addendum. *Industrial and Labor Relations Review,* 1963, 16(2):221–234.

Griesinger, Frank H. Pros and Cons of Leasing Equipment. *Harvard Business Review,* 1955, 33(2):75–89.

Harlan, Neil E. *Management Control in Airframe Subcontracting.* Harvard Business School Division of Research, Boston, Mass., 1956.

Higgin, Gurth. *Communications in the Building Industry.* Tavistock Institute of Human Relations, London, England, 1963.

Higgins, Carter C. Make or Buy Re-examined. *Harvard Business Review,* 1955, 33(2):109–119.

Hirshleifer, J. On the Economics of the Divisionalized Firm. *Journal of Business,* 1957, 29(3):172–184.

Ito, Taikichi. Structural Peculiarities and Labor Problems of Small Business in Japan. In *Small Business in Japan.* The Japan Times Ltd., Tokyo, 1960, pp. 147–170.

Jacobs, Paul. *Dead Horse and the Featherbird.* Center for the Study of Democratic Institutions, Santa Barbara, Calif., 1962.

Jewkes, John. Factors in Industrial Integration. *Quarterly Journal of Economics,* 1930, 44(3):633.

Justin, Jules. How to Preserve Management Rights under the Labor Contract. *Labor Law Journal,* 1960, 11(3):189–215.

Kahn, Mark. Jurisdictional Developments in Organized Labor. In *New Dimensions in Collective Bargaining.* Harper & Row, Publishers, Incorporated, New York, 1959, pp. 19–21.

Kahn, Robert. The Arbitration of Disputes over Subcontracting, Discussants Comments. In Jean T. McKelvey (ed.), *Challenges to Arbitration.* Proceedings of the Thirteenth Annual Meeting of the National Academy of Arbitrators. Bureau of National Affairs, Washington, 1960, pp. 72–77.

Kaldor, Nicholas. The Equilibrium of the Firm. *Economics Journal,* 1934, 44(1):60–76.

Karsh, Bernard, and Solomon B. Levine. Present Dilemmas of the Japanese Labor Movement. *Labor Law Journal,* 1962, 13(7):541–548.

Klassen, E. T. Preserving Management's Responsibility to Manage. *Problems and Practices in Industrial Relations.* American Management Association Report No. 16, New York, 1958.

Knight, O. A. On Contract Maintenance. *IUD Digest,* 1961, 6(4):31–35.

Koontz, H. D., and C. J. O'Donnell. *Principles of Management.* McGraw-Hill Book Company, Inc., New York, 1959, pp. 175–196.

Kuhn, James W. *Bargaining in Grievance Settlement.* Columbia University Press, New York, 1961, pp. 144–190.

Leontief, W. W. *The Structure of the American Economy.* Harvard University Press, Cambridge, Mass., 1941.

Levine, Solomon B. *Industrial Relations in Postwar Japan.* University of Illinois Press, Urbana, Ill., 1958.

Lipstreu, Otis. Management Rights: Conflict or Cooperation? *Labor Law Journal,* 1956, 7(9):558–63.

Lunden, Leon E. Subcontracting Clauses in Major Agreements, Part I. *Monthly Labor Review*, 1961, 84(6):579–586.

———. Subcontracting Clauses in Major Agreements, Part II. *Monthly Labor Review*, 1961, 84(7):715–723.

Maintaining Production for America. Construction Industry Joint Conference, Washington, D.C., 1959.

Make It or Buy It: Which Pays Off? *Business Week*, July 3 and Aug. 13, 1954.

McPherson, W. H. Grievance Settlement in Western Europe. *Proceedings of the Fifteenth Annual Meeting, Industrial Relations Research Association.* Madison, Wis., 1963, pp. 26–35.

Meyers, Frederic. Job Protection in France and Britain. *Labor Law Journal*, 1962, 13(7):566–575.

National Association of Manufacturers. *Preserving the Management Function in Collective Bargaining.* Employee Relations Department Information Bulletin No. 24, New York, May, 1956, p. 12.

Northrup, Herbert R. The UAW's Influence on Management Decisions in the Automobile Industry—an Outsider's Point of View. *Proceedings of the Seventh Annual Meeting, Industrial Relations Research Association.* Madison, Wis., 1955.

Ornati, Oscar A. *Jobs and Workers in India.* New York State School of Labor and Industrial Relations, Ithaca, N.Y., 1955.

O'Shaughnessy, James B. Management Rights: Control or Anarchy. *Labor Law Journal*, 1957, 8(1):25–27.

Oxenfeldt, A. R., and M. Watkins. *Make or Buy: Factors Affecting Executive Decisions.* Consultant Reports on Current Business Problems. McGraw-Hill Book Company, Inc., New York, 1956.

Paton, William A., and R. L. Dixon. *Make or Buy Decisions in Tooling for Mass Production.* Michigan Business Report No. 35. University of Michigan Bureau of Business Research, Ann Arbor, Mich., 1961.

Raskin, A. H. Labor Is Cheered by Reuther Pact. *New York Times*, Jan. 27, 1959, p. 41.

Rees, Albert. *The Economics of Trade Unions.* University of Chicago Press, Chicago, 1962, pp. 136–150.

Report of Proceedings of the Fiftieth Anniversary Convention of the Building and Construction Trades, A.F.L.–C.I.O. Building and Construction Trades Department, A.F.L.–C.I.O., Washington, D.C., 1958.

Robinson, E. A. G. *The Structure of Competitive Industry.* University of Chicago Press, Chicago, 1962.

Rogers, David, and Ivar E. Berg. Occupation and Ideology: The Case of the Small Businessman. *Human Organization*, 1961, 20(3):103–111.

Sayles, Leonard R. *The Behavior of Industrial Work Groups.* John Wiley & Sons, Inc., New York, 1958.

Schedler, Carl R. Subcontracting under the Labor-Management Agreement. *Arbitration Journal*, 1955, 10(3):131–137.

Slichter, S. H., J. J. Healy, and E. R. Livernash. *The Impact of Collective Bargaining on Management.* The Brookings Institution, Washington, D.C., 1960, pp. 280–316.

Sobel, I., and L. Brown. *A Review of the St. Louis Construction Industry's Market.* St. Louis Construction Industry Joint Conference, St. Louis, Mo., 1961.

Starr, Albert R. Using Outside Contractors. In L. C. Morrow (ed.), *Maintenance Engineering Handbook.* McGraw-Hill Book Company, Inc., New York, 1957, pp. I-89–I-81.

Steelworkers vs. Warrior and Gulf Navigation Co. *Daily Labor Report* 119. Bureau of National Affairs, Washington, 1960.

Stieber, Jack. Work Rules and Practices in Mass Production Industries. *Proceedings of Fourteenth Annual Meeting, Industrial Relations Research Association.* Madison, Wis., 1962, pp. 399–412.

Stigler, George J. The Division of Labor Is Limited by the Extent of the Market. *Journal of Political Economy,* 1951, 59(3):185–193.

———. The Economies of Scale. *Journal of Law and Economics,* 1958, 1(3):54–71.

Strauss, George. Tactics of Lateral Relationship. *Administrative Science Quarterly,* 1962, 7(2):161–186.

Tannenbaum, R. Managerial Decision-making. *Journal of Business,* 1950, 23(1):22–39.

Thorp, Willard L. *The Integration of Industrial Operations.* U.S. Bureau of the Census, 1924.

———, Walter F. Crowder, and associates. *The Structure of Industry.* Temporary National Economic Committee Monograph No. 27. Government Printing Office, Washington, 1941.

Torrence, G. W. *Management's Right to Manage.* Bureau of National Affairs, Washington, 1959, pp. 17–33.

Turnbull, John G. The Small Business Enterprise and the Management Prerogative Issue. *Industrial and Labor Relations Review,* 1948, 3(1):33–49.

Van de Water, John R. Growth of Third Party Power in the Settlement of Industrial Disputes. *Labor Law Journal,* 12(12):1135–1160.

Verge, Pierre. *Contracting-out Issues in the Province of Quebec.* M.A. thesis. McGill University Industrial Relations Centre, Montreal, Canada, 1962.

Weber, Arnold R. The Craft-Industrial Issue Revisited: A Study of Union Government. *Industrial and Labor Relations Review,* 1963, 16(3):381–404.

Wirtz, Willard. The New Role of Government in Collective Bargaining. *Qualified Contractor,* 1963, 28(2):49–50.

Woods, H. D., and S. Ostry. *Labour Policy and Labour Economics in Canada.* The Macmillan Company, New York, 1962.

Woodward, Joan. *Management and Technology.* Department of Scientific and Industrial Research, London, England, 1958.

Young, Stanley. The Question of Management Prerogatives. *Industrial and Labor Relations Review,* 1963, 16(2):240–253.

#

Index

Abbott Publishing Company, NLRB decision, 239

Abegglen, James G., 17

Acceptable work, cultural definition of, 180–181

Account-poaching, in the Soviet Union, 22
  in the United States, 154, 162

Adelman, M. A., 53

Airline industry, contracting-out in, 171–172
  disputes, pilots and flight engineers, 182, 187
  technological change and rights issues in, 171–172

Alger, Chadwick F., 7

Anonymity and neutrality as goals of contractor, 136

Arbitration awards, 79–81, 203–212, 252
  assessment of, 208–209, 212, 252

Arbitration awards, assignment of fair shares in, 212
  decision criteria, 205–209
    impact of technological change on, 211–212
  division of work between inside and outside forces, 208, 212
  effect on parties in dispute, 79–81
  prediction of outcome, 209–212

Arbitrators, changing role in contracting-out disputes, 204–205
  effect of Warrior-Gulf decision on, 204–205

Automatic process control effect on maintenance cost calculations, 43

Avoidance defense, managerial, 91–95
  avoiding coercive comparisons, 92, 93

Avoidance defense, managerial, frequency of use, 92
  restructuring work and work force, 93–95

Bacon-Davis Act, as a jurisdictional wedge, 251
  and missile site disputes, 233–235
Barter defenses, managerial, definition of, 89
  equalizing conditions for inside and outside forces, 102–103
  firms using only, 105–107
  frequency of use, 97–98, 101, 103, 104
  letters of intent, 103–105
  notification of union, 97–100
  old versus new work, 100–102
  weaknesses of, 116
Bendix, Reinhard, 32
Berg, Ivar E., 11
Bergen, Harold B., 87
Berliner, Joseph S., 15, 22
Bid-shopping, 131
Black, white, and gray formula, assessment of, 196–198
  definition of, 192
  division of work between inside and outside forces, 192
Blough, Roger M., 100
Blue label shop, 123
Bogus work and Typographical Union, 184
Brandt, Floyd S., 43, 52
Bridgeport Pact, 195
Brown, Emily C., 22
Brown, Leo C., 45, 87
Building Trades Department, AFL-CIO, 194
Bureau of Labor Statistics, survey of agreements on contracting-out, 217–218, 223–224
Business cycle factors, effect on contracting-out, 38
  and vertical disintegration, 38–39
  and vertical integration, 38–39
Bussard, B., 17

Buyer-vendor model for outside relations of the firm, 10, 149, 162

Canada, arbitration in, and legalism, 64–65
Caples, W. G., 85
Centralization of services, effect on management and workers, 152
Challenge, control of (*see* Protest, control of)
  prescriptions for avoiding, 290–291
Chalmers, W. E., 74, 90
Chamberlain, Neil W., 73, 75
Chandler, Margaret K., 11, 13
Client departments' relations with service departments, 153–156
Collective bargaining, 213–232
  assessment of, 214, 219, 253
  assignment of fair shares by, 213–214, 217–219, 232
  contrast with interunion pacts, 231
  contributions of, 229–232
  criteria specified in contract clauses, 219–224
  degree of permanence of agreements, 78–79
  division of work between inside and outside forces, 219
  major negotiations, 225–229
  structure of, 213
Communications Workers, dispute regarding established work relationships, 200
Competition between inside and outside forces, assets of inside forces, 173–174
  assets of outside forces, 173–174
  blocks to information flow, 44
  cost aspects of, 44–47
  degree of freedom in, 172
  effect of technological change on, 53, 173–174
  future developments, 175–176
  stronghold of inside forces, 173
  stronghold of outside forces, 173
Consensus, managerial, 297–302

Construction Associates, specialty contractors' joint venture, 145

Construction Industry Joint Conference, 128, 129

Construction industry subcontract system, 35

Construction work, contracting-out of major projects, 31
contracting-out of minor projects, 31

Contract clauses on contracting-out, incidence of, 107, 217–219
and management defenses, 107–108
restrictions imposed by, 107

Contract maintenance, definition of, 36, 131
project agreements, 129–130, 197
promotion of, 128–129

Contracting-out, in airline industry, 171–172
business cycle factors and, 38
interest in research on, 33
organizational explanation for, 156–157, 160–164
facilitation of procedural changes, 163
responsibility for employment relationship, 163
as a rights issue, 7–8, 88, 187
structure of group relationships for, 121–122

Contractors, basic orientation, the construction philosophy, 132–134, 137, 147
the maintenance philosophy, 136–137, 147
anonymity, and neutrality as goals, 136
fair share of work, 247–250
historic functions, 33, 127
relations with inside management, 11–12, 160–164, 248–250
norms for, 132–137, 161–163
reciprocity, 162, 248–250
sources of support for contractors, 248–250
tenuous position of contractor, 161

Cost, degree of precision in calculations, 42
as a factor in decision-making, 272
management disagreement about the nature of, 300
relative wage rates as a significant element in, 45–47
rigorous calculation and union challenge, 42
selective bias regarding, 44–47

Cost and feasibility criteria, contract clauses concerning, 220–221
frequency of occurrence, 219

CPM (Critical Path Method), 43

Craft and industrial union pacts (*see* Interunion pacts on contracting-out)

Craft and industrial unions, historical relations between, 190–191

Craft splinter movements, attitude of industrial unions toward, 214–215
attitude of management toward, 215
incidence of, 215
prospects of, 216

Crawford, Donald A., 179, 187, 204–205, 207–208, 211, 230

Crowder, Walter F., 33

Culliton, James W., 258

Cultural definition of acceptable work, 180–181

Cumulative Series Analysis, data, 284–288
definition of, 283

Cyert, R. M., 270

Dalton, Melville, 153, 156

Dash, G. Allan, Jr., 80, 204–205, 210

Davis, Louis E., 173

Decentralization of service facility, consequence of, 156

DeChazeau, M. G., 37

Decision factors, order of, 272–274

Decision-making process, and differential cost calculations, 272

Decision-making process, flow chart analysis, 261–263
  group pressures on, 263–268
  ideal model of, 258–259
  information needs in, 296–297
  main units of analysis, 259–261
  management consensus, 297–302
  order of factors, 272–274
  organizational model, 259
  relation to technological factors, 293–294
  role of staff specialists in, 295–296
  spacing and timing, 271
Decision structure, degree of centralization, 294–295
  management disagreement on nature of, 298
Derber, Milton, 74–75, 90
Detroit Pact, 193–194, 203
Diversification and integration, 34–35
  research on, 33
  and specialization, 35
Dobe, H. Donald, 98
Drucker, Peter F., 85–86
Dunlop, John T., 66

Edelman, Milton, 74, 90
Emerging union structures, liabilities of present structure, 174
  superunions, 174–175
Empire-building, managerial, 37–38, 153
Employment relationship, changes in, 168–169
  failure to recognize changes, 168
Equity, concepts of, 179–187, 243–254
  definition of, 179
  and differences in union officers' and members' goals, 216–217
  interrelated systems of, 185–187
Erosion model for loss of management rights, 66–68
Established work relationships pact, 198–203
  assessment of, 203

Established work relationships pact, conflict subsequent to, 202
  definition of, 199
  dispute settlement formula, 198–202
    specific cases under, 200–201
  division of work between inside and outside forces, 192

Fabrication industry, definition of, 41
  management disagreement in, 302
  management rights in, 51–52, 76–77, 110–111, 297
  policy on contracting-out, 49
  position on cost of contracting-out, 50–51
  proportion of work contracted-out, 49
  size of maintenance force in, 48–49
  size of plants, 48
Fair shares, concepts of, and arbitration, 212
  assessment of various means for determining, 250–254
  and collective bargaining, 213–214, 217–219, 229, 232
  the contractor's, 247–250
  definition of, 179–181, 271
  the inside workers', 218–219, 246–247
  the inside service department's, 244–246
  and inter-contractor relationships, 144–145
  interrelated systems of, 185–187
  and legislation, 232–233
  and methods for sharing work, 184–185
  at the missile sites, 234–235
  and the National Labor Relations Board, 236–237
  principal parties in determining, 182–183
  of services in the plant, 152
Featherbedding, definition of, 180
  feasibility of, 185

Featherbedding, and work-sharing, 223

Featherbedding-type contract clauses, 202, 224–225
  management initiation of, 224–225

Feigenbaum, E. A., 270

Fibreboard decision, NLRB, 236–242
  the initial version, 237
  reversal, 238
  NLRB member's dissent, 239

Field, A. W., 20

Fixed base operators, 172

Flow chart analysis, management decision, 261–263

France, management rights in, 20–21
  political challenge to, 21
  and rival unionism, 21
  and union structure, 20–21, 23

Franklin, Roger, 43

Fruits of the Bargain Theory, 205

Fueling contractors, 172

Fujita, Wakao, 16n.

Garment manufacture, sub-contract system, 35
  work-sharing agreements in, 223–224

General contractor, relation to specialty contractor, 131

Gort, Michael, 34–35, 49–50

Greenbaum, Marcia L., 204–207, 210

Group pressures on management decision, 113–114, 263–266
  (*See also* Pressure group model for decision)

Hawaii Meat Co., NLRB decision, 239

Healy, J. J., 74

Higgin, Gurth, 131

Higgins, Carter C., 258

Holland Report and missile site disputes, 233–235

Human Relations Committee, steel industry, 225–227

Indianapolis Pact, 195

Industrial relations managers, disagreement, on extent of union influence, 301
  on nature of costs, 301
  on nature of policy, 299–300
  on nature of practice, 298
  relations with outsiders, 10
  role in decision process, 152, 296

Industrial Union Department, AFL-CIO, craft secession from, 196

Infant industries, recent changes, 36
  vertical integration in, 34, 36

Information needs (*see* Decision-making process)

Inside forces, definition of, 121–122, 167–168
  extent of support by managerial groups, 150, 159
  future prospects, 173–176

Inside-outside relationships, flaws in traditional concept of, 10–12

Inside relationships, flaws in traditional concept of, 6, 10–11

Inside service departments' fair share of work, 244–246
  regarding quality of work, 244
  regarding scope of function, 245–246

Inside worker's fair share of work, 218–219

Integrated contractors, definition of, 137
  scope of organization, 138, 146–147

Integrated management, 150–151

Internal profit and loss control systems, 50

International Brotherhood of Electrical Workers dispute regarding established work relationships, 200

Interunion pacts on contracting-out, Bridgeport Pact, 195
  Detroit Pact, 193–194, 203
  diagram showing division of work, 192

Interunion pacts on contracting-out,
   Indianapolis Pact, 195
      local craft-industrial union pacts,
         195
   Miami Pact, 192
      (*See also* Miami Pact)
   plant level agreements, 202–203
   Youngstown Pact, 195
Ito, Taikichi, 17

Jacobs, Paul, 180, 185, 187
Japan, 16–19, 23–25
   contrast with the United States,
      23–25, 180–181
   inside security system, 24–25
   management rights, 18
   new developments in employment
      relationship, 18, 19
   outside forces, 8, 16–19, 24
   permanent employment relation-
      ship, 17–18, 24–25
   relations between inside and out-
      side forces, 8, 16–19, 24
   subcontracting, 17, 23, 24
   temporary workers, 17–18, 23
   union position on management
      rights, 18
   union structure, 18
Jewkes, John, 38
Joint ventures of specialty contractors, 145
Jurisdiction, absence of in long term
   relationship, 125
   concept of, effect of interunion
      pacts on, 194
   and the Miami Pact, 198
   and past practice concept, 201–
      203
   as a problem in era of automa-
      tion, 126
   rejection of as a means for dis-
      pute settlement, 251
   contractor-inside manager differ-
      ences on, 124–125
Jurisdictional issues between craft
   and industrial unions, historical
   basis, 190–191

Jurisdictional issues in intra-company relations, 149, 160
   the inside union's role in, 159
   in inter-divisional relations, 158–
      159
   the service department's role,
      157–158
Justin, Jules, 85, 86

Kahn, A. E., 37
Kahn, Robert, 231
Karsh, Bernard, 18
Klassen, E. T., 68, 73
Knight, O. A., 170
Koontz, H. D., 153, 154

Labor contractors, in England, 32
   in India, 32
   modern, 138–139
   role in early industrialization, 33
Layoff, men on, contract clauses
   concerning, 219–220
   frequency of occurrence, 219
Legalism in contracting-out disputes,
   252–254
Letters of intent, frequency of use,
   104
   management attitude toward,
      103–104
Levine, Solomon B., 15, 18
Limitations on subcontracting, contractors' protests about, 195
Lipstreu, Otis, 87
Livernash, E. R., 74
Local craft-industrial union pacts,
   195
   (*See also* Interunion pacts)
Lunden, Leon E., 218, 223–224

McDonald, David, 128
Machinists Union, Lockheed contract, 1963, 202
   organization of outside forces, 170
   position on contracting-out, 172

Machinists Union, railroad negotiations, 227

McPherson, M. H., 20

Maintaining Production for America, booklet, controversy over, 128–129, 196

Maintenance and construction departments, expected behavior patterns, 149

  proportion with craft organization, 153

  proposed changes in, 151–152

    centralization, 151–152, 156

    institution of controls, 152

    relations with client departments, 153–156, 157

      jurisdictional conflict, 157

      poor service, 154

      reciprocity, 154–155

Maintenance work, changes in nature of, 48

  contracting-out of nonroutine, 31

  contracting-out of routine, 31

Make or buy problems, and business cycle factors, 38

  interest in research on, 33, 258

Management-controlled defenses, avoidance defense, 91–95

  avoiding coercive comparisons, 92–93

  restructuring work and work force, 93–95

  and company position on management rights, 95–97

  definition of, 89

  frequency of use, 90–96

  and industry type, 95

  "no discussion" defense, 90

Management defenses of rights, defenses of ability to contract-out, 88–89

  goals of, 83

  strategies, 85

    human relations, 86–87

    legalistic, 86

  unintended consequences of, 84

  and union influence, 112–113

Management disagreement, influence of technological factors on, 302

  contrast between fabrication and process industries, 302

  on nature of, costs, 300

  decision policy, 298–299

  decision practice, 298

  decision structure, 298–299

  union influence, 301

Management rights, changing nature of issues, 69–70

  and defenses, 95–97

  and distinction between insiders and outsiders, 10

  erosion model, definition of, 66–67

    and doctrine of individual responsibility, 67

    and permanence of union-management agreements, 78–79

    and union penetration, 68

  issues in public arena, 70–73

    public attitude toward, 71

    public relations campaigns, 71

    relation to collective bargaining, 70–71

    symbolic content of, 72–73

  organizational meaning of loss of, 114–115

  research on, 4, 73–75

  structural factors, influence of, 77–78

  and technological factors, 51–52, 76–77, 110–111, 171–172, 186, 297

  traditional approach to, 67–68

  traditional roles of parties in conflict, 170–171

  in United States, 4, 21

  in Western Europe, 19–20

Managerial competition within the firm, 157–160

Managerial consensus, 297–302

Managerial groups, support, of inside forces, 150, 159

  of outside forces, 150, 248–250

Manufacturer-contractors, competition with construction craft contractors, 140
competition with inside forces, 141
definition of, 140
services offered, 140–141
assembly-line repair shops, 141
package programs, 141
March, J. G., 270
Meany, George, craft-industrial union relations, 190–191
Meyers, Frederic, 21
Miami Pact, assessment of, 198–199, 203
NLRB decision under its terms, 201
provisions of, 192
reaction to, 193
subsequent conflict over contracting-out, 195–197
utility of, 198
Minimum surrender, principle of, definition of, 191
Missile sites, craft-industrial union disputes, 130, 197–198, 251
manufacturer-construction industry disputes, 140, 233–235
Modernization work, contracting-out of, 31

National Construction Association, building trades agreement, 127
National Labor Relations Board, definition of management defense and offense, 84
division of work between inside and outside forces, 237
and notification of union, 183, 238
role in contracting-out disputes, 183, 236–242
NLRB decisions, 236–242
effect of, 239–242, 250, 252, 266
on management rights, 239–242
(*See also* Abbott Publishing Co.; Fibreboard decision; Hawaii Meat Co.; Town and Country decision)

"No defense" firms, membership of group, 89–90
"No discussion" defense, definition of, 90
frequency of use, 91
Nonwage issues, resolution of, 120
Notification of union, contract clauses concerning, 221–223
frequency of occurrence, 219
management attitude toward, 97–100
frequency of management-initiated notification, 97–98
methods employed in, 99–100

O'Donnell, C. J., 153–154
Oil, Chemical, and Atomic Workers Union, organization of outside forces, 170
contract provisions obtained, 170
position on contracting-out, 170
Organizational developments within the inside and outside forces, 169–170
contrast between old and new elements, 169
shifting boundaries between, 169–170
Ornati, Oscar A., 4, 32
O'Shaughnessy, James B., 85
Ostry, S., 64
Outside forces, advantages of craft organization of, 127
definition of, 121–122, 167–168
future prospects, 174–176
impact of automation on, 173
labor problem focus, 123–126, 147
marketing problem focus, 127–129
problems of craft organization, 126
structure of, 122–125, 169–170
worker-management relations, 150–159
Overhead charges for maintenance and construction work, in fabrication industries, 50

Overhead charges for maintenance and construction work, in process industries, 50
  size of, 46
Oxenfeldt, A. R., 38, 181, 258

Past practice criterion, consequences of use, 203
  operational definition of, 270–271
  problems of, 184
  tendency to favor insiders, 201
  use in black, white, and gray formula, 192–193
  use in craft-industrial union disputes, 201
Pennsylvania Railroad strike, 1960, 70, 228
Permanence of effect of decisions, arbitration, 79–81
  collective bargaining, 78–79
PERT (Program Evaluation Review Technique), 43
Plant employment size, future trends in, 57
  and industry type, 48–49
  and proportion of maintenance and construction work contracted-out, 53–55
  large plants, 56–57
  middle-sized plants, 56
  small plants, 55–56
Plant engineer, attempts to institute controls, 152, 155
  estimate of union influence, 301
  relations with outsiders, 10, 134
  defense of relation with contractor, 162
  preferential attitude toward contracting, 162
Plant level contracting-out agreements between inside and outside unions, 202–203
Powers, Bertram A., 184
Pressure group model for decision, 267
  data required, 268
Process industry, definition of, 48

Process industry, management disagreement in, 302
  management rights in, 51–52, 76–77, 110–111, 171–172, 297
  modern plants and contracting-out, 52–53
  policy regarding contracting-out, 49
  position on cost of contracting-out, 52–53
  proportion of work contracted-out, 49
  size, of maintenance force, 48–49
  of plants, 48
Program Evaluation Review Technique (PERT), 43
Protest, control of, 288–290
  flaws in managerial approach, 289
  prediction of, according to work group type, 276–277, 279
  and amount of money involved, 282
  and decision patterns, 278–279
  and number of men on layoff, 282–283
  outside forces', 279–280
  and special agreements, 281–282
  prescription for avoiding, 290–291
  rate and timing of, 278
Purchasing, contractor and in-plant manager differences over, 124
Purchasing managers, relations with outsiders, 10
Putting-out system and early industrialization, 32–33, 35–36

Railroad industry, management rights battles in, 71, 95, 227–229
Railroad negotiations and Transport Workers Union, 227–228
Railroad shopmen's strike, 29
Red tape, contractual, impact on contracting-out, 230, 239, 242

Research design, management de-
cision process, 267
    variables investigated, 268
    seventy-four plant survey, 13
Reserved rights theory, 205
Reuther, Walter, 128
Rights issues, problems of settle-
ment, 179
    (*See also* Management rights)
Rogers, David, 11

Sayles, Leonard R., 13, 276–277
Schedler, Carl R., 229–230
Schlissel, F., 17
Secession threats, AFL-CIO, local
level, 194
    Skilled Trades Society, 194
    national level, 194, 196
Senate Labor Subcommittee hear-
ings, February, 1959, 195
Service departments (*see* Mainte-
nance and construction depart-
ments)
Slichter, S. H., 74, 257
Smith, Adam, 34
Sobel, I., 45
Soviet Union, account poaching in,
22
    contract work in, 22
    cost calculations in, 22, 42
    inside and outside interests in, 22
    management rights in, 4, 21, 22
Spacing and timing of decisions, 271
Specialty contractors, attitude toward
contract maintenance, 130, 142
    entry into new markets, 141–146
        resistance to, 143–145
    joint ventures of, 145
    relation to general contractor, 131
Staff specialists, role of (*see* De-
cision-making process)
Starr, Albert R., 98
Steel industry negotiations, 1959,
70, 225–227
    Human Relations Committee,
225–227
    management rights issue, 70

Steel industry negotiations, Section
2-B, 70
    1963, 70, 225–227
        experimental agreement on con-
tracting-out, 225–227
Steelworkers Union, position on con-
tracting-out, 128, 193, 196
Stigler, George J., 33–34
Strauss, George, 158
Superior-subordinate model for in-
side relations of firm, 9, 149
Superunions, definition of, 174–175
Symbolic content of management
rights issues, 72–73

Taft-Hartley Act, controls on construction industry, 127
Tannenbaum, R., 68
Teamsters Union, and craft secession, 194
    and Town and Country decision,
237
Technological factors, impact, on arbitration decisions, 211–212
    on bargaining position of par-
ties, 43, 53, 126, 173–176
    on rights of parties, 51–52, 76–
77, 110–111, 171–172,
186, 297
    and management defenses, 95
    and union influence, 109–111
Third party role in contracting-out
disputes, 252
Thorp, Willard L., 31
Torrence, G. W., 45, 67, 85–86
Town and Country decision, NLRB,
236–242
    and good faith bargaining, 238
Transport Workers Union and railroad negotiations, 227–228
Tsuda, Masume, 17 *n.*
Turnbull, John G., 73
Typographical Union and bogus
work, 184

Union influence, definition of, 108–
109

Union influence, and management defenses, 112–113
and management disagreement on, 301
and organizational structure, 109
plant size, 109
proportion of total force in maintenance and construction, 109
and technology, 109–111
fabrication industry, 109–111
process industry, 109–111
and union structure, 111–112
craft, 111
craft-industrial, 112
industrial, 111–112
Union officers' and members' goals, differences in, 216–217
United States, management rights in, 4, 21
and class divisions, 20, 24
contrast with Canada, 65, 204
contrast with Japan, 23–25, 180–181
contrast with Western Europe, 19–20
and union structure, 21
United States government, interest in contracting-out, 183, 235–236
ambivalence of position, 183, 236

Verge, Pierre, 65
Vertical disintegration, and business cycle factors, 38
failure to materialize, 37
Vertical disintegration, research on, 33
and stages of industrial development, 34
Vertical integration, and business cycle factors, 38
and diversification, 34, 35
research on, 33
as a self-bounding process, 36–37

Warrior-Gulf decision, effect of, 183, 204–205, 230, 239, 261, 266
Weber, Arnold R., 215
Western Europe, management rights in, 19–20
Wirtz, Willard, 180
Woods, H. D., 64
Woodward, Joan, 294, 302
Work of industrial firm, organization of, 30–31
fringe activities, 30–31
hard-core activities, 30–31
variable activities, 30–31
and stage of industrial development, 34
Work-sharing agreements, 223–224, 232
Worker protest groups, types of, 276–279

Young, Stanley, 73
Youngstown Pact, 195